Why Are There OUGHTS?

Why Are There OUGHTS?

The Nature of Moral Necessity

STEPHEN E. PARRISH

Foreword by ANGUS J. L. MENUGE

WIPF & STOCK · Eugene, Oregon

WHY ARE THERE OUGHTS?
The Nature of Moral Necessity

Copyright © 2026 Stephen E. Parrish. All rights reserved. Except for brief quotations in critical publications or reviews, no part of this book may be reproduced in any manner without prior written permission from the publisher. Write: Permissions, Wipf and Stock Publishers, 199 W. 8th Ave., Suite 3, Eugene, OR 97401.

Wipf & Stock
An Imprint of Wipf and Stock Publishers
199 W. 8th Ave., Suite 3
Eugene, OR 97401

www.wipfandstock.com

PAPERBACK ISBN: 979-8-3852-6111-6
HARDCOVER ISBN: 979-8-3852-6112-3
EBOOK ISBN: 979-8-3852-6113-0

Scripture quotations are from The Holy Bible, Revised Standard Version, copyright 1971 by Division of Christian Education of the National Council of the Churches of Christ in the United States of America.

Permission has been granted by the Editor of Philosophia Christi to republish a revised version of the essay, "Defending Theistic Conceptualism," which first appeared in Philosophia Christi 20 (2018) 101–17. Additional information is available at www.epsociety.org.

To my grandchildren,

Conor, Kyrah, Mila, Bailey, Emmeline and Jonathan,
and any others that might show up,

For bringing hope for the future.

Contents

Acknowledgments ix
Foreword by Angus J. L. Manuge xi
Introduction xv

1. Approaching Metaethical Theory 1
2. Divisions of Metaethical Theories 17
3. Relevant Issues 30
4. Categories, the Nature of Ethics, and Beauty 47
5. Abstract Entities, Propositions, and Necessity 63
6. Antirealism 89
7. Weak Realism 114
8. Strong Realism 128
9. Some Strong Realist Theories 141
10. Theistic Antirealism, Absolute Creationism, and Theistic Conceptualism 165
11. Perfect Being Theism 198
12. The Trinity 217
13. Conclusion: The Best Reason for Ethics 244

Bibliography 247
Index 261

Acknowledgments

I WOULD LIKE HERE to acknowledge several people who made major contributions to this book. First is my wife, Dr. Elenn' Parrish, who edited, re-edited, and re-re-edited this book, turning a mass of confused writings into something intelligible. She may truly be thought of as a second author of the book.

I (and my wife) would also like to thank Dr. Dale Kratt for his very helpful insights and recommendations. He thoroughly critiqued the book and offered many valuable suggestions in organizing the thoughts. I should mention that Dr. Kratt's doctoral dissertation, "A Theistic Critique of Secular Moral Nonnaturalism," is an excellent resource for those interested in this subject.

Dr. Angus Menuge, an esteemed and deeply appreciated colleague, graciously read the manuscript and made several important contributions, including the forward to this challenging treatise. Thank you, Angus.

Dr. David Baggett has been very supportive with his encouragement of my work. His books on the subject have been especially helpful in my research and writing through the years.

Special thanks to Dr. John Restum and Professor Timothy Scarbrough of Moody Bible Institute in Plymouth, Michigan, for their thoughtfulness and going out of their way to aid me in finding needed resources.

I deeply appreciated the leadership of Concordia University Ann Arbor, which was always very supportive of my literary efforts. Thank you, fellow professors, for your encouragement through the years.

Foreword

THERE IS NO DOUBT about it: moral obligations and duties are strange things. They seem to have a compelling authority that overrides other considerations. For example, few would take seriously the idea that it was wrong to save a person from choking in a restaurant because the technique employed was considered bad manners by other diners. We seem to know that moral obligations—at least the fundamental ones—have an inescapable claim on us, a kind of normative necessity, that etiquette and other merely conventional systems of norms do not have.

This might suggest that moral obligations are like the laws of logic. No one thinks that the obligation to think logically is overridden by the various factors (tiredness, inattention, bias, and so on) that lead us into sloppy thinking, or that standard rhetorical practice in the political world has the same authority as logic. There is a necessity to logical systems: we can show that their axioms are tautologies, and their rules of inference are truth-preserving. So, one might think that moral obligations have the same kind of prescriptive necessity as logic.

However, this does not seem to be true. Suppose one grants that murdering children for fun is absolutely wrong, and our obligation not to do such a thing has universal normative necessity. Still, there is no obvious way to derive a formal contradiction from the statement "murdering children for fun is not wrong," and so if one denies the corresponding moral obligation, we cannot show that one's view is self-contradictory in the way we can if someone denies a law of logic.

If apparent moral necessity cannot be reduced to narrowly logical necessity, then we are left with some basic questions. Is moral necessity illusory? Or if it is real, what is its grounding if it is not pure logic? Can it be derived from human nature? Could some version of Platonism explain the source of normative necessity? What about God? Does it make a difference whether or not God exists? If so, does it matter what attributes

God has, and whether he is unitarian or trinitarian? These and many other related questions are answered in Stephen Parrish's systematic and insightful investigation of metaethical options.

Parrish's contributions to philosophy (in epistemology, metaphysics, and philosophy of mind, as well as ethics) are marked both by a tightly focused examination of foundational questions and a systematic thoroughness in their consideration of possible answers. The present work is no exception. It is tightly focused on just one question, arguably the most important question in metaethics: what should we make of the apparent normative necessity of moral obligations? And it offers a meticulous, exhaustive evaluation of all of the main metaethical theories to see how well they answer this question.

In this important work, Parrish first makes a compelling case that moral obligations really do exhibit normative necessity, and that neither the various forms of antirealism nor weaker versions of moral realism can accommodate this fact. Rather, he contends, the only viable option is "Strong Realism," which affirms categorical imperatives that are characterized by necessity, universality, and person-relatedness.

Yet if Strong Realism is true, we are left with the question of *how* it can be true, given that the necessity of moral norms is not reducible to that of pure logic. Moral necessity must have some independent ontological grounding, and in the rest of the book, Parrish explores what that grounding might be. He considers and rejects the atheistic moral Platonism of Erik Wielenberg, theistic antirealism, and absolute creationism. He concludes that the best available option is a version of theistic conceptualism, which locates the source of moral obligations in the mind of God. This position is defended against a range of standard and contemporary objections.

Going further, Parrish argues that the necessity of moral imperatives must ultimately be rooted in God's nature, and that this is best explained on a Trinitarian view of God. For the Trinity means that God *is* love (love is not merely an attribute, or quality of God), since there is a community of loving persons within the Godhead. As a result, some moral imperatives flow of necessity from the kind of being God is. Ethical propositions are made true or false because God either affirms or denies them, and at least some of these propositions are necessarily true because, due to His nature, God necessarily affirms them. As a result, we can see why the Euthyphro dilemma is no dilemma at all, because these necessary truths are neither arbitrary nor independent of God but grounded in His nature. Moral necessity is explained, therefore, as something that derives from the very being of God.

As readers may surmise, Parrish's case provides strong support for the moral argument for God's existence. If Strong Realism is true, and can only be true if God exists, then God exists. To be sure, a lot is at stake here, and we should expect such a bold thesis to be challenged by a variety of critics, both theists and non-theists. But Parrish has succeeded admirably in articulating the questions that need to be answered if we are adequately to account for the apparent inescapable authority of moral obligations. This book will help both scholars and general readers to gain a clearer view of the metaethical landscape, and it will make them think deeply about what our moral obligations ultimately tell us about the nature of reality.

Angus J. L. Menuge
Professor and Chair of Philosophy,
Concordia University Wisconsin

Introduction

THE PURPOSE OF THIS book is to provide a secure foundation for ethics. Many of the major disputes that exist in the world today are ethical or at least contain ethical issues. Except for a small minority of sociopaths, moral concerns seem vitally relevant to human beings. (I shall use *ethics* and *morality* as synonyms).[1] It is easy to see why. Much of what human beings think and debate about are related to what to do, and how to do it. There has been in our civilization over several centuries a loss of morality as a form of knowledge, which has led to uncertainty and many debates.[2] A large portion of these debates revolves around the ethical implications of these actions. Abortion, euthanasia, war, crime and punishment, sex, and the environment are all moral issues. However, these days there is less agreement about what is ethical than previously was standardly understood in our society, largely because there is less agreement about what reality is like.

What is ethics? Do ethical rules necessarily exist or are they something we invent? How do we know what is right? Issues like these cause endless confusion and disagreement. Building upon a secure foundation, therefore, is fundamentally necessary.

Reaching for that strong foundation, in this work I will examine the nature of ethical necessity—what it means and its implications. There are a lot of related issues that must be discussed before a firm conclusion can be drawn. However, there are two major tasks which will be essential for addressing all the others.

---

1. About this Scott B. Rae writes, "Technically, morality refers to the actual *content* of right and wrong, and ethics refers to the *process* of determining, or discovering, right and wrong. In other words, morality deals with moral *knowledge* and ethics with moral *reasoning and justification*." Rae, *Moral Choices*, 15. Since I am dealing with both, I will keep things simple and use ethics and morality interchangeably as synonyms.

2. Willard, *Disappearance*.

First, the question of whether there are necessary ethical propositions will be examined—that is, propositions that are necessarily true, in the same sense as the basic propositions of arithmetic are true. In other words, are there laws of ethics that are binding on us whether we like it or not? It will be argued that necessarily true ethical propositions do, in fact, exist, and significantly impact us and our world.

Second, it will be argued that given necessarily existing ethical truths, there are only two conceivable foundations for their existence. One is Platonism, and the other is theism. That is, if there *are* necessarily existing ethical truths, do they exist as ontologically independent (Platonism), or do they depend for their existence on something else (as in theism)? It will be argued that in the second case, the only plausible candidate for this ontological ground is the God of Perfect Being Theism (PBT).[3]

It is doubtless true, as Linda Zagzebski writes, that there is a lot more to ethics than this.[4] This is not an attempt to be a comprehensive examination of the whole field, but an attempt to get at a central, core question, which is, "Are there *categorical imperatives?*", and to explore the implications of their existence, if they indeed do exist. To state the question another way, "Are there *absolute 'oughts', 'shoulds', or 'must not do's'*"? Though my focus will be narrow in some sense, for clarity in the examination several important aspects of various relevant philosophical issues will also be covered, and therefore the discussion will be broad.

Although this book is shorter than my other books, it has been the most difficult to write. This was not because of intractable problems with my thesis, but because there were so many issues to examine, and it is therefore difficult to write about one topic without writing of others. This made it difficult to decide which issues were to come first. Among these themes are different kinds of ethical theories, the nature of necessity, the nature of abstract entities, categories of being, and the existence and nature of a relevant God.

The resulting outline of the chapters' contents is:

1. Approaching Metaethical Theory
2. Divisions of Metaethical Theories

---

3. Though I note that there is disagreement about what properties a perfect being God would have.
4. Zagzebski, *Divine Motivation*, 6.

3. Relevant Issues: Human nature and its limitations, autonomy, reason, and motivation.
4. Categories, the Nature of Ethics, and Beauty
5. Abstract Entities, Propositions, and Necessity
6. Antirealism: Theories that ethics are *invented*.
7. Weak Realism: Theories that ethical truths are *derived* on some aspect of human nature or reason.
8. Strong Realism: Theories that ethical truths *exist necessarily* and are not created by human beings.
9. Some Strong Realist Theories
10. Realist Theories of Theistic Antirealism, Absolute Creationism, and Theistic Conceptualism.
11. Perfect Being Theism: The only concept of God that can account for God's being the ontological foundation of ethics.
12. The Trinity: How the Trinity overcomes the Euthyphro objection to theistic ethics, among other things.
13. The Conclusion: The Best Reason for Ethics.

This book is written for both scholars and lay people who are interested in the subject of the *foundation of ethics*. Have you ever pondered and questioned *why* we have moral thoughts and ethical systems? Welcome to a deep dive into the fathoms of ethics.

Some background knowledge of the subject will be helpful. One final point is that philosophers sometimes use the same words for different concepts than the meaning that other philosophers attach to them. I have essayed to clarify definitions where misunderstandings could cloud the discussion.

CHAPTER 1

Approaching Metaethical Theory

WHY ETHICS EXIST

ETHICS, AS A SUBJECT of study, exists because human beings are not only rational beings, but also beings that think there are ways that societies *should* exist in certain manners, and that these conventions are somehow binding on us. It seems that considerations of morality are bound up in the fabric of human nature, as every society has *rules* that they consider should be followed, even though the rules may differ greatly from society to society. That the whole world is now interconnected causes more confusion as to *what is right or wrong*.

THE NATURE OF ETHICAL VALUES

Put simply and traditionally, ethics is the idea that there are actions we *ought* or *ought not* to do in certain situations. There are, in effect, rules that ought to be followed. And traditionally, these rules are of the deepest and most important kind. They are rules that bind us whether we like it or not. That is, these rules have an inescapable authority unlike optional conventions such as etiquette.

This notion has come under a great deal of criticism in the last century or so, and the debate rages as to what is the true concept of morality.

This brings us to the ontological question: in what manner does ethics exist? Is it something we invent, or is it somehow contained in our nature, or does it exist apart from us and thereby would exist even if human beings had never existed?

This is a key part of metaethics—the study of ethics at its most basic level.[1] What ethical statements fundamentally are, is what is meant by the *ontological* status of ethical propositions. In what way do they exist and how do they relate to the rest of reality? Included in this examination are three interrelated terms: ontology, necessity, and categoricity. Why do morals[2] have the content that they do? How can they be understandable by human (and any other finite rational) minds is another problem. In addition, what is the relation of ethics to God, if any?

Here at the beginning, the different theories of morality investigated will be defined. *Ethical theory* is, like most things that have been examined in depth for a long time by a plethora of philosophers, very complex. There are many different but legitimate ways in which metaethical theories may be divided. To make things manageable, metaethical theories will be divided into three basic concepts: antirealism, weak realism, and strong or robust realism. This is a useful way to categorize these theories, though certainly not the only way.

First, in *antirealism*, ethics is ultimately based upon what people desire. Most people want to have secure lives with a certain amount of freedom and, so, antirealists think that we should adopt rules that allow most people to have that security and freedom. It is not that we are obliged to follow these rules, it is just that this makes it easier to create a situation wherein we can get what we want. For example, most people want to live safely, so having laws against murder, theft, and rape is deemed necessary. This is considered so even though on antirealism there is nothing intrinsically wrong with murder, theft, and rape. For antirealists, an ethical system which is obligatory is a concept that does not exist but is *invented* by human beings. *Nihilism* and *extreme nihilism* are also defined as forms of antirealism.

Second, *weak realist systems* are based on some feature of reality regarding human beings, or perhaps rational creatures in general. A weak realist will typically look at human nature, see that it is objectively built in a certain manner, and from this deduce that a certain way of acting is the right or ethical way. On this rationale, one *decides* a certain way in which life ought to be lived. For example, the weak realist will build a case for ethics founded on the fact that human beings desire happiness, or on

---

1. A standard introduction to metaethics is found in Miller, *Contemporary Metaethics*. For a major reference work on the subject, see McPherson and Plunkett, *Routledge Handbook of Metaethics*.

2. *Morals* and *ethics* are used interchangeably in this book.

the ability to flourish, or because they are intermittently rational beings, or even just on a desire to live. In effect, then, in weak realism ethics are *derived* from some aspect of human nature or from the nature of reason. Hence, weak realism makes ethics contingent, even though founded on objective concepts.

Thirdly, with a *strong realist system* there are necessary laws of morality dictating that one *ought* to act in accordance with one's nature—whether one wants to do so or not. In other words, in strong realism, ethical truths are *necessary* in the same sense that fundamental mathematical truths are necessary. By *necessary*, what is meant is "existing in all possible worlds." In short, with strong realism, ethical truths are *discovered*. They are a part of the fundamental architecture of reality.

This theory may also be called *robust realism*. Sometimes the term robust realism is reserved for non-theistic theories, or for some form of Platonism in ethics. However, this term encompasses all theories that hold that metaethical truths are *necessarily true*. This necessity derives because, in some way, to deny these truths entails a contradiction, but how this happens in the case of ethical propositions is complex.[3]

It is this concept of *the logical or absolute necessity of morality* that I will ultimately attempt to vindicate. As stated above, these morals are true in all possible worlds, whether there are beings in those worlds or not. It will be shown that the only concept of morality that can provide for categorical imperatives is strong realism. Antirealisms and weak realisms, by contrast, fail in the end to be full-blooded concepts of morality.

To more clearly address these major categories of ethical theory, it will be necessary to delve into a deeper examination of pertinent matters affecting the discussion of these respective theories.

Inventory of Ethical Theories

There is a very wide variety of ethical theorizing, based on what different theorists believe is *the nature of ethics*. This may be one reason why there is so much dispute about the issues. Various theorists attach different meanings to the same words, while also operating from their own worldviews, that vary in ideas about what constitutes evidence and truth. There are many terms used to analyze ethical propositions. Though these

---

3. See chapter 8 on this point.

may be expressed with differing terminology, the most basic division in ethics is between strong realist theories and everything else.

Let me now attempt to show how the alternative theories examined represent an exhaustive inventory of ethical theorizing; every concept of what ethics is, is in fact covered by my mapping. There are other legitimate ways of dividing up metaethics. In the bullet list directly below, how each of the different theories are derivable is outlined, noting the polar opposite concepts of necessity and contingency. Start with this question: "*Are there objective ethical truths?*"

Here is my list, which is inclusive of all (or at least most) of the possibilities.

1. *Strong Realism:* Ethical truths are necessarily true, and exist independently of any contingent, finite minds. *Non-Naturalism* is another name for theories where ethical propositions exist apart from the natural world.

    a. *Platonism:* Ethical truths exist necessarily and independently of any other being. They are abstract entities.

    b. *Theism:* Ethical truths are dependent upon God, but not in a voluntaristic sense.

        i. Absolute Creationism: God creates ethical truths, which then exist as abstract entities outside of his mind. These truths are based on his nature, and since God's nature does not vary from possible world-to-world, at least some of them are necessarily true, but others might only exist in some worlds.

        ii. Theistic Conceptualism: Ethical truths are ideal objects, which exist necessarily in God's mind, and are affirmed by God. This is the same as Absolute Creationism, except that God does not create ethical truths. Rather they are propositions that God necessarily thinks and affirms.

2. *Weak Realism:* Ethical truths exist but depend for their existence upon finite truths or facts about contingent reality.

    a. *Naturalism*: Ethical truths exist based on some aspect of human nature, or the natural world itself. Moral truths are mind independent, objective facts, but are natural facts. For example, happiness and flourishing would be natural facts.

    b. *Rationalism*: Ethical truths are based on the nature of reason, such as Kant's deontological metaethics. Any appeal to the notion that reason itself provides a basis for ethics would go here.[4] Another form of rationalism might be Derek Parfit's theory.[5]

3. *Antirealism*: Antirealists either hold there are no ethical truths or hold that ethical truths are grounded in our evaluative attitudes and not in independent moral norms. The whole category of ethics is empty or is entirely reducible to another category of being.

    a. *Cognitivism*: Ethical statements are beliefs chosen by some individual or individuals. They cannot be reduced to non-ethical ideas but have no truth value other than what some persons want or desire.

        i. Subjectivism (often called relativism): Ethical propositions are meaningful, but do not describe an additional aspect of reality.

            1. Individual Subjectivism: Ethical propositions are simply what everyone would think is morally right or wrong. Morality therefore varies from person to person. Individual subjectivism seems somewhat redundant, but here it will be used to separate it from the following positions.

            2. Inter-Subjectivism: Ethical propositions

---

4. Ethical rationalism is a view in which moral truths are knowable a priori, by reason alone.

5. Parfit is somewhat difficult to place. In three large books Parfit has defended a theory that has deservedly received much attention. Parfit, *On What Matters*. He is a realist and rejects naturalist theories but also rejects Platonism. Parfit might have thought that his theory is a form of strong realism, but it has been put in the weak realist category. Martin Jakobsen argues that Parfit is a rationalist. Jakobsen, *Moral Realism*. See also Smith, *Moral Problem*.

are simply what some groups of people, such as a tribe, culture, or nation, believe is morally right or wrong. Inter-Subjectivism is therefore, in a way, simply subjectivism writ large.[6]

    3. Theological Voluntarism: God creates ethical truths, but contingently. In the actual world, God commands kindness as a good, but He could have made cruelty a good, though of course he may never have wanted to.

b. *Noncognitivism*: There are no ethical propositions as such. In other words, moral propositions are not really propositions, though they may be expressed as such, but they are fundamentally non-propositional forms of speech. These include the following:

    i. Reductionism: Ethical propositions are reducible to non-propositional ones.

        1. Emotivism: Ethical propositions are merely expressions of emotions.[7]

        2. Prescriptivism: Ethical propositions are merely prescriptive; they express what individuals or groups are expressing as what they would *like* to be the case.[8]

        3. Expressivism: Individuals or groups are merely expressing what they *feel* should be the case.

    ii. Eliminativism: Propositions are eliminated.

        1. Nihilism (Error Theory): Ethical truths

---

6. For an argument against relativism from an empirical standpoint, see Gairdner, *The Book of Absolutes*. Alasdair MacIntyre argues that rationality only makes sense in terms of a tradition. He argues that only when this is understood, can there be meaningful dialogs between different traditions. I am not certain if this is relativism or not. MacIntyre, *After Virtue*; and MacIntyre, *Whose Justice?*

7. Ayer, *Language, Truth and Logic*.

8. Hare, *Language of Morals*.

do not and cannot exist. People either mistakenly think that there are or pretend to think that there are ethical truths. Morality is therefore an empty category.[9]

2. Extreme Nihilism: This category is one where ethical propositions are meant to be true, but in fact are entirely meaningless. They mean nothing and cannot be reduced to anything else. For example, the "Grabled musskips are tennlific," is meaningless and cannot be reduced to anything else.[10]

One point should be made here at the outset. The term *naturalism* has more than one meaning. We will delve into this in more detail, but here are briefly mentioned two common meanings. First, as implemented above, naturalism refers to the natural world we live in. Second, "natural" can refer to non-normative statements. The term naturalism will mainly be used in the first sense in this work. If the term "naturalism" is used in the second or some other sense, the appropriate clarification will be used.

A case can be made that nihilist theories should be placed in the Cognitivist category, as they are purportedly about ethical propositions, even if they really are not. However, they have been put in the non-cognitivist section because ultimately, given these theories, ethical propositions are not really about anything.

In this mapping, there are therefore three fundamental ways to divide up metaethical theories, corresponding to the division made between strong, weak, and antirealist theories. How they are divided then will be structured with reference to how they are being presented, i.e., what questions are being asked about them. In the above, ethical truths are divided as being either 1) *necessarily true*, 2) *contingently* but objectively *true*, or 3) *not true* and reducible to some other facet of reality, or meaningless. It may be seen, though, that the lines between different categories are sometimes thin. The line between weak realism and antirealism is especially attenuated.

---

9. Mackie, *Ethics*.
10. Morris, *Believing Philosophy*, 45 n. 6.

This is not to claim that this division of theories is the only way that metaethical theories may be categorized. For example, Angus Ritchie divides the field into Error Theory, Moral Quasi-Realism,[11] Constructivism,[12] Anti-Anti-Realism,[13] Objectivism,[14] and Naturalism,[15] all of which are in a non-purposive or secular account of the universe. There are purposive accounts of the universe, which include theism and axiarchism.[16]

Ritchie's is a useful listing, though not as detailed as mine. Under my classification, error theory would be antirealism, while quasi-realism through Naturalism would be a weak realist theory, and theism and axiarchism (which is a particular version of Platonism) are strongly realist. There are indeed many forms of weak realism, but ultimately, they all appear to suffer from the same malady. They are all based on contingent aspects of reality, as will be discussed below. Still, although metaethical theories may legitimately be divided according to different classifications, the list is a useful one for our purposes.

WHENCE COMETH THE "OUGHT"? ORIGINS OF NORMATIVITY

Normativity and Necessity

Normative Truths

Normative truths are (to put the matter very simply) true statements in which some things necessarily follow from other things, or in which they are supposed to follow. A *norm* is an action guiding rule that imposes a necessity, requirement, or outcome upon an action. For example, if one is doing logic, and is using the rule of inference known as *Modus Ponens*, then one will see that if A is true, and that if A then B is also true, it necessarily follows that B is true. The truth of B follows from the two premises via the logical rule of inference, and if one does not see that B is derivable from the two premises given, one is thinking irrationally in some respect.

---

11. Gibbard, *Thinking How To Live*; and Blackburn, *Essays in Quasi-Realism*.
12. Korsgaard, *Sources of Normativity*.
13. McDowell, *Mind and World*.
14. Scanlon, *What We Owe*.
15. Foot, *Natural Goodness*.
16. Ritchie, *From Morality to Metaphysics*, 3; Leslie, *Value and Existence*.

So, it is a normative truth that in Modus Ponens, the conclusion follows with necessity from the two premises. *Thus, normativity is a kind of necessity, with necessity being a foundational concept.* Normativity puts the "ought" in the conversation.

The same point is true for many other subjects, such as mathematics. If one understands the laws of basic arithmetic, for example, then one will see that if Anya adds two plus two together, necessarily the result is four, and if Anya instead obtains the answer of five or even one hundred and thirty-seven and a half, then something has gone very wrong. Again, in both logic and mathematics, the conclusions flow necessarily from the premises. There is an "ought" located somewhere in the problem.

Similarly, in ethics, if one thinks, for example, that stealing is morally wrong, then if John steals something from Emmeline, one should be able to see that John has done something morally wrong. Morally wrong things are, by definition, things that ought not to be done. Thus, there is an important normative aspect to ethics just as much as there is in logic and mathematics, though what kind of normativity is a controversial matter. In ethics, there is an additional factor that moral and immoral actions supervene on personal and physical actions.[17]

Necessary Truths

As argued above, in logic and basic mathematics, one is dealing with necessary truths. They are necessary truths in the sense that they are true in all possible worlds. That is, a statement is *necessary*, if there are no possible worlds in which it is false. The same is true for entities. An entity has a *broadly logical* or *absolutely necessary* existence if and only if it exists in all possible worlds.[18] Prima facie at least, the same thing seems to be true of ethical statements. That one ought not to steal, nor murder, seems to be a truth that could not be false, and is therefore absolutely necessarily true, just as much as two plus two equals four is true. This much is true in at least any strongly realist metaethical theory. Weak realist and antirealist theories would have to give a different response, as will be argued below.

However, *necessity* is something of a puzzle in the case of ethics. For while in logic and mathematics the conclusions follow necessarily

---

17. The whole notion of normativity has received criticism. This will be briefly covered in chapter 6.

18. Hale, *Necessary Beings*. See also Pruss and Rasmussen, *Necessary Existence*.

from the premises, the same cannot be as easily done in ethics. Modus Ponens (briefly annotated would appear as $P \supset Q, P, \therefore Q$) and $2 + 2 = 4$ are both necessary truths, and it is obvious that *to deny them will sooner or later entail a contradiction.* Having said that, it is also a fact that other necessary truths in logic and mathematics do not follow as easily or obviously as these simple examples do. In many of them, demonstrating their necessity may be beyond human abilities to accomplish, even with the aid of computers. Only God could demonstrate their truth.

Logical rules of inference and simple mathematical statements are therefore logically necessary truths and are such because of the *law of non-contradiction*. Other necessary truths are not called logically necessary truths because they are not reducible to first order logic. Sometimes necessary truths are called logically necessary or metaphysically necessary truths. Such truths include propositions such as, "Nothing is colored both red and green (in the same place and way, and at the same time)"; "Red is a color rather than a number"; "All physical objects have temporal extension"; "Everything has one beginning"; and so on.

My belief is that these true ethical propositions are true in all possible worlds because of their essence and the law of non-contradiction.[19] It will be useful here to discuss essences: what they are and why they exist. By essence, what is meant is simply that for any particular thing, substance, property, event, etc., it must have a certain set of properties to be that kind of thing.[20] A thing cannot be a dog without being a mammal. A thing that was made of plastic in the shape of a credit card would not be a dog. A geometrical figure without three sides cannot be a triangle. A number cannot be prime if it is not odd, except for the number two. In short, to be something, there must be a minimal set of properties that defines that kind of thing. It is difficult to deny this minimal definition of essences without falling into absurdity. A dog cannot be a reptile or an insect, let alone a number or a color.

Necessary truths that are purely logical are called *logically necessary*. Necessary truths that are so because of their essence and the law of non-contradiction are also logically necessary in a sense, though this

---

19. By "essence" all that is meant here is those *properties* that an object must have to exist as the kind of object that it is. See Oderberg, *Real Essentialism*. See also Ross, *Thought and World*.

20. For a full defense of essentialism, see Oderberg, *Real Essentialism*.

corresponds with Plantinga's broadly logically necessary truths.[21] Possible worlds are indeed possible because they contain no logical contradictions.

Though not directly reducible to logical forms as Modus Ponens is, the examples given above can be shown to be necessary because their denial results in a contradiction. To be colored green is to exist in a certain way, say *G*. To be colored red is to exist in some other way, say *R*. To be colored green and red at the same time, place, and manner, would therefore be to exist as both red and green in the same way, time, and place. Since *G* and *R* are different from each other, a contradiction is generated.

Something similar may be said about such necessary truths that water is H_2O rather than *XYZ*. Suppose that as far as their macro properties went, H_2O and *XYZ* were identical. That is, they looked, tasted, and acted the same. The difference between the two would only become apparent after the ability to see things at a molecular level was developed.

Then why is water *necessarily* H_2O? Before and after the discovery of water's chemical nature we understood this stuff to be water. Because of the law of identity, everything is necessarily itself. Therefore, if water is H_2O, then it is necessarily H_2O. Even were human beings to discover on some other planet that the water-seeming-stuff there was really *XYZ*, we would know that it is actually not water because water, considered at a micro level of existence, is *necessarily* H_2O.[22]

Therefore, necessary truths, which are propositions that are true in all possible worlds, are all absolutely necessarily true. Logical truths are necessarily true because of their logical form. Metaphysically necessary, broadly logically necessary, or absolutely necessary truths are true because of the application of the law of non-contradiction to the essence of the objects at hand. In all cases, the truths are necessarily true because ultimately, the law of non-contradiction applies to them. *Absolutely necessarily true* is a generic term that covers all necessary truths whose denials entail a contradiction, whether human beings can demonstrate the contradiction or not.

Some philosophers today think that there are *Brute Necessities*. They think that these are things that are necessarily true but are ultimately true for no reason, simply by chance. It will be shown that the concept of Brute Necessity is self-contradictory and thus incoherent.

---

21. Plantinga, *Nature of Necessity*, 1–9.
22. Kripke, *Naming and Necessity*.

Ethical Paradigms of Necessity

Take, for example, two paradigm ethical propositions. Proposition T = torturing for fun is wrong, and S = stealing for personal gain is wrong. These are introduced here to simplify this discussion throughout the book. There is a difference between the two as far as being part of fundamental ethics. T seems to be necessarily and always true, while S is normally and almost always true, but it seems that there may be exceptions to it in unusual circumstances where it is the lesser of evils.

Necessity and Non-contradiction

Non-contradiction is the key to understanding the concept of logical or absolute necessity.[23] The same is not true for ethics, or at least their derivation is not as straightforward as it is in simple logic or math. Suppose that John takes money from Emmeline without her consent. Under normal circumstances, we would call this stealing, and stealing is immoral. However, the immorality does not flow immediately from the concept of taking Emmeline's money without her consent. One also needs the concept that stealing is morally wrong. Of course, stealing is by its very concept something that most people take to be morally wrong. Actually, stealing is wrong by definition, by the meaning of the word.

However, why is this true? Unlike the cases of Modus Ponens and $2 + 2 = 4$, there seems to be no contradiction derived from denying the simple concept that taking something without the owner's permission is ordinarily unethical. Stating that taking something from someone without their permission is not morally wrong does not seem to be contradictory in the same way that denying truths of logic or mathematics seems to be contradictory.

If "stealing is wrong" is a conceptual truth, wherein lies the necessity; from where does the necessity arise? Where does the normativity against stealing come from? One cannot just define things as being necessarily so. For example, one could define "schtealing" as taking something from someone *with* his or her permission, and declare that schtealing is morally wrong, as the word is defined. However, doing this hardly proves that taking something from someone with his or her permission is therefore

---

23. Parrish, *God and Necessity*, 1–21.

morally wrong. One cannot prove that something is unethical simply by defining it as being so.

In other words, stealing is to take something from another person without his or her permission and is immoral. However, why is taking something without their permission immoral, while taking something from someone with their permission is not? Saying that stealing is not wrong contradicts the meaning attached to the concept of stealing. *However, where does the wrongness itself come from?* This is a key question. The necessary "wrongness" of stealing is not derived directly from the law of non-contradiction, unlike the examples in math and logic given above. Where then does the "wrongness" come from?

WHENCE COMETH THE "WRONGNESS"? THEORIES

It is at this point that we come to the major categories of answers to this question that were mapped under the inventory of ethical theories above.

Antirealism

Antirealism gives the answer that there is really no problem here, as stealing is not wrong in any objective sense of the word, because nothing is "really" wrong. There is no absolute "ought not." Anyone or any group may come up with some code to follow, but it is strictly a matter of choice if anyone chooses to follow the code. Here, things boil down to a simple *choice*, usually based on some idea of what will make either the individual or the group happy. In this case, stealing is wrong simply because a group of people has decided to ban stealing.

Weak Realism

Another answer to the origin of ethics is that of *weak realism* wherein ethical right and wrong depend upon contingent factors in the universe, such as the existence of human beings and the nature that they have. To give an analogy: in chess the pawn moves only one space per turn, except on the first turn where it may move forward up to two spaces and moves diagonally when capturing another piece. Therefore, if one wants to play chess correctly, then one must only move a pawn in such a manner as described above. There is no logical necessity in doing so, in the sense that one can easily imagine a game wherein the rules could be somewhat different, such as pawns' being able to move three spaces on their first turn. However, strictly speaking, such a game would not be chess (though we might consider it a chess variant).

Similarly, in weak realism, normativity flows from some contingent aspect of the universe. Of course, most ethical propositions are more important than the simple matter of how far a player can move a pawn. If pawns could move three spaces on their first move, it would change the game of chess, but nothing else of importance would follow.

In contrast, if a society decided that stealing, rape, or murder were now morally acceptable, it would make huge changes in the whole fabric of that society, quite possibly destroying it. Still, none of the changes in that society would entail a logical contradiction. Because this is so, ethical commitments in the different forms of weak realism are in effect a *choice* to buy into the normativity. In this sense, weak realism resembles antirealism, and indeed, it seems that in the final analysis, the two positions are not that far apart. The biggest difference between antirealism and weak realism is the fact that in weak realism, the choice is based on some objective fact about human nature, such as being rational, rather than on more subjective features which antirealism appeals to. Even here, the difference between weak and antirealisms is not that great, as most antirealists will try to develop a moral code that leads to greater flourishing of some sort.

Strong Realism

In *strong* or *robust realism*, there is, by contrast, a necessity in ethics. Ethical normativity flows from a strong kind of necessity. Ethical truths are, by this definition, *broadly logically or absolutely necessary, and therefore are true in all possible worlds.* Hence, given the analysis above, *to deny the truth of true ethical statements is to somehow or other entail a contradiction.* Finding where the contradiction is becomes the main problem. However, when we come to ethical statements, one can stare at them and their denials until one is blue in the face and still see no derivable contradiction.

This is one of the major questions for strong realism ethics: *how do ethical statements receive their normativity*? Alternatively, where does the necessity of ethics come from, if indeed, there is a normativity of ethic which is just as strong in its own way as that of logic and mathematics? The normativity of necessarily true mathematical equations is derivable from the law of non-contradiction. 2 + 2 = 4 because 2 can be broken down into 1 + 1, and 2 + 2 = 4 can be reduced to 1 + 1 + 1 +1 = 1 + 1 + 1 +1. In other words, it is reducible to a tautology and hence is logically necessary. The point here is that this equation is necessarily true because of *logic*.[24]

Graham Oppy disagrees. He writes, "Given that 2 + 2 = 4, it is necessary that 2 + 2 = 4, but there is nothing that explains why it is necessary that 2 + 2 = 4. . . . [W]e have no explanation of why it is necessary that 2 + 2 = 4. . . . While all necessity is 'brute', only 'primitive' necessities are theoretical costs."[25] I beg to differ. It seems clear that necessity is explained by the fundamental laws of logic—identity, and non-contradiction—combined with the natures of the entities involved. Oppy opts for the position that necessities are brute. The whole notion of 'brute necessity" is incoherent and is examined in chapter 9.

Relationship to Logic

To be clear,

(1.1) The denial of logic entails a contradiction and is therefore the commission of a logical wrong.

(1.2) The denial of mathematical truths entails a logical contradiction and therefore the commission of a logical wrong.[26] The logical contradiction may be difficult or impossible for finite minds to demonstrate, but it must be there.

(1.3) The denial of robust or strong ethical truths entails a contradiction, but this contradiction does not seem to flow directly from the nature of the ethical statements, and hence, must come from somewhere else.

---

24. Beyond simple truths that are based on fundamental logical principles, mathematics is often based on axioms that are debatable.

25. Oppy and Pearce, *Is There a God?*, 105.

26. Mathematical truths do not depend on empirical postulates or debatable conventions. For example, I do not know if 756,327 is a prime number. But necessarily it must either be or not be a prime number. If it is a prime number, then to maintain that it is not will somewhere entail a contradiction.

The above (1.3) may be questioned. Why, it may be asked, does the denial of a robust ethical truth entail a contradiction? The basic reason is simple: a robust or strong ethical truth (if there are any) are necessary truths, true in all possible worlds. Possible worlds are based on fundamental laws of logic, specifically the laws of identity and non-contradiction. That is, a world is possible if and only if there are no contradictions in it. Thus, if a strong ethical truth could be denied, there would be a possible world where it fails to be true, and this contradiction rules out its status as a necessary truth.

It should also be noted that not all mathematical and even logical truths are necessary in this sense. Otavio Bueno argues that some are instead contingent, depending upon the axioms and systems that are chosen.[27] When it comes to some high-level mathematical theorizing, he is correct. However, at the most basic level, when dealing with rational numbers and simple arithmetic operations, it seems obvious that there are, indeed, necessary truths. As was just argued, 2 + 2 necessarily equals 4, and we can understand why this is the case. The same is true with countless other mathematical equations.

It will be shown below that like them, ethical truths in the strong sense are also based on the law of non-contradiction, but *indirectly* rather than *directly* so. They may entail contradictions, but in thinking about them, we cannot "see" their full implications and therefore may not see the contradiction that they entail. This will be explained in chapter 5.

---

27. Bueno, "Contingent Abstract Objects," 91–109.

CHAPTER 2

Divisions of Metaethical Theories

MAJOR DIVISIONS

Strong Realism—Platonism and Theism

As has been noted in the "inventory" above, in strong realism, ethical truths exist independently ontologically (Platonism) or else exist dependently in the mind of God (Theism), or possibly are created by God.[1] This position has at times been called *Intuitionism*.[2] Intuitionism is, however, more a term that comes from a description of how strong realist moral truths are *accessible*, than of their ontological status.[3] Strong realist theories have also been called *dualist*, because they hold that there are two kinds of statements—necessarily normative ones, and ones that are merely descriptive in some sense.[4]

---

1. Different defenses of theistic metaethical theories include Adams, *Finite and Infinite Goods*; Baggett and Walls, *Good God*; Evans and O'Neill, "Moral Argument"; Flannagan, "Divine Commands"; Copan and Wolf, "Another Dimension," 123–40; Gamwell, *Divine Good*; Hare, *God's Command*; Henry, *Christian Personal Ethics*; Murphy, *God and Moral Law*; Smith, *In Search*; Baggett and Walls, "Moral Argument"; Owen, *Moral Argument for Christian Theism*; Bales, *Communism and Moral Law*; Beck, *Does God Exist?*; and Linville, Mark D., "Moral Argument," 391–448. Another brief argument is given in Linville, *Is Everything Permitted?* For a classic defense, see Taylor, *Faith*. For a history of the Moral Argument see Baggett and Walls, *Moral Argument History*; and Hare, *God and Morality*. For a different approach see Coppenger, *Moral Apologetics*.

2. Huemer, *Ethical Intuitionism*.

3. Another defense of intuitionism is Audi, *The Good*. Audi is a theist rather than a Platonist.

4. A defense of a non-robustly real form of intuitionism may be found in Kauppinen, "Humean Theory."

Everything Else—Monism

The other division in metaethics is sometimes called *Monism*. Monism holds that there is only one kind of statement in existence—the descriptive or non-necessarily normative kind. In other words, according to monism, there are no necessarily true or false value statements over and above statements of facts.[5]

No one believes in the truth of every purported ethical statement, as there is potentially an infinite number of them and some of them contradict others. Still, a strong realist will believe there is at least one ethical statement that is necessarily true. Because of this, there is a category of ethics that has real existence, given strong realism.

This question is being approached from my own standpoint. There is nothing intrinsically wrong with this; indeed, it is inevitable. It is simply that one must be clear about what one thinks about the matter and must define the meaning of the significant terms used. What will be defended here is strong or robust realism. For me, only this approach will give a "real" ethical system. From this viewpoint strong arguments in its favor will be given. Here are summarized six different ways that metaethics may be approached.

THEORETICAL CATEGORIES OF WHY ETHICS EXISTS—FROM SUBJECTIVE TO OBJECTIVE

To evaluate strong or robust metaethical theories, a few points must first be discussed. Since in strong theories, ethical propositions, at least many of them, are necessarily true, the question of how that can be the case must be discussed. The following is a subjective to objective scale, starting with fully subjective. For example, both 2.1 and 2.2 are forms of antirealism; 2.1 is subjective, while 2.2 is intersubjective, which makes it perhaps somewhat more objective.

(2.1) Antirealism, subjectivism: These theories define values as concepts that are held by some person or group of persons who accept them without any sense that they are necessary. They simply accept them because they think that at some time and place these values would be useful. In this group the purest forms of subjectivism are found. Here values are arbitrary and have no weight other than that

---

5. Huemer, *Ethical Intuitionism*, 7–8.

some people believed in them at some time. Ethically, this is something like the "creation of values," wherein the creation is simply the adoption of these values because of personal preference.

(2.2) Antirealism, intersubjectivism: Ethics exists because some individual (or group of agreeing individuals) live in such a manner that they will inevitably (though not from logical necessity) accept and promote a certain set of ethical values. Here the set of values exists because the code is ingrained in a particular society. Because the values here are simply those that are traditional for a society, there may be a little more objectivity here than in (2.1), but they are ultimately still subjective, though the subjectivity is that of a whole society. This may be called inter-subjectivism.

(2.3) Weak Realism, Naturalism: They exist because they can be *derived from human nature*—from the way that human beings are made and the values that we necessarily have in order to exist and flourish, or simply because it seems that human nature needs to exist in a certain manner. Here we reach a level wherein there is something more objective than those listed above. One might say that because of human nature, all people have the right to live, and any of the necessities that go along with this.

(2.4) Weak Realism, Rationalism: Ethical propositions exist because they can be *derived from the nature of rationality*, and what it is to be a rational being. That is, the very nature of being a rational being imposes ethics on those beings. Here we have reached a level that applies not only to human beings, but to any rational creatures that could exist. For example, it might be argued that because human beings are by nature rational creatures, they need ethics in order to exist as rational beings. Since only rational beings are concerned with ethics, any axiom of thought based on the nature of rationality will concern them and them alone, though of course would not be only about these rational creatures (that it is wrong to torture animals would concern animals, though the non-human animals would, of course, neither know nor understand anything about ethics).

(2.5) Strong Realism, Platonism: Ethics exist necessarily apart from any finite mind. In Platonism, ethics is ontologically independent of anything else. Related to this is Absolute Creationism, wherein God creates ethical abstract entities. At this level, there is maximum strength. Ethical values necessarily exist apart from anything that finite beings like us think or even of which we are aware.

(2.6) Strong Realism, Theistic Conceptualism: On this theistic theory, the axiom would be based on God's nature in some manner. Ethical propositions, though necessarily true,[6] exist necessarily in the mind of God rather than as independent abstract entities. Again, here ethical values have maximum strength.

The Nature of Ethical Values

There are, thus, different theories of the nature of ethical values. Numbers (2.1) through (2.2) are forms of *antirealism*. It will also be argued that (2.3) and (2.4) are forms of *weak realism*, as they are objective, but based on contingent factors in the universe. This leaves number (2.5) and (2.6) as the form of what is here called *strong or robust realism*. It will be argued that there is a fundamental distinction between (2.5) and (2.6) and the others. The distinction is that for (2.5) and (2.6) ethics is *necessary in an absolute sense*, while not so for any of the other theoretical forms. *This is a key to ethics.*

With this in mind, three fundamental kinds of metaethical systems will be discussed—naturalism, reductionism, and rationalism—in their relationships to these theories of realism—antirealism, weak realism, or strong realism.

METAETHICAL SYSTEMS—NATURALISM, RATIONALISM, REDUCTIONISM

Naturalism

Naturalism defined

This section calls for careful distinctions in terms. *Naturalism* is a word that has several different meanings. In a scientific sense, naturalists typically believe that the physical universe is the only concrete thing (or collection of things) in existence. David Armstrong writes about this, "Naturalism I define as the doctrine that reality consists of nothing but a

---

6. This is something of an oversimplification. In some versions of theistic conceptualism, not all ethical propositions are necessarily true.

single all-embracing spatio-temporal system."⁷ Theists on the other hand think that besides the physical universe, there is another being in existence, God, who is not limited to being an object in the spatio-temporal physical universe. (However, due to God's omnipresence he does exist in some sense in the universe, but not as a whole or part of it).

Naturalism, when regarded in ethical theory, or metaethics, refers to the view that ethical truths are dependent for their existence on some aspect of reality that in itself is not ethical. In other words, *ethical propositions are dependent for their existence on non-ethical things.* That these other things are usually conceived of as part of nature means that there is a good deal of overlap between the two definitions of naturalism. However, in this general sense, according to some philosophers, if ethical propositions are considered dependent upon something else for their truth, this view is a form of naturalism, even if it is God, a "supernatural" being, on which the ideas are dependent.⁸ Undoubtedly, this terminology is somewhat confusing.

Naturalist and non-naturalist ethical theories

To make things clear, a distinction will also be made between naturalist and non-naturalist ethical theories. *Naturalist* theories depend upon the nature, that is, the *essential properties* of entities that exist in our universe, such as human beings. Theories that depend upon a supernatural being, usually conceived of as God, will be referred to as *supernaturalist* theories. There can be other theories that are not reducible to nature or God. Some theories are dependent upon the nature of reason itself; these, therefore, can be termed *rationalist*.

Naturalism reduced

For decades, in recent philosophy, there have been attempts to develop naturalist theories of just about everything. As Kelly James Clark writes, "In the last several decades, there has been a flood of work under the

---

7. Armstrong, "Naturalism, Materialism," 261–62, quoted in Goetz, "The Argument," 286.

8. I dislike the term supernatural. However, it will be used here to distinguish between ethical dependence upon some aspect of the natural or physical world, and dependence upon something not part of the natural or physical world. When specifically discussing theories involving God, they will be labeled as theistic theories.

banner of 'Naturalism,' with philosophers applying naturalistic approaches to virtually every area of human inquiry, including epistemology, rationality, jurisprudence, consciousness, ontology, and morality."[9]

What this fundamentally means is that all the terms in Clark's list above, according to naturalism, are to be reduced to the physical aspects of reality. Many naturalists in this sense of the word are also physicalists of one variety or another.[10] What Clark means is that ultimately, everything concrete that exists is physical or composed of physical things; there is no non-physical entity. When the goal proclaimed is to naturalize something, ultimately all the terms are to be defined by physical entities, properties, and processes.[11]

This is a form of reductionism. *Reductionism* has been long and widely argued about in philosophy, but there is no doubt as to its influence.[12] It should be mentioned here that reductionism does not automatically mean that everything can be explained in terms of the most basic parts of which it is composed. For example, biologists study living creatures, who cannot be described merely as a bunch of quarks, even though all living creatures' bodies are composed of quarks and other subatomic particles. Their being and activities cannot be reduced to talking about these particles.

Naturalism in ethics

What does *naturalism in the case of ethics* entail? What it comes down to is that in strict naturalism, ethics is considered completely reducible—*explicable without remainder*—to "natural" entities and properties. Strict naturalists will say that ethical properties are identical with physical properties. Natural entities and properties are those that are studied

---

9. Clark, "Naturalism," 7.

10. Some naturalists are property dualists, and seemingly, an increasing number are panpsychists. By these terms, what is meant is that there are conscious properties in addition to physical ones. However, this still can be a form of naturalism because the conscious aspects are simply part of the natural universe and have nothing to do with God. Panpsychism is the view that all (or many) of the basic components of reality have both physical and conscious properties. Property dualism is similar but may reduce conscious properties just to brains and similar items. On presentations and defense of panpsychism, see Goff, *Galileo's Error*; and Goff, *Consciousness and Fundamental Reality*.

11. Gordon and Dembski, *Nature of Nature*.

12. See for example, Jones, *Reductionism*.

by the natural sciences and are thus physical. This definition may seem to be rather circular, but the natural sciences study nature, and therefore naturalism considers reality to be this physical universe and the things that exist within it. This eliminates any purportedly supernatural beings such as God.

However, it does not necessarily eliminate Platonic abstract entities.[13] Broad naturalists may accept the existence of abstract objects like numbers, but to remain consistent in the realm of ethics, ethical naturalists must reject the existence of abstract moral entities. The natural universe includes things like space, time, energy, and material and biological objects. Different scientific disciplines such as physics, chemistry, geology, astronomy, and biology study these different aspects of reality. In naturalism, both morality and the study of morality are one with the above—like the others, they study one aspect of nature. Also, in naturalism, metaethical properties are held to supervene on natural ones. They may be irreducible physically, but still natural in a broad sense of the word.[14]

Write Owen Flanagan, Hagop Sarkissian, and David Wong about what a naturalistic ethical theory entails,

> Let us call an individual a *scientific naturalist* if she does not permit the invocation of supernatural forces in understanding, explaining, and accounting for what happens in *this* world. An *ethical naturalist* (assuming this person already accepts scientific naturalism) applies the same principled restriction to describing, explaining, recommending, endorsing, prohibiting, and justifying values, norms, actions, principles, and so on. In other words, the complete warrant for any norm or value must be cashed out without invoking the views or commands of a divinity.[15]

Put this way, naturalism in ethics simply seems to be an atheistic ethical theory. However, to quote Ira Gershwin, "It ain't necessarily so." There are some atheists or non-theists who reject naturalistic ethics and accept some form of ethical Platonism. In addition, it is possible for an ethical naturalist to believe in the existence of a god or gods so long as they are part of nature. Ancient pagan religions believed this, as does

---

13. By this what is meant is such entities as numbers, universals (like colors), and propositions. For a full discussion, see chapter 7.
14. Angus Menuge outlined this argument to me.
15. Flanagan et al., "Naturalizing Ethics," 17.

the modern religion of Mormonism.¹⁶ Further, a naturalist in morality might believe in a transcendent God if the naturalist's ethic is not based on this God. In this sense, someone who accepts a naturalist theory of ethics need not be an atheist (though in the current intellectual milieu they probably will be) but only hold that ethics are not directly based on God.[17]

Rationalism

Other theories may be difficult to place in naturalism, even though they make no appeal to God or Platonic abstract objects. Such theories may best be thought of as forms of *rationalism*. These theories appeal to other criteria than what is generally considered best for human beings. Such theories might appeal to things like *contractualism*, where what is ethically right is decided by what rules people agree on. Another example might be Kant's *deontological moral system*, wherein what is right is based on the *categorical imperative*.[18] This imperative is not a Platonic entity, but rather it is based on what Kant thought a rational being would self-legislate.[19] These theories would best be placed as rationalist theories because they ultimately appeal to the nature of rationality, and what they think rational creatures should decide based on their nature as rational creatures.

---

16. On Mormon theology, see for example, Paulsen, "Comparative Coherency." It should be noted that Mormons do not agree on every aspect of their theology.

17. One may believe that God created human beings with a certain nature, and that ethics is based upon that nature, but that we can know and justify ethics apart from God or belief in God.

18. Kant, *Foundations of Metaphysics*.

19. A view of Kant is given by John E. Hare. He writes, "All rational agents are subject to the universal laws which they themselves make, and these laws require them to treat each other as ends in themselves. They thus together comprise a kingdom constituted by these laws. This Kingdom, says Kant, has members and a head. The head is also a member, being a rational agent himself; but he (unlike the others) is an infinite rational agent, being a maker of laws but not himself 'subject' to the will of any other." Here God is a maker of laws. Given this interpretation, Kant's theory might be considered a theistic theory in a way that is often ignored. It would then be a form of strong realism. But I leave it here because it seems for many that Kant's ethics is based on a non-necessary choice.

Reductionism

Naturalism and Rationalism could both be considered to be reductionistic. In *ethical reductionism*, moral statements, when looked at properly, are reducible to non-ethical statements.[20] Reductionism reduces these ethical statements such that there is no remainder. Nothing is left over and above whatever they are being reduced to. Ethically reductive statements are held to be reducible to natural statements—statements about physical objects, properties, or states of affairs. Thus, in the final analysis, some ethical statements are just natural statements. Some theistic philosophers would reduce them to supernatural objects, properties, or states of affairs. Reductionist philosophers think that this analysis is the proper one to give to moral propositions. They are explicable in, and reducible to, statements about some other category of reality than ethics proper.[21]

For example, an ethical action in a *consequentialist* theory is an action that will cause the most happiness or pleasure in the world. In this sense, morality is reducible to that which causes the greatest amount of happiness, to the greatest number, with no remainder. It is nothing over and above that greatest amount of happiness that results from the action. Happiness is not something that is conceptually reducible to the physical objects in the universe, for it is a mental state. Suppose that what is making a person happy is the thought of the profound truth of some statement. The concepts involved in being happy in this instance cannot be reduced without remainder. Profundity is not composed of space or mass or forces, the way that physical things are. However, if one is a physicalist of some sort regarding the mind, then happiness can be ontologically reduced to the physical. This would be the case even though we have no concept of how it could be done. Further, things that make for happiness would all be physical.

To give one simple example of how reduction works, a painting is nothing more than the physical components of which it is composed. Any pictures that one sees in the painting when one looks at it, are supplied by the mind, for in the artistic renderings there are materials which are colored in a certain way and arranged in a definite manner. The viewer supplies the picture, presumably the picture that the painter intended. However, in a very real sense, the painting is nothing more than paint on a canvas.

---

20. An example of this is Jackson, *From Metaphysics to Ethics*.
21. For categories, see the discussion in chapter 4.

To give another example. Take materialist or physicalist theories of the mind. In these theories, the mind is somehow ontologically reduced to the brain (and nervous system and body in general), and also, perhaps, the light rays and sound waves that connect us to the external world.[22] For simplicity's sake, let us say that a mind is reducible without remainder, with nothing left over, to the brain, which is of course a physical object. There is nothing—no kind of stuff or being, or even properties—left over when the mind is thus reducible to the brain.

This reductionism cannot be right; reductionism cannot adequately explain the existence and origins of ethics. These kinds of theories leave out the essence of what it is to be ethical. The *essence* of something is the set of properties without which that thing could not exist. Some of the essential properties of the number seven, for example, are 'oddness' and 'primeness.' These properties are conceptually part of the number seven, whereas Gertrude's favorite number is not.[23]

Where do reductionist theories fit?

Where do reductionist theories like naturalism and rationalism fit into my threefold division of moral theories—into robust realism, weak realism, or antirealism? Naturalist and rationalist ethical systems seem to fit best into weak realism. These ethical systems are supposedly based on *objective features about human beings*, and while they thus avoid the subjectivism of antirealism, at the same time, they are not unconditionally necessary, but at best only conditionally necessary. They are not something that already exists, and thus are discovered by human beings, and hence cannot be considered a form of robust realism.

THE CATEGORICAL NATURE OF ETHICS—THE ESSENCE IS MORALITY

To try to reduce without remainder ethical statements to non-ethical ones by definition leaves out an essential part of ethical statements, which is their *categorical nature*.[24] What is omitted is the "moral" part of the moral statements. It is what makes one say not only that doing X will cause the

---

22. Schulz, *Wednesday's Child*.
23. For a defense of this notion of essentialism, see the discussion in chapter 1.
24. The Categorical Imperative will be discussed in chapter 8.

greatest amount of happiness, but that one *ought* to do X because it will cause the greatest amount of happiness. If "oughtness" is simply reducible to the statement that X will cause the greatest amount of happiness, then the concept that there is an obligation to perform it is lost.

It is true that in some sense moral statements supervene upon non-moral natural ones.[25] Something immoral, like theft, is only possible because there are natural objects that can belong to someone and can be taken without the owner's permission by someone else. If the thing stolen is something like a diamond or some other jewel, what is stolen is very much a natural object, and of course, the person who steals and the person or persons from whom it is stolen are in some sense natural objects. There is also intellectual theft, where ideas are being stolen. Nevertheless, these still only have significance because they have an impact in the world of physical objects.

So, for this to work, it must also be true that not only are physical objects like jewels natural objects, but so are human beings and their mental states. These things are also natural objects in the world, though whether they are entirely physical is debatable. They are natural at least in the sense that they exist in the physical universe, and in some way, interact with the unquestionably physical objects in the universe.

For something to be a theft, for example, there must be the institution of the owning of property. Property ownership is not a physical object like ice cream, or a roller skate. It can only be defined in terms of conscious, intentional agents, who, because they are reasoning creatures living in a society, develop complex systems of rules, such as property rights, in order to function and flourish.

Derek Parfit writes that there are two kinds of naturalist ethical theories—analytic and non-analytic. He writes, "According to *Analytical Naturalists*, all normative claims can be restated in naturalistic terms, and such claims, when they are true, state natural facts. According to *Non-Analytical Naturalists*, though some claims are irreducibly normative, such claims, when they are true, state natural facts."[26] In either case, the basic problem is that natural facts are by themselves, non-normative, and can only be made normative by the addition of some other factor.

---

25. Supervenience basically means, "A set of properties A supervenes upon another set B just in case no two things can differ with respect to A-properties without also differing with respect to their B-properties. In slogan form, 'there cannot be an A-difference without a B-difference.'" McLaughlin, "Supervenience," 1.

26. Parfit, *On What Matters*, vol.2, 10.

An example of one way in which naturalism could work is the following. All human beings wish to be happy. What might make human beings happy differs *significantly* from person to person, but the desire for happiness seems universal. It is true that there are people who do not *seem* to wish to be happy—some may commit suicide, or some may be masochists, for example. However, a person who commits suicide is usually in great pain, physical or emotional or both, and sees no way of escaping the pain except by dying; they seek a less unhappy state. A masochist is actually trying to achieve happiness, though in a perverted sort of way. So, even these situations reflect attempts to be happy.

It is also true that human beings differ on the scope of how much happiness they desire. That is, they might wish for happiness for themselves, or for their family and friends, or perhaps for the entire human race. A narcissist will have quite different desires than a saint will have. However, besides wishing happiness for others, even saints will almost certainly desire happiness for themselves, even if they do not think about it.

This desire for happiness seems to be a part of human nature. Further, those animals with consciousness also seem to seek happiness in whatever way in which they are made, though they probably do not think in such terms. Indeed, it is difficult to imagine sentient beings who do not desire happiness, however they may conceive of it.

Happiness is not the only naturalist ethical starting point. *Flourishing* of a human being, or of society, could be taken as another factor. These states of affairs will usually produce both individual and societal happiness. Here I will simply take happiness as a state of well-being that includes pleasure, but is not simply reducible to pleasure. It includes not only pleasure, and mental and physical well-being, but also flourishing. This would include the possibility that people have the ability and opportunity to engage in many worthwhile pursuits, with attendant rewards. It is, to put it another way, a life that is well lived and enjoyed.

The basic problem here in both cases (individual and social) is that there is no conceptual link between happiness and normativity—between the desire to be happy and "oughtness." That is, the fact that happiness is what most people or everyone desires does not entail that therefore there is an *obligation* to try to be happy, let alone that one should help other people to be happy. A basic problem here is that ontological reduction seems necessarily to involve the concept of necessity itself. To make matters more complex, there are several *different kinds of necessity*.

If reduction involves necessary relationships between concepts, then we need an examination[27] of what kind of necessity is relevant. Not all kinds of necessity are pertinent to the problem. What is needed is what is sometimes called a broadly logical or absolute necessity, which is a necessity in all possible worlds.[28]

For purely natural objects, all that is required for reduction is the physical parts of which they are composed. For manmade objects like a chair, there is also the intention of the people creating the object. This conscious intentionality is existentially required for normative statements, which will be argued below.

Naturalist theories start with the *nature of human beings*, and our desire to flourish, for example. So also, *rationalist* theories start with the *nature of rational creatures*. There is therefore an overlap between naturalist and rationalist theories. Indeed, in a way they are similar because ethics becomes *reductive* in at least some sense.

It should also be noted that there is a moral system that is somewhat based on human nature, but which is not atheistic, and classically often has been theistic. This is the *natural law theory*, wherein what is right is based on following human nature. Historically, this has been an extremely important moral theory. It can be traced at least as far back as Aristotle and it was a major component in Western thought right up to the nineteenth century, when, at least partly due to Darwinism,[29] it was displaced. It was a major intellectual force in the founding and growth of the United States, among other things. Though natural law theory lost a lot of influence with the coming of Darwinism, it may be making something of a comeback.[30]

Therefore, it seems that a totally reductionist view of ethics, by its very nature, leaves out the very essence of what it is to be ethical. It leaves out the *oughts* and *shoulds* that set apart ethical statements from others. At least it does not give an adequate explanation for these moral imperatives. This will be discussed in more detail in chapter 6.

---

27. This will be discussed in chapter 5.

28. On this concept of necessity as pertaining to all possible worlds, see Plantinga, *Nature of Necessity*; and Hale, *Necessary Beings*.

29. Regarding this history and its far-reaching ramifications, see West, *Darwin Day*.

30. For studies of natural law ethics, see Angier, *Natural Law Ethics*; and Budziszewski, *Written on the Heart*.

CHAPTER 3

Relevant Issues

BEFORE GOING ON TO the main metaethical positions, it will be useful to clarify some of the relevant issues.

HUMAN (AND OTHER) NATURE

Human beings are the kinds of things to which ethics directly relate. So are angels, Klingons, Hobbits, and other kinds of rational entities, were they to exist. Yet human beings and angels have very different natures. Why would ethics be relevant to both? If one does not want to include angels in the discussion, one can easily imagine other possible creatures to whom ethics would be directly relevant. Suppose that there were a race of sentient mushroom-like creatures who reproduced by spores rather than sexually.[1] This would be strange but does not seem to be beyond the realm of possibilities. These beings would be very different creatures than we are in some ways, but they would be both rational and highly intelligent. How would having a different nature affect the relationship of ethical truths to these creatures, and how and why would it be different from the one that human beings have? For example, it seems that mushrooms, because of their sporish nature, would not have any ethics regarding sex. If such creatures could exist, then any ethical laws that apply to human beings, such as the wrongness of rape or adultery for example, would be irrelevant, because of the nature of these beings. Other ethical principles would have to apply to them regarding such matters as reproduction.

---

1. Obviously, these creatures would also have to have some animal characteristics, such as having muscles.

To get to the crucial point: human beings are creatures with a specific, though somewhat flexible, nature. There metaethical theory known as *natural law* has been very important, including in the history of the United States. This theory has fallen on hard times of late. For one thing, the idea that there are fixed natures, at least among living creatures, is no longer widely held to since the advent of Darwinism. Nevertheless, it hardly seems possible to get rid of natural law entirely, and yet still hold on to a plausible ethical theory. Ethics only applies to rational beings of the kind that human beings are (at least usually are). Ethics, considered as a demand on beings to act in a certain specified manner, does not apply to other animals, plants, or any non-living objects. To be subject to ethical statements, it is necessary that one have moral understanding—that one can recognize what ethical statements are, and what are the demands that they make on rational beings. Of course, there is more to human nature than just being rational. We exist as beings who live, eat, reproduce, and do countless other things according to the way we are made. But because of what we are, we cannot choose to reproduce by spores or eat concrete for nourishment.

Other, even stranger creatures are easily imaginable. Suppose that there were a race of rational insects, where at some point in their life cycle the females decapitated and ate the males of the race, such as is the case with praying mantises. That such creatures could exist is at least imaginable. What would this do with the ethical principles that murder is wrong?

Alternatively, how about a race made of sentient beings where the females, after giving birth to several offspring, then immediately died? In that case, to perpetuate the race would involve a sort of murder. If one reads enough science fiction or fantasy, or has a good enough imagination, one can think of all sorts of odd, alien, but quite rational, races of beings—rational in the sense that they can use reason, language, are self-aware, and have all the hallmarks of rationality. Again, sentient races like these are imaginable, even if they are not possible, for biological or theological reasons.

The basic point being made here is that human beings, as well as any other possible sentient species, have a nature. We can do certain things, not do certain other things, desire certain things, and dislike certain things, though at the same time, many of the abilities and desires and dislikes differ from individual to individual. That there is a wide difference in human beings is itself a part of human nature. Still, almost everyone enjoys various pleasures, and hates a variety of pains. The few individuals who do not are abnormal and malfunctioning.

What things we enjoy largely depend upon our nature. Further, what seems right also depends to a certain extent upon our nature. For example, monogamy is clearly preferable to polygamy, if for no other reason than the fact that the number of males and females is roughly equal. Polygamy, on the other hand, has historically resulted in rich and powerful men taking many wives, leaving poor men without a chance to be married, frustrating their nature, and leading to anti-social behavior.[2] Therefore, rationally, monogamy is preferable.

Of course, this line of reasoning may be questioned; these days almost everything is being challenged. Nonetheless, it seems obvious that what morality human beings accept depends largely upon their culture. Also, of course, much of what we do with our time hinges on our culture. If one had been born British, then one might have appreciated the game of cricket. We all like or dislike certain foods, clothes, games, jokes, styles of social interaction, religion, and much else, depending largely upon the culture in which we were brought up. Again, human nature is flexible enough that it allows for wide differences in cultural expression, much more so than in animals. But the morality a culture accepts may be very different from "real morality," assuming it exists.

Humans, by our very nature, are flexible enough to develop variations in culture. Animals, on the other hand, act largely according to instinct. If they have different cultures in the wild, the differences between them are very small compared to the differences in human cultures. Those creatures that live with us, like pet cats and dogs, do act quite differently from those in the wild, but that is obviously because of their interactions with humans. In the West, dogs are thought to be loyal and loving pets, and act like such in our families. We often consider them family members. In the Middle East and other lands, in contrast, dogs are often considered filthy scavengers and are vicious. They act differently because they have been treated differently, but the reason that they do so is because they are possessed of a certain nature.

One may think that other sentient races of beings would also need to have a large amount of this flexibility. A race of beings, however intelligent, that did not have flexibility in creating culture, would never rise above the level of their inbuilt character. Cultures depend much upon

---

2. Tucker, *Marriage and Civilization*.

creativity, and it seems obvious that creatures without creativity would never progress much. Therefore, a certain amount of creativity and flexibility would have to be "built into" any race of sentient beings capable of developing a civilization.

Having said that, there could be a large variance in the natures of species of sentient beings. The Mushroom race mentioned above, which reproduced by means of spores, probably would not have the institution of marriage, nor have any of the complex social behavior associated with human sexuality. A species of sentient insects (not the head biting ones) that all lived communally together with different castes (like ants and termites), and who reproduced via one or several queens as ants and termites do, might not have the concept of private property, or much in the way of individual freedom, at least for the lower castes. A species where females outnumbered males by five to one might take polygamy for granted. And so on. The point here is that all sorts of different sentient species seem to be possible, and if they were to exist, they could have natures that would be in some ways very different from ours.

In describing ethics for human beings, significant notice of the way that human beings actually *are* should be taken. This has been challenged historically by what can be called the "Blank Slate" view of human nature. Promulgated by John Locke and many others through the last few centuries, this is the view that the minds of human beings at birth are blank slates, upon which almost anything may be written. The *Blank Slate* has been very influential in the history of the twentieth century, as all sorts of visionaries were sure that they could cure human ills by educating and conditioning people in a manner that they, the visionaries, considered rational. It was thought that this would produce the perfect society, or at least one far better than the ones that human beings have created so far. For this to be possible depends upon the notion of the blank slate.[3]

It is not unfair to say that this project of utopia has been, overall, a miserable failure. Indeed, even the fact that there are those who accept the idea that human beings are blank slates upon which almost anything can be written implies that human beings do have a nature—in this case, according to their views, a blank slate nature. The fact is that human beings *do* indeed have a nature, and whether anyone likes it or not, this nature consists of considerably more than just a blank slate upon which reformers and revolutionaries can make what they want, and the truth is

---

3. Pinker, *Blank Slate*.

that attempts to circumvent this obvious fact have caused a great deal of damage to the world.[4]

Human nature does unquestionably have an important role to play. We are rational beings. We have this rationality as an essence, and it is therefore unchosen. We cannot opt, for example, to be the kind of creature that does not have the ability to choose. We have no choice but to be that kind of being. It is not just rationality, however, that describes our essential nature. As was discussed earlier, one can imagine rational creatures who are otherwise quite different from us. We are material beings, divided into two sexes, omnivorous, with all the feeling and emotions that human beings possess, having senses of sight, hearing, taste, touch, and smell, but not radar or sonar, or other conceivable modes of perception.

Human beings do not choose their fundamental nature, the same as everything else. Even God could not have chosen to be other than what he essentially is, like choosing to be a beach bum. Selecting our essential nature is something that is beyond our control. The important point here is that having a specific nature that is beyond our control limits our *autonomy*. We can, granting that some version of free will is true, choose within limited bounds. To this extent, existential philosophy which denies that we have a nature is in error.[5] We *do* have a nature and understanding that nature is an important part of ethical theory.

AUTONOMY

So, what does *autonomy* therefore mean? It means that, given that human beings have some form of *free will*, we can choose within bounds—bounds that are not set by us, but by whatever or whoever created us. However, even this does not guarantee a viable conception of autonomy.

Today, many philosophers are physicalists of one kind or another. *Physicalists* believe that all human beings (and other animals) are entirely composed of *matter*. Matter acts in accordance with the laws of physics. Therefore, if human beings are entirely composed of matter, no matter how intricately arranged, their behavior is governed by the laws of

---

4. Marxism has been the main driver of utopian ideas. As Leszek Kolakowski writes, "Marxism has been the greatest fantasy of our century." Kolakowski, *Main Currents of Marxism*, 1206. For an examination of the consequences of Marxism, see Rosefielde, *Red Holocaust*.

5. See Molnar, *Sartre*.

physics. One might object that there is much more to it than that, that the behavior of human beings is also guided by thought. However, as strange as it may sound, given physicalism, the mentality of human beings is completely reducible without remainder to matter, and hence is ultimately subject to the laws of physics.

Some try to avoid this by adopting a form of non-reductive physicalism. I have argued at length that this also does not work, though that argument will not be presented here.[6]

The laws of physics are not amenable to free will.[7] Hard determinism is the view that human choices are caused by external events over which we have no real control. This is true regardless of whether the laws are deterministic or only probabilistic. Given hard determinism, human beings can have no freer will than a can opener does. They are simply much more complicated than can openers, and for some reason (which is very difficult to explain with materialism, in my opinion), also have consciousness. Still, given hard determinism, human beings are no more than automatons—machines that are made of meat and bone rather than metal and plastic.

With all of this, it seems that if we are truly automatons, any concept of autonomy or self-determination would be an illusion. We may think that we truly make decisions. It may feel like we are making decisions. But, in fact, all of the real work is being done at the level of physics, chemistry, and biology. Granted, given that we are complex organisms, things are much more intricate than just the laws of physics themselves, at their most fundamental level, being responsible for our behavior.

For example, iron atoms have a certain set of properties. An iron atom by itself will not move around in circles. However, if there are very many iron atoms, and they are formed in the shape of a wheel, they will, if rolling downhill, move around in circles. So, when the basic components are put together in more complex patterns or constructions, behavior may happen that is not caused by the properties of any of the individual atoms of which the patterns or objects themselves are composed.

---

6. Parrish, *Knower and the Known*, 47–53.

7. One could argue that there is free will in quantum physics, where it seems that most scientists believe that there is genuine indeterminism in the activity of sub-atomic particles. However, even if this be true, the indeterminate behavior of quarks, for example, is basically randomness within limits. Free will should not be thought of as essentially random.

Similarly, some have argued that because humans' brains are complex objects, it is not the basic laws of physics that cause our behavior. Rather, our mental life supervenes upon the complex brain instead. Thus, some allege, given materialism or physicalism, the behavior of human beings is not just "dictated" by the laws of physics, but is even partially dependent upon other things, such as choice.

One may grant all of this, but it does not change the fundamental issue at hand. Just as a wheel made of iron may act differently than an individual iron atom, or just an undifferentiated mass of iron atoms, the fact that it will roll downhill is dictated by the laws of physics. When these laws are applied to a mass of iron atoms shaped in the form of a wheel, the form of the group is the reason why the wheel rolls downhill rather than just sitting there.

So, it seems that there is no escape from hard determinism for the physicalist. My point here is not to argue against either materialism or hard determinism, but to instead point out that if these theories of reality were true, then we would have no genuine autonomy. In effect, we would merely be machines, which *unaccountably* have consciousness and the feeling that we are making choices based on beliefs and desires. For physicalists, chemicals in the brain are pulling the strings.[8]

Some philosophers reject theism partly because theism supposedly interferes with their autonomy.[9] Yet, many non-theists are physicalists of one variety or another, and in view of the above argument, they cannot have autonomy anyway. The discussion on free will seems like a good place to point this out.

In fact, there is a deeper problem than this. For if there is no autonomy in any sense, and we really are just machines made from meat and bone, it is difficult to see how there could even be any ethics at all which are relevant to human beings. A car's transmission is amoral, and can do nothing wrong (even though it might aggravatingly appear to have it in for us sometimes), because everything that it does is dictated by its nature and the environment it exists in. If human beings are machines, then it seems we have no more control over our actions than a transmission does over the car's movements.

---

8. Angus Menuge pointed out in a private conversation that this is echoed in Wegner, *The Illusion of Conscious Will*, wherein we preview actions our brains make us do. For a partial rebuttal, see Egnor and O'Leary, *Immortal Mind*.

9. See the discussion in Pojman, *Ethics*, 242–43.

It will be protested that human beings are conscious, and therefore very different than car transmissions. While this is certainly true, given physicalist theories of the mind, it is difficult to see how consciousness as such has any role in causing or affecting our behavior. This is because in physicalism, joined with the causal closure of the physical, consciousness is epiphenomenal, and does no useful work. This being the case, then we and our consciousnesses are irrelevant, and we really are just machines. Which means we are not autonomous, but rather are automatons. Further, if consciousness is epiphenomenal, then there is no reason to think that our thoughts have anything to do with reality, as what we think is irrelevant to what we do. There is a deep problem with physicalism here, as it has no adequate account for the nature of the mind.[10]

LIMITS ON HUMAN NATURE

We have seen that our response to ethical issues depends upon our nature, and that our essential nature is not something that we can control. How does this affect what we can believe about our ethical choices? What can we choose, and what is beyond our capacity to choose, even given the limits placed upon us by our nature?

That there are limits can easily be seen. Some *tastes* are acquired. For some people, coffee is an acquired taste. When they first drank it, they did not like it, but persevered, and after a certain amount of time grew to enjoy it. Some things that are liked may be enjoyable the first time that they are tried by a person, and yet there may be other things which some people will never learn to enjoy, no matter how much they try, even though some other people seem to enjoy those things from their first experience. Besides human nature, every human being has an individual nature which forms the basis of much of what he or she likes or dislikes.

However, there are certain likes and dislikes which are in-built in us which cannot be changed. To take the major example, pain seems to be, by its very nature, something that we dislike, and the more pain that there is, the more we dislike it.

For most people, pain is something bad. This badness is built into pain. It is something that by its nature is uncomfortable and we dislike and do not want. In some odd cases, this may be overridden by other

---

10. Parrish, *Knower and the Known*.

factors, but still, it seems that pain is intrinsically, by its nature, something *bad*. We cannot just choose to like pain, or to hate pleasure.

Pleasure is the opposite of pain. By definition, a feeling of pleasure is something we like. We are made to want pleasure—it is in our nature. What gives us pleasure may differ to a certain extent from individual to individual, but nonetheless, pleasure is something that we like and therefore is considered a *good*. Again, these likes and dislikes may occasionally be overridden by other factors—one may feel great guilt for some pleasure for example—but pleasure is, by its nature, something that we enjoy.

Pleasure and pain may be considered primitive terms; they cannot be broken down into something else more basic than they themselves are. However, though both pleasure and pain have many different aspects, and come in many different forms, there is still a common denominator to both that cannot be further reduced.

Many things cannot be reduced to something more basic without their losing their essential natures and thus cease to be themselves. In another work, for example, it was argued that philosophers cannot reduce phenomenal consciousness to the physical without losing their essential properties, despite the widespread acceptance of physicalism today. Similarly, ethical statements cannot be reduced to any other aspect of reality without losing themselves, so to speak. *Morality is, in this sense, a primitive term, even though ontologically, the truth about ethical statements is dependent upon something else.* Moral statements, dependent on other things for their existence and truth, are in a unique ontological category of being.

REASON AND RATIONALITY

Philosophers often appeal to reason.[11] Indeed, that is what philosophers primarily do. A closely related term to *reason* is the term *reasonable*. Being reasonable is considered a virtue. Being unreasonable is a vice. A lot of our behavior is ethically subject to the concept of whether it is reasonable or not. *Reasonable* has much to do with reason, but it is not the same thing.

Ethicists sometimes put forth principles such as, "That which is ethical is what no one can reasonably refuse to do." Ethics is something

---

11. Related to reason is science. For a critique of theories that attempt to base ethics on science, see Hunter and Nedelisky, *Science and the Good*.

that can make a reasonable claim on us. However, is there an objective way to define what reasonable is in regard to ethics? Here are several formulations of the *dependence of ethics on reasonability*. Several of these are listed here to show the comparison. They are:

- *The Kantian Contractualist Formula*: Everyone ought to follow the principles whose universal acceptance everyone *could rationally will*.[12]

- *Kantian Rule Consequentialism*: Everyone ought to follow the principles that are optimific, because these are the only principles that everyone *could rationally will* to be universal laws.[13]

- *Formula*: It is wrong for us to act on some maxim unless *everyone could rationally* consider it to be true, because they believe that such acts are morally permitted.[14]

There are many others. So, what is it to be rational and reasonable? At a minimum, the law of non-contradiction and other laws of logic must not be violated.[15] This is true but does not give us many specifics in the case of ethical behavior. One might think that it is perfectly right to torture innocent people for fun, simply because one enjoys hearing them scream.[16] There seems to be no law of logic that is violated by such a belief, morally horrible and reprehensible though it unquestionably is.

Looser definitions of what it is to be rational and reasonable can help. One can argue that it is irrational to act in a way against one's own best interest. For example, suppose that a man desires a certain career, and the only way to obtain that career is to go to college and do well there, and that the man believes that this is the best way for him to have a happy life. Indeed, if he does not manage to accomplish this, he knows that he is almost certainly destined for a career in a field in which he

12. See Parfit, *What Matters*, 20.
13. Parfit, *What Matters*, 23.
14. For Scanlon's own work, see Scanlon, *What We Owe*.
15. There are a few philosophers who deny the absoluteness of the law of non-contradiction. About them Jason Waller writes, "While 'para-consistent logics' exist, which can admit contradictions without exploding, these are very weak systems that can prove very little because they need such weak rules of inference to avoid exploding." Waller, *Cosmological Fine-Tuning*, 22. For a detailed examination of the laws of logic, see Meixner, *Ontic Modalities*.
16. Although I put in "innocent people," to make the case stronger, it is wrong to torture *anyone* or *anything* for fun. Indeed, it is controversial whether torture is *ever* justified.

has no interest, and which pays a great deal less. In this case, it would be irrational for him to goof off and party during college, not get good grades, or even flunk out, because this would be against his own long-term self-interest.

Going back to the original question, what would count as being rational in the ethical sense as stated, for example, by the Kantian Contractualist Formula, Scanlon's Formula, or the Kantian Rule Consequentialism standard? All three of these formulas make an appeal to being rational or reasonable, and what everyone *could rationally will*. What do these formulas mean, and what specifically is meant by rational?

The problem begins with the premise that everyone ought to follow principles that, for example, *everyone could rationally will*. Why are there such principles, and why could everyone also rationally support them? In addition, even if everyone could rationally will them in some broad sense of the word, could we, would we, expect that everyone does so?

Take an ethical rule that was already mentioned and which most individuals would consider to be reasonable—that no one should torture innocent people for fun. What about this rule makes it reasonable or rational, and why would everyone wish it to be a universal law? Or why is it a principle to which no one could reasonably object?

What is being said here is that *there must be some standard of normativity* by which we can judge things rationally or not. *Rationality, above all things, cannot be arbitrary*—there must be some sort of *rational standard* by which things can be judged rational or not. So, *what standard is to be used in ethical statements?* Further, what kind of rationality is ultimately applicable to ethics, and how will it relate to other kinds of standards of rationality?

Criterion for Rationality

First—the laws of logic

The first and most basic criterion regarding rationality is *the laws of logic*, especially identity and non-contradiction. Simply stated, *something is irrational if it entails a contradiction*. Nothing contradictory can exist. Examples are easy to come by. It cannot be raining and not raining, if raining is precisely defined, at the same time, place and in the same manner. For the situation to be raining or not raining one may substitute just about any other example, as long as one has *A* and ~*A* (not A). This most fundamental standard of rationality is rock bottom.[17]

Second—rational beings

The most plausible candidate for this narrower criterion of what is rational in the case of ethics seems to be related to those beings that are concerned with ethics in the first place—*rational beings*, such as human beings. So, the most plausible criteria for the rationality of the ethical principles to which Kant, Parfit, Scanlon and many others refer, is the nature of human beings' capability of using reason.[18]

Although the nature of human beings necessarily includes rationality, it is of course much broader than that. This second level of rationality is related with being in accord with the nature of the creatures involved—how they are made. Therefore, there is a limit to what these creatures could value, in the sense that nothing could contradict being rational in the broad sense of the word, but quite different in other respects.

Since this is a philosophy book, we can make up pretty much anything we want, as long as it has some sort of consistency. We can conceive of creatures that, although being rational in the sense of not offending logical consistency, would have very different notions of rationality in ethical concerns than countless other creatures might. This is because the nature of these alternative creatures is different from our nature. What is rational in this second sense of the word is that which conforms to the nature of the beings involved.

Third—culture

There is still another third level of rationality. This is not in accordance with the creature's nature as such but has to do with *culture*. It is an obvious fact that although there is a generic human nature, there is a wide latitude in how this nature may be expressed.

We in modern Western society generally think that war is awful and should be a last resort. Other cultures, such as the Spartans, Vikings, and Mongols living in the ancient world or during the Middle Ages, thought differently. We tend to think that men and women are equal, with equal

---

17. See chapter 3, footnote 15.
18. See for example Parfit, *What Matters*, 111–29.

rights. This has not been the case for many, if not most, other cultures that have existed around the world over time. For example, in Muslim culture law, a man may have as many as four wives at once and may beat them if they are disobedient, or even if he only suspects disobedience.[19]

We think that burning widows (or anyone else) alive is abhorrent, but some Hindus for many centuries thought that Sati, widow burning, was a sign of love, devotion, and piety. Widows that refused to be burned alive were looked down upon, ostracized, and subjected to various restrictions and prohibitions. This contrasts greatly with the biblical command to take care of widows and orphans. The difference could hardly be starker.[20]

Why do cultures differ so much from each other? There are of course many reasons, but one very important one is the different *worldviews* that people accept. Worldviews that have been accepted by people over the centuries are often wildly divergent from the worldviews which are accepted at the present. Some are theistic, some are naturalistic, and some are pantheistic, to mention only one important difference between them.

If one thinks that sacrifice of newborn babies is pleasing to the gods, one will have a very different value structure from one who believes that God thinks that such a thing is an abomination. If one thinks that marriage is ordained by God, one will probably have a different attitude towards divorce than if one thinks that marriage is simply a human institution that people came up with to arrange society. Neither may think that divorce is generally a good thing. However, the person who thinks that marriage is ordained by God may think that divorce should be less readily available, if available at all, than the person who thinks marriage is not sacred and is just a convenient way to order some relations and raise children.

The point is that what people believe as to the nature of reality, and of the place of human beings in it, will, within the bounds established by human nature, be largely dictated by what form of culture will be created and sustained. The opposite is also true: the form of any particular culture will be a part of what worldview *is believed.*

To make the point here sharply, the reason that the Aztecs attacked other tribes, took captives, and then cut out their hearts was to feed the sun god. We think such a belief system is maximally bizarre and

---

19. The Qur'an 4:34, Spencer, *Critical Qur'an*, 70.
20. Narasimhan, *Sati*.

odious—but the reason that we believe this is that we have very different ideas from those of the Aztecs as to what reality is and the place of human beings in it.

Fourth—the individual

Below culture, there is another level of what can be considered to be rational standards. This has to do with the *individual*. Individual human beings vary greatly amongst themselves. How much of this is inborn and how much of it is environmental is something that we do not know and may never know. Be that as it may, individuals differ in a myriad of ways. Hence, something may seem rational to some persons, while seeming quite irrational to others.

What standards should be used?

This being the case, it appears that those standards which *everyone* thinks are rational may in fact be few and far between. *So, what standard should be used in deciding the rationality of some moral principles?* The standard cannot be simple logical consistency, because that would allow any ethical standards, no matter how abhorrent, so long as there was no contradiction. All things rational fall under the fundamental laws of logic. The realm of rational consistency therefore is all of reality. However, while its application is wide, the judgements that it makes are narrow. Therefore, the standard of rationality must be from some other criterion than simple logical consistency.

This can be demonstrated easily with some simple illustrations. For example, a man might be able to will without contradiction that he would capture, kill, cook, and eat any neighborhood children if he is certain that he would not be caught. This is, of course, morally horrific, but there seems to be no problem as such with the law of non-contradiction—nothing directly contradictory is being asserted. It is not like basic mathematics. Everyone can and should rationally accept the principle that two plus two equals four, or that six is not a prime number, while seven is. The truth of these concepts necessarily follows from the nature of the notions involved and the law of non-contradiction. However, since the denial of ethical principles does not normally violate the law of non-contradiction, all sorts of horrible things could be considered acceptable.

Simply put, logic is about *the relations of ideas to each other*. By itself, logic has no content, being purely formal. So, if we take Modus Ponens for example, we have If $P \supset Q$, and P, then we also have Q. This is a necessary truth. However, what P and Q are does not come from logic; their meaning must be supplied from somewhere else. So, the first criterion, that of logical consistency and coherence, is too broad to give us what we need. Of course, this does not mean that the laws of logic are irrelevant; it just means that for our purposes they are *insufficient*.

MOTIVATION

Let's investigate what affects our reasoning and conclusions and look at the concepts of internalism and externalism.

Internalism and Externalism

Internalism is defined as *the theory about the relation between human beings and ethics* that, as Mark van Roojen writes,

> . . . are necessary connections between moral judgments or truths, on the one hand, and reasons and/or motives, on the other. For example, an internalist about the relationship between moral judgments and motivation might think that such judgments necessarily motivate those who accept them. Also, similar views about the relation between reasons and motives.[21]

Therefore, *in internalism, moral truths, when understood, necessarily are motivating people to accept them.*

In contrast, *externalism* is the view wherein, as van Roojen also writes,

> Someone could deny that moral judgments have any *necessary* or *conceptual* connection to reasons and motives for acting and give some other explanation of the sense in which ethics is practical. These people would not be internalists; they'd be *externalists*, as we label those who deny internalism.[22]

Hence, let it suffice to say that *internalism* necessarily *involves the effect of moral propositions on people*, individually or collectively, and their

---

21. van Roojen, *Metaethics*, 294.
22. van Roojen, 54–55.

thoughts about ethics, while externalism does not. Internalism is allied to the view that *ethics depends upon human beings and their inclinations.*

Internalism is, as was explained above, the view that morality only makes sense in the fact that it includes the *motivation* of the individual.[23] That is, ethical propositions are statements that are inherently or necessarily motivating to the individuals who grasp them. This view has the advantage of explaining, in some way, the fact that ethical statements do seem to motivate people to act in certain manners. A moral individual, for example, will be motivated by the sight of someone being tortured to stop the torture, or at the very least not to take part in it. By being the correct sort of human being or rational creature, this kind of response should automatically take place under normal circumstances. An example of this is the outrage expressed by many people to the school tragedy in Uvalde, Texas, where hundreds of police on site did nothing for over an hour while children were dying at the hands of an active shooter.

So, is ethics intrinsically motivating or not? It depends upon what is meant. If it means that ethical truths ought to be motivating to persons with the ability to understand their nature and in the correct situation, then ethics is intrinsically motivating.

Motivation examined

What we ordinarily mean by motivating something is simple enough in concept and is something that we all experience frequently in ordinary life. In essence, it is the one thing X (fact, object, idea or possibly something else) that gives a subject S a reason for doing some action Y. For example, the fact that one is hungry gives one motivation, a reason, for going into the kitchen to get something to eat. This basic fact is simple enough, and countless other examples could be put forth, but in essence the idea is quite simple.

What makes moral motivation different from other motivations? That is the fundamental question. The real reason is the *categorical imperative*, the idea that one has *a moral duty* to perform some act. This is the heart of the concept: a truly rational creature would understand and agree with the concept of a purely moral obligation, and being moral and rational, would be motivated to fulfill it. In that sense, a categorical

---

23. See Hume, *Enquiry Concerning Morals*. For a critique of Hume, see Anderson, *Hume*, 22–25.

imperative has inescapable authority: we see by reason that we are "under" the law, making our inclinations and wants morally irrelevant.

This is quite different from other motivations, as it is the difference between *categorical imperatives* and *hypothetical imperatives*. If one recognizes the existence of categorical imperatives, and acknowledges the necessity of obeying them, then he or she will obey. Some of these imperatives may be very deeply rooted in human nature. Nonetheless, given weak realism, as we shall see, simply because ethical propositions are not logically necessary (not true in all possible worlds), they therefore can never be absolute or *categorical imperatives*. So, though people who hold to a weak realist theory of ethics may feel obligated to do something, in the end they do it for another reason. Hence, their feelings of obligation and morality are based on an amoral choice that logically is not necessarily motivating, though psychologically it may be. It may *seem* to the rational individual that morality is an obligation, though logically, in weak realism, it is not actually necessary.

Lastly, for theists, whose *categorical imperatives* are genuinely tied to God, ethics is both intrinsically motivating and external. Intrinsically, because for theists obedience to God is a major motivating factor, and externally because the ultimate motivation comes from God. For theists, the whole debate between *intrinsic or extrinsic motivation* is not much of an issue. This will be further discussed as we delve deeper into weak realism in chapter 7.

CHAPTER 4

Categories, the Nature of Ethics, and Beauty

CATEGORIES

Much of my argumentation in the notion of ethics is that ethical truths (among other things) are in an *irreducible category of existence*. First, what is a category in philosophy? Writes Jack Meiland about this point, "[A]n ultimate class. Categories are the highest genera of entities in the world. They may contain species but are not themselves species of any higher genera.... If a set of categories is complete, then each entity in the world will belong to a category and no entity will belong to more than one category."[1] Though there is much truth in this quotation, the situation is more complex than what is stated.

There have been several attempts by philosophers to give a complete list of categories to represent reality. Prominent among them are Aristotle and Kant. One thing that is interesting, however, is that the lists are quite different from each other. They are not all describing the same level of things.

- Aristotle's list

  » Substance (primary), Substance (secondary), Quantity, Quality, Relation, Where, Position, When, Having, Doing, Being affected[2]

---

1. Meiland, "Category," 108.
2. Aristotle, *Works of Aristotle*, 7–37.

- Kant's list

  » Quantity, Unity, Plurality, Quality, Reality, Negation, Relation, Inherence and Subsistence, Causality and Dependence, Modality, Possibility, Existence[3]

Other philosophers have made lists of categories that differed from Aristotle and Kant. One of my teachers, Lawrence Powers, gave the following list when discussing Aristotle's list.

- Lawrence Powers's List

  » Bodies, Minds, God, Universal, Space, Time[4]

Indeed, so different are the lists that it seems that they are about different things. More recently, philosophers have given other lists of categories, such as E.J. Lowe, with four categories.[5]

My conclusion is that reality may legitimately be divided up in many ways. Some may be better than others—more comprehensive, clearer, less redundant, and so on. Nevertheless, the basic point stands: reality may be legitimately divided in many ways. For example, assume that God exists. Could reality be divided into only two ultimate categories–God and everything else? Alternatively, could the categories not be abstract objects and concrete objects? How about consciousness entities and non-conscious entities? Or a distinction between real entities and fictional ones, that is, ones that have existence only as a thought? Each of these seems a legitimate way of dividing reality, though these lists may not include in them everything that exists.

The point here is that there are many legitimate ways to divide reality into categories. Having clarified this, *ethical truths will be defined as a category of reality*. For this, the theory of categories developed by the Dutch philosopher Herman Dooyeweerd is helpful. Instead of categories, he calls them modal aspects, which are irreducible to one another. In this section, the terms *categories* and *modal aspects* or *spheres* are interchangeable. By doing this, it is not being assumed that Dooyeweerd's theory is ultimately correct. Rather, in at least a limited context, it is both

---

3. Kant, *Critique of Pure Reason*, 113.

4. Powers, *Non-Contradiction*, 39:76. I should note that though Powers lists God, he adds "if any." In fact, Powers was a militant atheist and put God in only to cover all the bases, so to speak.

5. The categories are substantial particulars, non-substantial particulars, substantial universals, and non-substantial universals.

legitimate and useful. The Ethical aspect is the next to last in the list below and is in bold.

- Dooyeweerd's list
    » Quantitative aspect, Spatial aspect, Kinematic aspect, Physical aspect, Biotic/Organic aspect, Sensitive/Psychic aspect, Analytical aspect, Formative aspect, Lingual aspect, Social aspect, Economic aspect, Aesthetic aspect, Juridical aspect, *Ethical aspect*, Pistic aspect. [6]

As can be seen, the list starts with the most basic aspects of reality and then moves to higher ones. It is not necessary to accept the whole list as given. One may have a different list of the aspects into which reality may be divided. *For my purposes all that is needed here is to show that there are aspects of existence, which include the ethical and the aesthetic, that are irreducible to anything else, though they can be included in other, more fundamental categories.*

Granting that reality is, in some sense, composed of irreducibly different yet necessarily interlocking aspects, what does this show about the nature of ethics and ethical statements? How then can the argument for strong realism be understood given the above discussion? Consider the proposition which states that ethics is a mode or aspect of reality that is understandable and irreducible.

THE NATURE OF ETHICS

Ethics is not reducible

Any attempts to reduce ethics to some other aspect of being seems to fail based on the nature of the concepts that are involved. Aesthetics seems to be the other aspect of being that is most like ethics, as they are both concerned with normativity, and both involve value. Yet aesthetics is distinguishable from ethics, as they have different subject matters, the former's subject matter is *beauty*, and the latter's subject matter is the *good*. Although the good may be beautiful, and to be beautiful is a good, they

---

6. Dooyeweerd, *New Critique*. Adapted from Vol. 2; 3–413. An interesting question is how information fits in with the different categories. I would have to say that information is somehow adapted to use in the different categories seeing as how different they are. For a work on the nature of information see Dembski, *Being*.

are not the same concepts. One cannot be reduced to the other without remainder.

If the above is true, then ethical concepts are irreducible to anything else at that level and hence form a separate aspect of reality. This aspect or mode of reality is something to which we seem to be intrinsically attuned, to think in terms of, and to feel. The question then becomes, "Is all this just an odd quirk of evolution, or are human beings made so that we can understand ethical reality just as we can the other aspects mentioned?"

Ethics is understandable and intuitive

First, it seems that ethics is *understandable*. Everyone, or at least the great majority of people, knows what it means to say that something is morally right or wrong. Take *T*, that it is wrong to torture people or animals for fun. Most people, almost all in fact, understand that torturing innocent people for fun is wrong, and this is apart from any other considerations. One understands that there is something wrong with torturing innocent beings for fun apart from how economically or socially debilitating it is; apart from how much fun it is; and apart from how much it appears to be unaesthetic. It is just wrong in and of itself. One may possibly disagree with this,[7] but it seems that human beings are able to understand it.

Further, we do not just understand the premise; rather we also feel it. When something pointlessly cruel is done, we normally feel revulsion. If someone does something heroic or benevolent, then we tend to feel admiration. Normal people have these feelings and emotions in the presence of either actual goodness or real evil. People who never have such feelings are sociopaths—who are mentally ill. Therefore, it seems that the understanding of and feeling for morality is built into human nature. Does this fact allow us to think that morality also exists apart from us, apart from our beliefs and feelings?

Are humans made to understand ethical reality?

Perhaps one way of approaching this question would be to look at the other aspects of reality. Does the fact that human beings seem to be able, by our very nature, to understand these different modes of being give us

---

7. As do psychopaths and some philosophers.

reason to think that they exist? Are we attuned to external reality, or are things just an expression of our minds?

The fact that we can understand different modes of being gives us a strong reason to think that such a mode of being, an external reality, exists. We are often wrong about the members of an ontological level, e.g., there are no phoenixes in real, living creatures. But it would be radical to call into question the very idea of living beings by claiming that there is no real difference between living and non-living entities.

Take for example, the lowest aspect on Dooyeweerd's list of categories: the *quantitative*. It certainly seems to be the case that things can be counted—that they necessarily exist in some number. Whether or not numbers exist as abstract objects, it is undeniably true that objects can either exist alone, or else in sets of more than one. Therefore, there is a quantitative aspect in reality that exists apart from human beings.

The next on the list is *spatial*. It certainly seems that there are physical objects—after all, we are surrounded by physical objects, and, indeed, in a way we ourselves are physical objects. Therefore, another aspect of reality that we can grasp seems to exist in reality apart from our beliefs about it. Whether or not space exists substantively, spatial modes of existence do exist.

The next on the list is *kinetic*. This aspect involves motion and change. Despite Zeno's paradoxes, it seems impossible to deny that motion and change clearly occur. Again, there is a link between the way that we perceive and understand reality, and the way that it actually is. Even if our perception of the external world is a delusion, there seems to be a change in our thoughts. First, we think of one thing, and then we think of something else.

I could go on, but the basic point is made: the aspects of being into which we divide reality seem to be built into reality itself. Take *logic*, which in itself appears to me to be wrongly placed on the list. (Dooyeweerd must have been thinking of logic in its actual role as a mode of human thought about reality, rather than logic in and of itself.) Logic is foundational to reality, as well as to thought. Everything that we can think about seems to be governed by the laws of identity and non-contradiction. Here, perhaps more than at any other place, thought and reality converge.

One objection to this is that the above examples all apply to physical modes of reality, which is different from the purely conscious, personal ones. However, these too seem undeniable. There is sensation, there is conceptualization, there exist economics and society. All these different modes exist in our human world, and they are readily recognizable and understandable. We see a piece of jewelry, we conceptualize that it is worth a lot of money, and realize that it would be illegal, as well as morally wrong, to steal it, no matter how desirable the jewelry is. *Indeed, it seems impossible to be able to understand a particular mode of being while that mode of being is necessarily empty of any examples.*

Given all of this, *the fact that ethics is a distinct and understandable mode of being is a strong reason for thinking that it is an intrinsic part of reality*, something that is there and would be there even if there were no human beings. If this is the case, then morality is real, and exists apart from our thinking, and hence ethical antirealism is false. I think that morality deserves to be acknowledged as the *default* position, and that it must only be unseated by very strong arguments. If the realm of ethics is a delusion, it is an enormously systematic and coherent one.

Thus, it seems that the existence of ethics is impossible to deny. Indeed, its existence appears to me to be luminous.[8]

Arguments against understanding. Kant, for example

What might be said in response to this argument? One response would be to take a Kantian approach to things. Simply put, our minds are indeed structured to form sensations, which we receive from outside ourselves, and put them into various categories. By itself, this may seem unproblematic, but what Kant seems to be saying is that the way our minds form our perceptions is quite different from the way that reality is. There is the thing, as we perceive it, and then there is the thing in itself, which exists unperceived by us and exists in a manner that we cannot comprehend. Because of this, reality is divisible into the *phenomenal*, which is how things seem to us, and the *noumenal*, which is how they are in themselves. Space and time themselves do not really exist apart from us—they are simply the way that we structure our outer (spatial) and inner (temporal) experiences.[9]

Whether or not this is the correct interpretation of Kant will not be discussed here. Certainly, it is a widespread interpretation and *seems* to be what Kant wrote. Some have said that Kant, when he revised his

---

8. Smithies, *Epistemic Role*, 345–79.

9. For a modern exposition and defense of Kant's epistemology, see Allison, *Kant's Transcendental Idealism*.

Critique, changed his mind about this, and moved to the position that our minds are structured to understand reality as it is.[10]

However, let us assume that Kant's real position was as outlined: that the mind categorizes things in a way that is radically different from the way that things are in themselves. What can be said about it? Here one must tread with caution, for Kant is one of the, if not *the*, most important philosophers of modern times, and a vast literature has grown up around his epistemic theories.

Why did Kant embrace such a counter-intuitive theory, for it really does seem odd that given his theory of knowledge, knowledge of reality as it truly is becomes impossible? Apparently, the main reason is that he was trying to combat skepticism. Hume had raised the problem of how we know that everything that happens will have a cause. Kant's answer was that because of the way that the mind is structured, and the way that it experiences reality, the mind will always supply a cause for every event. This is how we know that every event that happens will have a cause: necessarily the mind will supply one. Therefore, thought Kant, skepticism is avoidable. However, this avoidance of skepticism comes at a high price.[11]

One thing that seems to follow from Kant's theory is that we do not have much knowledge of reality. We may see a chair, for instance, and think that we understand it, but the chair as it is in and of itself, is different than the chair as experienced. Seemingly, the chair does not exist in space. This is skepticism, a rather global skepticism, which is rather ironic considering that Kant was writing partly to escape skepticism.

On Kant's view, external reality in itself is forever unknowable, because since our minds were formed in a certain manner, they will always form sense perception in a certain way that is different from the way that the things exist in themselves. This has the implication that we never really know anything outside of our own minds. This being the case, how can Kant know that reality is utterly unlike the way that we form it? Wouldn't he have to know what reality is like to know that we can never know what reality is like?

Indeed, isn't it far more plausible to think that our minds are structured in such a manner as to mirror reality as it exists in itself? After all, if we are dependent upon understanding to survive in the world, it would seem more likely to think that our minds are, in effect, a mirror of nature,

---

10. At least one of my professors, Dr. William Stine, thought so.

11. Altman argues that Kant's skepticism is not absolute, but relative. Altman, *Companion to Kant's Critique*.

since we live in nature. In fact, in the final analysis, theories that claim we cannot know reality undercut themselves, as they appear to know something about reality, which they claim we cannot know.[12]

It is true that the quantum world is very different from the world that we experience every day around us.[13] Physical objects are mostly empty space instead of being solid the way it seems to us. Phenomenal color is probably in our minds rather than in the external world. But the quantum world is also, at least to an extent, knowable. And, taking a holistic approach to things, the world of everyday experience is objectively ascertained and understood. So, given external reality, our perspective in that reality, and the sensory and cognitive faculties we have, we do sense the external world in an objective way. Unlike God, we do not experience things immediately as they are, but the understanding is mediated by certain faculties we have. So, to a certain extent, Kant was right. We can see things only according to our abilities. But he was wrong to say that therefore we cannot know reality. At the macro level, we do see things in a particular but objective way. And, by working on the sensory data we have, we can understand the micro quantum world that is the physical basis of the macro world.

Further, it seems that given his theory, Kant could not say anything about the minds of other people. The only mode of access that he has toward other minds is via sense perception, but as we have seen, Kant's sense perception gives him a picture of reality that is unlike reality in itself. This being the case, how does Kant know that other minds are structured, or for that matter, that other minds even exist? Kant seems

---

12. For an opposing view, see Rorty, et al., *Philosophy and the Mirror of Nature*.

13. See for example Hoffman, *Case Against Reality*. Hoffman argues that our minds structure reality based on an unknowable substratum. The objects we experience, like spoons or books, exist only in our minds and cease to exist when anyone stops observing them. They are based on an unperceivable and almost totally unknowable substrate, which is the "real" reality. His book is interesting but has, in my opinion, several weaknesses. First, he says that everything is the way that it is because of evolution, which is geared toward survival rather than to truth. However, based on his theory, wherein almost everything we see is a mental construction of our minds, how can he be sure that evolution is true? He writes about our brains, but for him, brains also are simply a construction of our minds. Hoffman seems to be very close to sawing off the branch upon which he sits, if in fact he has not already done so. Finally, the theist has what seems to be a much better answer as to why we can know the simple physical objects around us. The spoon or book does not disappear when we are not observing them because God always observes them. It can be said, as Husserl held, that the world we perceive is *the* or at least *a* real world, and that the things that physicists investigate are abstractions from it. See Husserl, *Crisis*.

CATEGORIES, THE NATURE OF ETHICS, AND BEAUTY 55

to think that he knows a lot about things that his theory does not permit him to know.[14] His theory thus fails the transcendental test.[15]

Kant is not the only philosopher who has taken a skeptical stance. Other thinkers are either dubious about knowing reality or at least some portion of it. Robert Nozick, for example, is skeptical about the notion of necessary truth.[16] The basic reason seems to be the belief that our minds evolved to help us survive in the world, and that therefore they might not be trustworthy when it comes to philosophical issues, at least some of them. Colin McGinn has argued for Mysterianism in the case of minds. He holds that although consciousness can be reduced to the physical, because of the way that our brains evolved, we can never understand how this can be.[17] Further, the logical positivists were skeptical about our ability to know anything not tautological or present to the senses.[18]

This attitude seems self-defeating. If we can't trust our minds to do philosophy, then why even try? To do anything, we simply must believe that our minds are capable, at least to some degree, of accessing and evaluating the different issues.[19] *We can understand the questions. Why is it assumed that we cannot understand the answers?*

Granted, we perceive reality in a limited way. We do not see the world as it is in every single respect. Though it is somewhat controversial, it seems obvious that phenomenal color, for example, is the way that the mind presents the external world and spectral reflectance to itself. Phenomenal colors do not exist in the external world. We see things differently than they are, because we see them with a certain perspective and with certain sensory capabilities. As Thomas Nagel has argued, a bat would experience the world quite differently than we do, and in a way that we can never experience.[20] A well-known, simple example would be the difference of perception for those who are "color blind."

---

14. About this general idea of unknowable things, see chapter 9.

15. The transcendental test asks, "Does the position in question allow for the existence of knowledge?"

16. Nozick, *Invariances*.

17. McGinn, *Mysterious Flame*.

18. The early Wittgenstein also thought that ethics was strictly speaking meaningless. See for example Wittgenstein and Russell, *Tractatus*.

19. For a defense of our ability to know ourselves and the world, see Meixner, *Defending Husserl*.

20. Nagel, "What Is It like to Be a Bat?"

In conclusion then, it seems both simpler and just all around easier and more plausible to think that our minds are fitted to external reality, rather than to accept Kant's Copernican revolution and believe that we fit external reality to our minds. Inevitably then, some things are left out. We do not have, and cannot have, a God's eye view of things, even if we adopt the view that our minds in general accurately represent reality to ourselves.[21] We perceive things from a particular perspective and with a certain set of sensory abilities. Doubtless other creatures with different sensory abilities might see things very differently. Successful collaboration and communication make it implausible that we do not access a shared public world.

Arguments against unique understanding. Postmodernists for example

There is another problem that may be raised here—one that has been raised by postmodernists. This is the notion that there are equally valid different ways of presenting and understanding reality. According to this, one may think that space, change, and physical objects exist, but it still may be thought that there are many ways that reality could be categorized, and that no system of classification is better than any other.

Here all that will be said is that if the basic data of experience is acknowledged as being real, this is all that is needed for the success of the argument. That is, *as long as the basic aspects of reality are acknowledged as existing, however they may be thought of in theory, then it is the case that we do understand, however imperfectly, how reality actually is.* Denying that we do have understanding undercuts all of scholarship, especially philosophy. If we cannot understand reality as it is, then all science, philosophy, and other scholarly disciplines are a waste of time, except for some possible practical benefits. For example, even if all our medical thought is wrong, by some odd coincidence, doing something for the wrong reason may have a good effect on health. In other words, the more skeptical that the theories are, the less plausible they are, while the less skeptical that they are, the weaker the disputation against the argument that I am making in this chapter.

In truth, in a broad sense, we do have an understanding of reality. Whether or not numbers exist as abstract objects, we understand them and the whole realm of mathematics, and we are able to use this in

---

21. See also Reid and Thomas, *Reid's Essays*, Chapter 14.

manipulating physical reality. The same may be said about logic. Even if phenomenal color is a way for us to represent surfaces to ourselves, it is still the case that physical surfaces exist. And so on.

Not only is a strong skepticism about our ability to know reality strongly counter-intuitive, but there seems to be no way to account for the rapid growth and high success that the sciences have in comprehending reality. That is, if we accept antirealism about the sciences and other scholarly disciplines, it seems to be an amazing coincidence that they have a growing success. At any rate, even given some form of antirealism concerning science and other disciplines, it is obvious that we are able to grasp and understand the existence of the fundamental aspects of reality like space, motion, logic, etc.

What about ethical intuitions?

The question now becomes, does the fact that in general our intuitions seem to match reality mean that our ethical intuitions also match reality? Although perhaps one cannot have a conclusion with certainty in this matter, it seems to me that we should assume that they do. Why should our epistemic intuitions be able to correctly see that there is space, time, solidity, number, and other matters in the universe, while our ethical intuitions are completely illusory? Indeed, ethical intuitions seem to be as strongly grounded as other instincts. They do not seem to be merely internal principles we have adopted, but principles that are binding on us. Any decent, sane human being would be opposed to setting a cat on fire for fun.

If we do grasp the basic aspects of reality, then the argument that I am making has weight. Put simply, we comprehend the other aspects of reality that are presented in the list above, and they all really exist. Therefore, since we understand ethics in both an intellectual and intuitive way, as well as in an emotional way, there is good reason to think that the ethical aspect of reality also exists, along with all the other spheres of existence. This is especially the case when given that ethics can be fitted in with the personal aspects on the list that Dooyeweerd gives.

In response, it might be disputed that our knowledge of such modal spheres or categories such as the spatial, kinetic, and the quantitative ones are more basic and fundamental, and that they are revealed to us through sense perception. The argument might state that with ethical intuitions (and aesthetics for that matter) we do not see something morally wrong in the same sense that we see that a baseball takes up space and has a numerical value.

This is true, but it does not appear to be much of an objection. Although they do not occupy space, or have colors, when one sees that something unethical is being done, one "sees it," in some sense. When looking at a bag of marbles, for example, one may sense that there are a certain number there, but one does not literally see a number. Rather, the number known is the result of an intellectual intuition. The same is true for an *ethical intellectual intuition*. Analogously, since natural science relies on logical and mathematical knowledge, it does not help to say ethical intuition is "spooky" since logical and mathematical intuition is similar.

Therefore, I conclude that the fact that we do experience, understand, and intuit the moral aspect of reality, gives us a strong reason to reckon that ethics exists, both at a rational level, and at a basic intuitive level.

Another argument for the existence of ethics and objective moral norms

Are there any other reasons for proving that ethics as a category exists? I think that there are, and they may be thought of as the following ones. Although this proposal is different, it reinforces the argument given above.[22]

(4.1) Our whole existence as human beings, including speech, incorporates moral concerns in itself.[23]

(4.2) Attempts to reduce morality to other aspects of reality all fail: Ethics is irreducible (as are the other aspects of reality).

(4.3) There is a pragmatic reason for accepting the existence of moral norms. Which is, to dismiss ethics and accept antirealism has some awful and strongly counterintuitive results. Although the fact that a particular theory has awful implications does not automatically

---

22. Arguments for ethical realism can be found in Huemer, *Ethical Intuitionism*; Kulp, *Knowing Moral Truth*; and etc. See also Audi, *Moral Perception*.

23. See also his book, Cuneo, *Normative Web*.

mean that it is false, it does give us reasons to examine the theory to see if it is true.

From each of these explanations, an argument can be developed that some form of realism gives the best understanding of ethics. I will now examine each of the above listed points one by one. This will not be an exhaustive analysis but should be enough to show the basic structure of the discussion.

Human existence entails ethical truths (4.1)

First, it seems that our whole existence, including such a basic phenomenon as speech, entails the existence of ethical truths. For example, Terence Cuneo argues that the very fact that we engage in speech with each other entails the existence of moral realism.[24] Relying on a response that Samuel Clarke made to Thomas Hobbes, Cuneo writes,

> Under a natural interpretation, Clarke's point is that if agents in the state of nature are to make a compact with one another—if they are genuinely to *promise* certain things to one another—moral obligations must already exist. To illustrate his point, Clarke adverts to the obligation that promises be faithfully performed. An obligation of this sort, Clarke intimates, is not generated by promising but is a condition of performing a promise in the first place. Accordingly, Clarke maintains, Hobbes' contractualism does not explain the emergence of moral norms. Rather, it presupposes their existence.[25]

Cuneo makes the extended argument that speech, or human communication in general, necessarily involved the presumption of morality. Speech cannot exist without a moral background being assumed. Since speech is an essential and integral part of human nature and existence, this provides an argument for moral realism, which ties into the one that was given above. This is true regarding both our social lives and our individual lives. Obviously, we use speech in our dealings with other people. However, we use speech—language—even when we are thinking to ourselves. If we cannot even exist as human beings, in a human fashion,

---

24. Zagzebski, *Virtues of the Mind*.
25. Linda Zagzebski also argues to the close relation of ethics to knowledge.

using reason and speech without presupposing the existence of morality, then we have good grounds for accepting moral realism.[26]

If someone is communicating with another person, then when she speaks, the person listening to her will have the assumption that she is being honestly communicative. Writes Cuneo, "Only if agents have the rights, responsibilities, and obligations of being a speaker . . . do their locutionary acts count as illocutionary acts."[27]

It is not only in speech acts, but most of human interaction presupposes that there are moral norms which are binding on us. Being ethical is part of being a person, which is why sociopaths are thought to be defective individuals. In fact, we often hear of their barbaric acts as being "inhumane." The assumption here is that to be human is to be humane, i.e., ethical.

Ethics is irreducible (4.2)

A major reason for accepting moral realism is that expressed in (4.2). Ethics, being a proper category, is irreducible to any other category of being. Being pleasant, being useful, being admirable, in many senses, are different things from being morally right or wrong. That it is something separate from anything else is shown by the fact that people sometimes do things that they find unpleasant, dangerous, or painful simply because they think that it is the morally right thing to do. This was argued at length in this chapter, but I want to re-emphasize this here.

Ethics is pragmatic (4.3)

Simply put, societies cannot exist without some system of morality. Further, being unethical causes many problems in human beings. Some people, believing that nothing is morally right or wrong, turn into monsters, as noted in chapter 6 on antirealism. This is dramatically exemplified by a quote from Ted Bundy. Most people would not go this far, but some would, and it seems that in the absence of real morality, standards of honesty, generosity, and loyalty would deteriorate.

26. This does not differentiate between what here has been called weak and strong moral realism. For a defense of moral realism that in my opinion ends up being a weak variety, see Brink, *Moral Realism*. For a collection of essays on moral realism, see Sayre-McCord, *Moral Realism*.

27. Cuneo, *Speech and Morality*, 76.

Therefore, it seems to me that strong realism is the natural position to take. It is a form of strong realism that will be defended in the following chapters. To show that ethics is not the only part of existence of which these things are true, another modal sphere will be briefly examined, to use Dooyeweerd's terminology. This is beauty.

AN EXCURSUS ON BEAUTY

Another realm of existence where there may be thought to exist *Categorical Imperatives* is *aesthetics*. Given a strong realist theory of beauty, one is doing something wrong if, in the proper situation, one does not find some individual thing or things—a painting, a mountain, a portrait of a human being—to be beautiful. In several ways, aesthetics is relevantly like ethics.

It is not part of the purpose of this book to argue for the objectivity of beauty, though I think that some form of robust realism about beauty is correct. Here, it is merely stating that if realism about aesthetics is true, then there is another realm of reality besides the ethical wherein there is a kind of categorical imperative. To be a certain kind of being in the correct situation and not to appreciate a truly beautiful thing means that some defect is present. In effect, given a normally functioning human being, in certain circumstances beauty will *force* itself upon that human being.

It is true that different people have different tastes in art and aesthetics generally. In addition, there are frequent times and situations wherein one is not able to cognitively appreciate the beauty of some work of art or of nature. Whether or not one appreciates something beautiful is quite dependent upon the situation in which one finds oneself. It is this fact that causes some to accept a subjectivist theory of aesthetics, wherein what one thinks is beautiful or ugly is entirely up to the person's viewing. "Beauty is in the eye of the beholder."

A defect in appreciating the beauty of a painting, for example, may be a lack of proper training, or a defect in the person's natural capacity, either at that moment, or perhaps as part of the person's permanent character. In this sense, one may think of a person who does not appreciate or have any interest in beauty to be in the same boat as someone who does not care about moral rights and wrongs—a sociopath.

We do not expect an animal to appreciate beauty any more than we rationally expect it to understand the nature of ethical truths. They are simply not equipped with the kind of mentality that would enable them to do so. Animals, even the highest and most intelligent, are simply not capable of understanding these kinds of things. If any of them were the kind of creatures that would be able to appreciate aesthetics or understand morality, we would think of them as persons of a sort.

So, to sum up, my argument here is that there seem to be at least two aspects of being in which, given a robust realism, there is some sort of *CI*, categorical imperative. These are ethics and aesthetics. Since ethics and beauty are both, in a real sense, the possessors of a *CI*, they are both real aspects of being. Further, they are both irreducible to any other of the modal spheres or categories, and most importantly, are not reducible to each other. They are different aspects of reality, though they have certain attributes in common. They are truly conceptually distinct.[28]

Given realism in both ethics and aesthetics, we have *an obligation* from both. If we are in a situation in which we have a moral obligation to act in a certain manner, then it is morally wrong not to do so. Our feelings and desires are irrelevant as to whether something is, in fact, beautiful. In both beauty and morality, we have a categorical imperative which one is obligated to obey.

With the above considerations, we have good reason to surmise that the ethical sphere is an objective part of reality that we discover, rather than invent.

---

28. A work on God and the existence of beauty is Wynn, *God and Goodness*.

CHAPTER 5

Abstract Entities, Propositions, and Necessity[1]

THE SUBJECTS OF THE basic theoretical concepts of this chapter are interrelated. Thus, just as a discussion of the "egg" requires understanding of the "chicken", so the ensuing explications will take some mental gymnastics to unpack.

Ethics is accessible to us in propositions (statements or axioms). If there are ethical propositions, then there are "abstract" entities, whatever that ultimately means. Moreover, disputes about the existence and nature of abstract entities are ancient and multifaceted. Thus, it is important to address these issues in more detail. That said, the arguments of various theories of abstracta do not weigh in heavily in the overall discussion of metaethics, save in the concept of propositions, which are vital in ethics. How else do we understand or process through ethics? The following discussion on abstracta is quite technical and could be skipped, with the assumption of the existence of propositions.

---

1. I shall usually refer to abstract entities as abstract objects here. Unless otherwise stated, the meanings will be identical with each other. Cowling states that a distinction can be drawn between entities and objects, but for the main part of my discussion there is no relevant difference. The term abstract objects is used to contrast them with the concept of ideal objects to be presented later. A short book on the subject is Bøhn, *God and Abstract Objects*.

ABSTRACTA

Do Abstract Objects Exist?

What are *abstract objects*? Do they even exist? Both the existence and the nature of abstract entities are highly controversial. According to Sam Cowling, traditionally abstract entities are thought of as being numbers, propositions, and universals or properties.[2] Further, the paradigm cases of abstract entities are also usually thought of as having the *properties of being acausal, spaceless and timeless, and accessible to intellectual intuition.*[3]

Abstract Object Theories

There are several different theories as to the nature of abstract objects. Some conceptions about the nature of abstract objects are that they exist only in the concrete objects[4] in which they are instantiated, or that they exist necessarily and eternally ontologically independent. This last is known as Platonism. Other theories hold that they exist in the Absolute (according to the philosophical theory known as Absolute Idealism), or in the mind of God, or that they exist separately from God but are created by God. In other words, abstract objects in some philosophical theories are not, strictly speaking, abstract objects according to the definition which has been given. This ambiguity can make the discussion difficult and give rise to confusion.

An anonymous reviewer of the manuscript of this book wrote that I was being unfair to Plato. He/she wrote, "For instance, on Plato's theory, the form of the good attracts all things like a magnet attracts iron. This suggests a possible Platonic basis for ethics." That is an interesting metaphor, but it does not explain how Plato's forms interact with each other and with the physical universe. At any rate, it should be noted that this conversation addresses modern theories of abstract entities, not classical Platonism, which is the theory developed by Plato himself.

---

2. Cowling, *Abstract Entities*.
3. Cowling, *Abstract Entities*, 2.
4. To clarify, concrete objects are things which occupy time and/or space, and/or have causal power (such as thoughts). See a further elucidation under "Realism" below.

How do Abstract Objects relate to Ethics?

How abstract objects relate to ethics is important for the argument about moral propositions. Ethics is accessible to us in propositions (statements or axioms). Propositions are prime candidates for being abstract objects, and these obviously include ethical propositions. So, this topic is not only important in and of itself, but also for the nature of metaethics.

However, not all alleged abstract entities have these properties (acausal, spaceless, timeless, accessible). Take, for example, entities like the equator, the orbit of Mars, fictional characters, and governmental, economic, and social entities like capitalism, socialism, and democracy. These do not share all of the three attributes of abstracta listed above.[5] Some philosophers hold that fictional characters like Sherlock Holmes are abstract objects. Further, some philosophers deny that abstract entities are necessarily acausal. For example, Matteo Plebani argues that books are abstract entities, and that they may have enormous causal impact.[6] This is true, of course, but it can be argued that it is the mind's realizing the character of books and other propositional entities that is the real cause.

The argument about Abstract Objects

The argument about abstract objects is ancient and complex. The basic division is between *realists* who accept their existence and *antirealists* who deny them. However, there are many divisions within both the realist and antirealist camps. William Lane Craig lists the basic possibilities in their divisions.

(5.1) The question is meaningless.

(5.2) Realism

(5.3) Antirealism[7]

---

5. Cowling, *Abstract Entities*, 69–105.
6. Plebani, "Recent Debates," 2.
7. Craig, "Response," 278.

Nihilism—Ethical Truth is meaningless (5.1)

The first, that either ethical truth or the nature of ethical truths is meaningless, is true only on *extreme nihilism*. Logical positivists (and others) deny the meaningfulness of ethical statements, but few philosophers these days hold to these positions. That there are normative statements and that ethical statements are normative statements seems apparent. The notion that ethical truths, or their ontological status, are meaningless, appears quite obviously false. It is evident that ethical statements are undeniably meaningful, even though the answer to the question of *what* they are may be difficult to find. After all, we clearly know how to use moral terms, and people can challenge us for misusing them.

Ignoring then "The question is meaningless," for it is outside the debate here, we have two basic divisions: realism and antirealism.

Realism (5.2)

In realism, abstract objects such as ethical propositions really exist, and are either true or false. There are two basic divisions in realism, and here we run into the terminological problem mentioned earlier. The first division is that abstract entities really exist as abstract entities, on their own, so to speak. This is Platonism, though there are other names for the position. On the abstract side, besides Platonism (where abstract objects are uncreated), we have absolute creationism, where the abstracta are created by God. In Platonism, abstract objects exist in a "Plato's Heaven," a third realm that is neither physical nor mental, where these entities all necessarily and eternally exist, uncaused by anything else. With Absolute Creationism, on the other hand, abstract objects are created by another "causal" entity, usually considered to be God.[8]

The other realist option is that functionally abstract objects may not, in fact, be strictly abstract entities (which is confusing, this whole discussion is apt to confusion), but rather are somehow concrete entities. The last may be surprising, for as was stated, abstracta are, by definition, not concrete. However, some philosophers hold that "abstract" objects do exist, and that they exist as concrete objects that play the same ethereal roles as abstract objects are defined to do. They can be thought of as physical objects, or as existing mentally in either human minds, or in

---

8. Gould and Davis, "Modified Theistic Activism," 51–79.

God's infinite mind, or for absolute idealists, they exist in the Absolute.[9] Concrete objects are things like physical or conscious ones. My cat Squirt, my dog Toffee, the planet Mercury, or Mount Rushmore are concrete.

On this "abstract objects as concrete" side, they are considered firstly as physical objects and secondly as mental objects. The mental objects category is further divided between *psychologism*, where they are objects in human beings (and other creatures), and *theistic conceptualism*, where they are thought of as being in God's mind. Other philosophers have called it scholastic realism.[10]

One can also possibly think that abstract objects only exist in material objects. For example, redness exists only in red objects. Trope theory says basically the same thing. Writes Sam Cowling on this,

> Where universal theory holds a property like *humanity* to be a single entity shared by many particulars, *trope theory* denies there is a numerically identical entity common to all humans. There is instead a plurality of particular property instances or *tropes*; one for each human.[11]

Giving what might be a simpler and clearer example, in trope theory redness is in those things that have the property of being red, but there is no "redness" that exists apart from any specific instantiation.[12]

Antirealism (5.3)

There are also antirealist theories, wherein abstract objects do not exist in the full sense of the word. These are sometimes classified under the name of *nominalism*. One antirealist theory holds that abstract objects are just a set of some particular things in the universe. In a world where there are no red things, for example, there is no redness. On the antirealist side, we have neutralism, free logic, fictionalism, ultima facie strategies, neo-Meinongianism, and pretense theory. There may be other additional antirealist theories.[13] However, all of them deny that abstract entities, however construed, really exist. There is something that is intuitively drawn to realism about abstract objects. But one must also take to heart

---

9. However, Absolute Idealists are scarce these days.
10. Peterson, *Scholastic Realism*, vol. 12.
11. Cowling, *Abstract Entities*, 34.
12. A good discussion of this is found in Kulp, *Metaphysics of Morality*, 141–88.
13. Craig, *God Over All*.

the standard objections to the classic theory of their existing in "Plato's Heaven."[14]

Abstract Objects summed up

To sum up, what is meant by the ontological existence of propositions, numbers, and other abstract objects is at least this: they *are things that can be thought of because they are fundamentally conceptual*. Many of them are also things that can be instantiated. It is eternally and necessarily true that, given the requisite kind of mind, one can think of abstract objects such as numbers and propositions. These propositions therefore exist as possible objects of thought, and as ways of categorizing objects in the world, like in obscure books of philosophy such as this.

For example, if numbers do not exist as Platonic objects, they are at least possible objects of thought. With numbers, one must consecutively count discrete conceptual objects such as one, two, three, etc. There are no, and can be no, prime numbers between eight and nine. These concepts exist necessarily and have necessary relations with each other. Thus, some sort of realism regarding numbers and mathematical operations seems to be true. The number seven, for example, has essential, necessary properties. It is an odd number and a prime number, which lies between the numbers six and eight.[15] Even if being concepts is all that numbers are, still they have necessary properties analytically included in their essential concept.

Concepts are things that are necessarily thinkable. Numbers, universals, and concepts are things that can be thought of by the right kind of minds. Therefore, a part of the essence of abstract objects is that they are necessarily thinkable by minds. It is necessarily the case that abstract objects have such a nature so that they are eternally, essentially, and necessarily understandable. This presupposes that the concepts in question are intelligible—that they mean something. Even if there are concepts that are too complex or alien for human minds to grasp, it seems possible that there could be different, more powerful minds that could think of

---

14. See chapter 7 about problems with Platonism.

15. See Husserl and Dummett, *Logical Investigations*, vol. 1, for a classic defense of the concept that we can understand abstract reality as it is. It includes a refutation of psychologism, which is the interpretation of things in subjective terms.

them. Given theism, God is eternally thinking them, for God's mind is, by definition, able to grasp any concept.[16]

Abstract objects should therefore be thought of as "concepts," or the equivalent of ideal objects.[17] Further, when they are in a mind, the thought is concrete. If the concept is somehow instantiated in physical reality, that instantiation is also concrete. Propositions are abstract objects that intend toward various concepts, whether the concept itself, or some object that instantiates the concept. Though the concepts themselves are also abstract, they can be instantiated in a sense in concrete reality. In this scheme, concrete objects exemplify concepts. Phenomenal green is a concept that can be exemplified in an object, though strictly speaking not the concept itself, but what the concept *is of* is exemplified.[18] Concrete objects are concepts that have been made "real," in the sense that they do not exist merely as being thought of in a mind.[19]

In conclusion, whatever else should be said about them, abstract objects exist as being thinkable. We can think about the number four, or the color red, or the proposition that pointless cruelty is wrong. At least in this sense, they are real and exist apart from any finite mind. If another possible world had been actualized instead of this world, without any human or other finite minds, abstract objects would still have existed in the sense that they *could* have been thought had there been the right kind of minds, and therefore, granting theism, abstract objects are being thought by God. That these concepts are understandable by the right kind of minds is a necessary truth, and in this sense at least, they are real.

Concentrating on propositions, they may be thought of as attempted descriptions of reality. That is, either they successfully describe reality the way that it is, or they fail. The situation is of course more complex than this, because, as in fiction, they are not used to describe reality. In fiction they are ways of describing reality as it could have been, or in some cases, could not have been. Nonetheless, propositions are intentional; they are geared toward some aspect of reality, whether they succeed or fail.

This discussion brings out a problem with Platonism. Platonism not only has the problem of how abstract entities like the number seven or redness can exist as abstract entities, but also how can humans and

---

16. At least in some sense, because God is omniscient.
17. This will be discussed below in chapter 8.
18. At least in some physical universes.
19. This does not imply that abstracta are not real, albeit in a very different way than concretes.

other minds access these entities? How is exemplification possible? How does a contingent, finite, mind existing in space and time access spaceless, timeless, acausal entities? With theistic conceptualism, there are no such problems, for abstracta exist in God's mind as ideas, and since we also have minds, we have the kind of thing to which "Platonic abstract objects," which are ideal objects, naturally belong.

Abstracta of Math and Propositions

To illustrate the above point, mathematical objects and propositions will be examined. Notice that in math, realists hold that mathematical things "like numbers" are objects. There does seem to be a certain initial amount of plausibility in thinking of the number four as an abstract object, something that eternally and necessarily exists. However, can the same thing be said about ethical truths?

This is obviously a difficult matter to consider. Nonetheless, it seems that it is easier to think of a number like four as being an abstract object than to think of ethical truths as objects. Now to be sure, some think of all propositions as being abstract entities, including ethical propositions. However, it may seem strange to think of propositions as objects just existing on their own. Because propositions have intentionality, and this is a property of minds, it seems that minds are the right home for propositions.

It seems easier to see that different abstract objects exist in different ways. Abstract entities such as redness or the number four can be best thought of as *things that can be thought—as concepts*. Propositions are abstract entities as intentional objects that are composed of concepts. For example, the propositions, "The door is painted red," and "There are four people in the room," are about things that are concepts. Both concepts and propositions seem to eternally exist as "things" that can be thought of by someone. Whether they are true or not is another matter entirely. A false proposition is a thinkable thing just as much as a true proposition is. In contrast, the number four just is, in a sense. It, like all other objects, is not *in itself* true or false—only propositions are.

Earlier, the concept that it is morally wrong to torture anything for fun was defined as proposition *T*. In the case of ethical truths like *T*, given realism, the question then becomes what makes them true? For example, the proposition, "My cat is sleeping on the bed," is true if there is indeed a cat sleeping on a particular bed, with the proposition said by the owner of the cat at a particular time and place. As was argued above, true propositions are thus looked at as descriptions of reality—the way that reality is. False propositions such as, "My cat is plotting to take over the world," are false because they are inaccurate—they do not describe the way that reality is. There is much more that could be said about the nature of truth, and regarding the long debates between correspondence theories and coherence theories of truth, for example, but for the purposes of the discussion at hand, we will determine that these propositions are made true or false by their congruence with reality.

If one considers how abstract objects could exist *in* some entity, then God's mind is the best candidate. In this theory, what abstract entities really are, are ideal objects in the mind of God, existing eternally and necessarily. They are thus fundamentally concrete objects, and God is the most concrete being, having necessary existence. However, to us and any other finite creatures, they seem abstract. In other words, *they are concrete to God but seem abstract to us*. This explanation fits especially well with the theory of *theistic conceptualism*, which will be explored in the last two chapters. However, there are many concepts of God, and not all of them provide a secure base for the existence of abstract objects.[20]

To sum up this section: there has been a long and complex debate among philosophers about the existence and nature of abstract objects. I think that they are best thought of as *concepts*. Which is to say, what abstract objects really are, are *concepts* that exist necessarily and eternally as things that may be thought of by the requisite kinds of minds and may in many instances be actualized in physical objects. In this manner, abstracta are objects that are eternally thinkable by some mind or minds. Regarding numbers, they too are best thought of as concepts. These abstract entities would exist in this manner even if no finite mind ever thought of them. Propositions are abstract entities that contain concepts and intentionality, though often the propositions are too vague to have a definite intentionality.[21] However, it will be argued in chapter 10 that they are also best thought of as existing as ideal objects in the mind of God,

---

20. For example, the Mormon god is a physical being and has the problems mentioned earlier that are associated with finite human minds. It should be stated that Mormons think there are two kinds of "matter"—the regular stuff we see, and spirit matter, which is somehow different.

21. For an interesting take on intentionality, see Mendelovici, *Phenomenal Intentionality*.

necessarily and eternally. However, some more needs to be said about the nature of propositions.

PROPOSITIONS

Ethical propositions

Require language

Human beings (and any other rational beings that might exist) are the only beings who can understand and appreciate ethical statements. A cat may think in some catlike way that her food bowl is empty, but try as she might, she cannot express this deplorable situation in a language, though she has other ways of making this situation known.[22] Still less can she understand such abstract matters as ethics.

Can contain events

An animal, a raccoon, for example, may see something as blue or square just as well as a human being.[23] That the raccoon is not rational, at least not in the same way that a human being is rational, does not mean that it cannot see a physical property such as some colors or shapes. However, ethical properties are not like this. They are apprehensible only by some minds under some circumstances. To an extent, they are like mathematical truths. A rabbit may see ten boxes, but does not see them as ten, while a person not only sees the physical boxes but also sees them as ten, even though the "ten-ness" is not a physical attribute in the same way that blueness or squareness is. Various *events* can have ethical properties. For example, torturing one's neighbor because one enjoys hearing him scream has the property of being unethical. Similarly, the moral rightness or wrongness of an act is not a physical property, though it will supervene on physical things. Whether expressed or not, the ethical truth regarding the act is only known propositionally.

As stated above, propositions are about things that are intentional. Therefore, if one states, "It is raining now," located at a particular time and place, the intention of the proposition is to identify a state of affairs

---

22. In the case of my cat, coming to where I am and staring at me.

23. Cats can apparently see some colors, especially blue and green, and perhaps yellow.

at that setting. However, if one simply says, "It is raining," and the statement is not about a particular location and time, then although it is understandable, it does not have the same intentionality. One could maintain that all that this second proposition states is that it is raining somewhere at that time. Alternatively, if one simply states, "It rains," all that this proposition expresses is that rain occurs at some time(s) and place(s). All propositions, to the extent that they have any meaning at all, are about the truth-value of something. (Any purported propositions that are too vague to have a meaning are therefore not true propositions with any real significance.) There is also the old philosophical problem about statements such as, "The present king of France is bald." Unless there has been a monarchist coup d'état in France in the last couple of hours or so, there is no present king of France. So, what is this statement about?[24] Such sentences are not relative to the foundational elements of propositions, so such issues will not be dealt with here.

What do ethical propositions intend?

The question regarding ethical propositions is therefore: what do the propositions intend? Ethical propositions are supposed to be *about* something. For example, "Murder is morally wrong," is about the concept of taking someone else's life without any justification. It is thus about an indefinite, indeed infinite number, of possible happenings. Murder exemplifies an act which would be considered universally and necessarily immoral. This entails that if John kills his neighbor, for example, he is doing something wrong.

Now, take the act of stealing. I have signified the proposition of stealing as being morally wrong as S. However, the proposition S is not just about individual acts of theft. It is about a *concept*, which itself is expressed in propositions. It is the *ascribing to a set of actions the attribute of moral wrongness*. One thing that this means is that a certain set of actions has a certain moral wrongness, common among the possible scenarios. What this further means is that there is an aspect of being morally wrong, and that therefore there is a *category of being* which is expressed. Ethical propositions are about ethical properties.

As mentioned above, a major point about ethical propositions like S is that they are not primarily about physical properties, though they

---

24. On matters like this, see Rosenberg and Travis, *Philosophy of Language*, 163–218.

supervene on them. Ethical propositions are about some aspect of reality that cannot be completely captured in physical things, or even phenomenally conscious things. They are about an aspect of reality that in itself is personal and rational, available only to some consciousnesses.

Truth and Intention

Assuming, for the sake of argument, that propositions do exist, then as explained above, their truth depends upon the nature of the entity or entities to which they intend. Given the nature of the concepts referenced in the propositions, and the laws of logic, the truth or falsity of the propositions follows as a matter of course. Statements regarding abstract objects are true only if they accurately describe reality as it is. For abstract entities, it seems that the truth of statements regarding them follows from their nature. All that one must do to understand that red is a color rather than a number, or that nothing can be older than itself, is to consider the nature of the abstract entities at hand.

Propositions necessarily have at least the appearance of being *about* something. "Thing" here may be understood in a very broad sense, as applying to anything—entities, objects, properties, events, states of affairs, the concrete or abstract, conscious or physical, real or fictional. They can even intend nothingness and meaningless states of affairs, though only with restrictions. These aspects of reality may be subsumed under the name *fact*.[25] Facts then simply are the way that reality exists in cases.

Propositions can be true or false or not about any specific situation. When precisely defined, they are *intentional*, that is, they are *about* things. What makes them true or false is what they say about reality. In other words, what the facts of the matter are determines the truth or falsity. This is also the case with ethical propositions.

---

25. On the relation between states of affairs and facts, see Peterson, *Scholastic Realism*, 75. Peterson writes, "Something is a fact f = df f is a state of affairs which subsists in and is known by the mind of God." Peterson denies the status of propositions, and instead replaces them with "facts." This is a deep topic which I shall not pursue here. I shall use proposition with the understanding that if Peterson is right, then what is really the relevant concept is fact.

Why Propositions are True or False

Most propositions "are made" to be true or false, contingent, necessary, or impossible by external reference. How then can ethical statements be true, or necessarily true? Looking at a different kind of necessary truth may be instructive. Take the case of a necessary truth: that 7 is a prime number is necessarily true, because of the nature of numbers including 7. The properties of being a number, being prime, and being the number 7 all come together to the truth that 7 is a prime number. The necessity flows from the concepts. To deny that 7 is necessarily a prime is to deny the logical laws of identity and non-contradiction. This can be easily seen in simple math problems, like the one here described, though more complicated ones would require much more work. In other words, this problem, like the other problems in logic and mathematics, ends up being a tautology, or else is analytically true, though what one means by the term analytically true is a matter of dispute, from which its necessity immediately follows.

Not all necessary truths are this easy to demonstrate, of course. Many of them are beyond the power of human beings to demonstrate, some beyond the power of any conceivable finite being to demonstrate. In many cases, complex necessities are derivable from simple ones. In addition, although the matter is somewhat controversial, it seems clear that human beings can understand some necessities just by intuition. A person may see, as did the slave boy in the Platonic dialogue *The Meno*,[26] that some truths must be necessarily true, and can be known by pure intuitive reason—in this case, how to find double the area of a square, while having no theoretical knowledge of geometry.[27] We are by our nature, capable of insight and understanding of modal and other necessary truths.

This being the case, if some ethical truths are necessarily true, why is there disagreement about them? Take, for example, abortion. Some will think that an abortion under a certain set of circumstances is morally acceptable, or perhaps even obligatory. Others deny this, holding that under the same set of circumstances abortion is morally wrong. Both

---

26. Plato, *Dialogues of Plato*, 353–484.

27. Although we should not accept Plato's position on this, there are better ways of accounting for it. See McGinn, *Inborn Knowledge*. He does a good job of dismantling empiricism but has no answer to why we are born with the ability to understand things. Theists, on the other hand, can argue that it is because we have been created in God's image.

sides are looking at the same set of facts—the same action was taken. Yet the judgment is different, indeed opposite.

It seems clear that the opposing judgments are made from different theories of what right and wrong are. An egoist may think, for example, that there is nothing wrong with abortion, if the woman having it would be better off because of it. A natural law theorist may in contrast think that the abortion is morally wrong because it goes against human nature—as it involves a woman destroying her own child, which is the opposite of what mothers are, based on their nature.

Therefore, it is *judgments* that themselves come from ethical theories, which tell one whether something is morally right or wrong. The truth of ethical judgments depends upon the truth of ethical theories. In realism, it seems that the theories must be necessarily true for the ethical statements themselves to be necessarily true. As we have seen, the necessary truth of ethical statements is not *analytically* necessary, for one can deny their truth without having an immediate contradiction.

To conclude here, if some ethical statements are necessarily true, they are necessarily true in virtue of some sort of synthetic necessity. They are made true by something deeper. The question then becomes, "What kind of synthetic necessity is there that can make ethical statements true?" Propositions are "made" true or false by the nature of the objects or concepts they intend. If ethical statements are made, we must ask the question as to what is the nature of the object that makes them necessarily true.

What does it mean for an Ethical Statement to be True?

Without going into detail on the long debate about what it means for something to be true, let me say that I accept a version of *correspondence theory*.[28] Put simply, a proposition is considered true when it *corresponds to some reality*, when talking about material or conscious entities, for example. If one says that the cat is sleeping on the bed, the statement is true if the cat is in fact sleeping on the bed. If one is thinking that it's nap time, the thought is true if it really is nap time. It seems that the *intentionality* is simply a thought or sentence describing some aspect of the world.

---

28. Rasmussen, *Correspondence Theory*.

So, "What is truth?", as Pontius Pilate asked Jesus?[29] The project of metaethics is about the truth of the different theories. All theories have proponents who think their theory is true.

If there are indeed ethical truths, then they must be about something. They have intentionality, like all other truths. What things they *intend* is the issue. Further, if there are ethical truths, then there are ethical propositions. Regarding the existence and essential nature of propositions, I will not attempt to defend the existence of propositions, and a correspondence theory of truth here but rather refer the reader to the work of William Alston[30] and Joshua Rasmussen.[31] Other theories include coherentism and pragmatism. Coherentism holds that propositions are true when they are in a coherent system. Pragmatism basically holds that what is true is what "works." After giving these very short definitions, the correspondence theory will be assumed wherein our beliefs are true if they correspond with reality.

There are other important philosophic disputes about the nature of truth, but I will concentrate on what is relevant to the topic at hand.

How can Ethical Propositions be Necessarily True?

Here, "true" is used in the strong sense that two plus two necessarily equal four. To do this, different suggestions as to how this all might be the case will be examined.

Take abstract entities as *concepts* in contrast to the classical Platonic abstracta. Platonic abstract entities include the paradigm cases of numbers, propositions, and universals. They exist in their own manner, necessarily, without spatial or temporal location, and acausally. Thinking of abstract entities as concepts reveals some interesting comparisons. Concepts exist necessarily and eternally in the sense that they may be necessarily thought of by the requisite kinds of minds in the right environment. They are acausal by themselves, but it seems that they may only exist in minds, or else be instantiated in the physical universe.

Do they have any other existence besides this? This is more difficult to say, but it is doubtful. However, positing theism does solve this

---

29. John 18:38. See also Hare, *God's Call*.

30. Alston, *Realist Conception of Truth*.

31. The existence of propositions is controversial. A realist stance toward them is taken here. See Alston, *A Realist Conception of Truth*; and Rasmussen, *Correspondence Theory*.

problem, though in a different manner than in classical Platonism. Here, in theism, all concepts exist in the mind of God, necessarily and eternally. In this case, there would be no abstract objects as such, as God's thoughts are in a sense concrete, although they would appear to be abstract to us, as they could be instantiated in different situations.

When writing about them without making a distinction between abstract and ideal entities, they will simply, for convenience's sake, be called abstracta or abstract entities. An important feature about the nature of many abstract entities, if they exist, is that they exist necessarily. Greenness exists necessarily in the sense that it is necessarily possible that green objects could exist.

To put things simply, thinking of abstract entities as fundamental concepts makes them easier to understand. It also has the implication that they *are fundamentally mental objects*, rather than ones living in a mysterious third realm of being (such as Plato's Heaven). Further, given theism, where God is the ultimate being, and God is essentially a mind, concepts have a natural home.[32] This is because numbers, propositions, logic, and universals are all conceptualizable; they can be thought of by the right kind of minds.

Most of the truths about the universe in which we live are contingent. In contrast, when speaking of many abstract or ideal entities, we are dealing with necessary truths.[33] Necessary truths are of all kinds. They especially exist in logic and mathematics, but also follow from the nature of concrete objects who may only exist contingently. For example, the planet Mars exists and has an orbit. Their existence is contingent. But the orbit of Mars exists eternally and necessarily as a concept that can be thought and instantiated.

James N. Anderson and Greg Welty write about the laws of logic, which is also true of all propositions:

> The laws of logic are necessary truths about truths; they are necessarily true propositions. Propositions are real entities, but cannot be physical entities; they are essentially thoughts. So the laws of logic are necessarily true thoughts. Since they are true in every possible world, they must exist in every possible world. But if there are necessarily existent thoughts, there must be a necessarily existent mind; and if there is a necessarily existence mind, there must be a necessarily existent person. A necessarily

---

32. Robert Adams writes that they *seem* like ideas. Adams, "Divine Necessity."
33. This is not true of all. See chapter 5 about Abstract Entities.

existent person must be spiritual in nature, because no physical entity exists necessarily. Thus, if there are laws of logic, there must also be a necessarily existent, personal, spiritual being. The laws of logic imply the existence of God.[34]

Given that the laws of identity and non-contradiction are the same in all possible worlds, necessary truths are true in all possible worlds. Indeed, these laws are what define possible worlds.[35] Thus, if robustly real ethical truths exist as necessary truths, they must be true in all possible worlds (even in those worlds which don't happen to contain creatures to whom the ethical truths are applicable). For example, "Murdering innocent human beings is wrong" is true in worlds without human beings, even as $2 + 2 = 4$ is true in worlds with only one object.

Therefore, necessary truths are truths that all minds which can understand them, and understand the reason why they are necessary, must affirm. Necessary truths have three mind-related features: They are:

(5.4) The right kinds of minds can *understand* their necessity.

(5.5) The right kinds of minds can *grasp why* they are necessary.

(5.6) The right kinds of minds can *affirm* their necessity.[36]

As a side bar it may be of interest to hear that abstract entities have an impact far beyond that of ethics. For example, the concept of abstract entities may also have a significant place in contemporary physics. In the Copenhagen and related versions of quantum mechanics, there are different ways in which quantum entities will behave, and these are not deterministic. To be more specific, in some theories there are quantum wave collapses, in which one of several possible happenings is actualized instead of the others. What are these possibilities before the wave collapses? They seem to be abstract of a sort. What kind of existence do they have before collapsing into one of the possibilities? The question then becomes, what causes this kind of abstract entity to become actualized?[37]

---

34. Anderson and Welty, "The Lord of Non-Contradiction," 336.

35. All of this is rather obvious, but sometimes philosophy consists in stating the obvious clearly.

36. This was suggested to me by Dale Kratt in a private correspondence. Dale Kratt, "Necessity," March 1, 2022.

37. For an interesting discussion of these matters, see also Koperski, *Physics of Theism*.

Further, how are they related to their kinds? In any event, abstract entities seem to be a very real part of reality.

NECESSITY

Necessity was discussed earlier in chapter 1, but some new points will be added here. To review, what is meant by necessity (and the related concepts of impossibility and possibility), is what is sometimes known as metaphysically, broadly logical, or absolute necessity.[38] With this concept, the *necessity* is *in all possible worlds*. Necessity and the related concepts are based on the laws of *identity* and *non-contradiction*. For something to be *necessary* means that its denial entails a contradiction. In contrast, *impossibility* means that something itself entails a contradiction. Depending upon the context, *possibly* either means that neither its existence nor non-existence in any way entails a contradiction, or it can mean that its existence is either necessary or possible in the sense that neither its existence nor its non-existence entails a contradiction.[39]

Given this, that the laws of identity and non-contradiction somehow entail necessary truths, and that the laws of identity and non-contradiction are the same in all possible worlds, *necessary truths are true in all possible worlds*. Indeed, these laws are what define possible worlds. Therefore, if robustly real ethical truths exist, they must be true in all possible worlds (including even in worlds without creatures to whom the ethical truths are applicable).

Specifically, if an *ethical proposition* is necessarily true, then *why* is it necessarily true? I have argued above that there is no *direct* contradiction in denying the necessity of ethical truths. However, if they are necessarily true, there must be a contradiction somewhere. The contradiction might not be in first order logic, but it must exist in some manner. Therefore, when dealing with such *necessary* truths, in seeking an explanation, one must seek out where a contradiction is. (Of course, something might be necessarily true without our ability to understand why they are necessarily true. Reality is much larger than our ability to understand it clearly and comprehensibly).

Sometimes, one can see the contradiction immediately. For example, one can intuitively see that a cube must have six faces. In other situations,

---

38. For a discussion of all this, see Hale, *Necessary Beings*.
39. In other words, it can have different meanings.

one can demonstrate where the contradiction is, and hence where the necessity lies. Seven plus five equals twelve because of the nature of the concepts involved. Since the equations on the opposite side of the equal sign are identical, a contradiction arises if one denies that two identical things are identical.

Other necessities cannot be seen so clearly or intuitively. Some necessary truths involve matters that are so complex that we cannot see their necessity, nor can we demonstrate them via logic and mathematics.

Necessary truths, however, are of different kinds. In earlier work, there were four different kinds of necessary truths, all of them derived from the law of non-contradiction and the nature of the entities involved.[40] This was my own scheme, and I am not claiming that it describes all necessary truths, or is the only scheme possible, or even the best, but it does have advantages and is useful in thinking about necessary truths. Here is also added a fifth concept, that of nomological necessity, which is the necessity of the laws of nature. They are universal and binding but denying them does not create a logical contradiction.

(5.7) Tautologically Necessary Truths

These propositional truths are of the kind that state that all bachelors are unmarried men. Another tautology is that all triangles have three sides. In effect, with tautologies one is saying the same thing with different words. Tautologies therefore do not give any new information, unless one is learning the meaning of words. By definition, the one is the same as the other. In denial of a tautology, a contradiction is entailed because, since the tautologous terms mean the same thing, to deny the one proposition is to deny the other.

It seems obvious that ethical propositions do not receive their necessity from being tautologies. For example, being immoral is not tautologous with any immoral act, such as stealing. Stealing is not immoral tautologically, when just considered as "Taking someone else's property without their permission,"[41] unless one adds the proviso that doing such a thing is wrong. Besides, as will be discussed below, "Taking someone's property without their permission" does not, just by itself, mean or entail wrongness. The wrongness must come from somewhere else.

---

40. Parrish, *God and Necessity*, 1–21.
41. See Moore on this. Moore, *Principia*.

(5.8) Analytically Necessary Truths

What is an analytical truth? This is a matter of some debate.[42] Some philosophers have questioned the whole notion of analytic truth.[43] Kant developed one of the first accounts of analyticity, though others had similar ideas. Here a particular notion about analytic statements will be added, with a certain definition.

This type of necessary truth is the kind that is illustrated in the example of a cube. It is necessarily true that a cube will have six faces and eight corners (at least in normal Euclidean space). The necessity is contained in the concepts involved but is more than merely giving a different name to the same concept. Having eight corners is necessary to *be* a cube but need not be included in the definition of a cube, though it is *analytically contained in the complete concept* of a cube. One may well understand what a cube is by playing dice or board games, without realizing that it necessarily contains eight corners. The essence of what a cube is, or any other entity, is not dependent upon our knowing the entire entailment of that essence.

Therefore, analytic truths can give new information, information that was not included in a particular definition. This takes us beyond tautology. In the case of the bachelor, by definition a bachelor is an unmarried man, and thus these two terms are tautologous. Looking further, however, being unmarried is *analytically contained* in the concept of bachelor. The difference here of *analytically contained* from being tautologous is that since women can be unmarried too, being unmarried is not identical with being a bachelor, but is analytically, necessarily included in the definition of bachelor.[44]

The same concept applies to scenarios that are vastly more complicated than these examples above. Take, for example, a specific geometrical figure that has one million sides. The angles between all the different sides will each have a determinate, necessary value, given the nature of the figure. However, no human being could directly grasp the necessity of values, though calculation might give the answer. It is simply too complex for that to happen. While not going directly into the ontology of the matter, it seems unquestionable that these kinds of objects have necessary truths. With this million-sided geometrical figure, whatever

---

42. See Juhl and Loomis, *Analyticity*.
43. Quine, "Two Dogmas," 20–46.
44. In response to Quine, see Grice and Strawson, "Defense of Dogma," 81–94.

the nature of the value of a particular angle in it, it is still the case that this value is necessary.

There are other ways of putting analytical necessity, but this should help with our discussion below. As already explained, to deny that 7 is a prime number, for example, is to affirm a contradiction, and contradictions cannot really exist. Similarly, though the contradiction is not as immediately obvious to us, to envision a cube that does not have eight vertices is to envision a contradiction. The necessity flows naturally and necessarily from the nature of the concepts that are involved.

Coming back to metaethics, wrongness is not analytically included in the concept of taking someone's property without his or her permission, unless one adds the concept of wrongness to it. Indeed, in certain unusual circumstances, taking a person's property without their permission may not be wrong. Therefore, analytic necessity does not seem to be the determining factor in establishing the normative involved here.

(5.9) A Posteriori Necessary Truth

I have also called this kind of necessity *metaphysical necessity*. This terminology, however, may cause confusion. Metaphysical necessity may be usable as a blanket term for all necessary truths apart from purely logical ones.[45] However, its main use is that of describing, logically enough, metaphysical truths such as that the past is unchangeable; a thing can only have one beginning; or, all colored objects have temporal extension.

---

45. What is the difference between logical and metaphysical necessity? This may be somewhat controversial. Stephen Maitzen writes, "I think of logical necessity as (predictably enough) the necessity imposed by the laws of logic. So, for example, it's logically necessary that no proposition and its negation are both true, a necessity imposed by the law of non-contradiction. But one might regard logical necessity as broader than that, since one might say that it also includes conceptual necessities such as 'Whatever is red is colored.'

Metaphysical necessity is a bit harder to nail down. Every proposition that's logically or conceptually necessary is also metaphysically necessary, but there may be metaphysical necessities that are neither logically nor conceptually necessary, such as 'Whatever is water is H2O' or 'Whatever is (elemental) gold has atomic number 79.' Nothing in logic or in the concepts involved makes those propositions necessary, but many philosophers say that those propositions are nevertheless 'true in every possible world,' which is the root idea of metaphysical necessity. Even if some proposition P isn't logically necessary, if P is metaphysically necessary then P is true in every possible world and the negation of P is false in every possible world." Maitzen, "What Is the Difference." To which I add, if gold is defined as having atomic number 79, then to call something that does not have atomic number 79 gold is to make a logical contradiction.

Here, to hold to standard convention, the term *a posteriori necessary truth* will be used, thereby avoiding possible confusion from different uses of the term "metaphysical." *A posteriori necessary truths* are truths such as that water necessarily is many H2O molecules acting together. From the concept of water at a macro level, one cannot derive that it is composed of molecules. Possibly, if one were smart enough, one could "see" that when you have many H2O molecules together, you have water. However, the opposite does not seem to be true, at least for human beings.

Again, this is a kind of necessity whereby new information is possible. Throughout most of human history, people knew a lot about water but were ignorant of its composition. That water is made of H2O was a discovery made long after humanity was familiar with the concept and importance of water. The sought-after contradiction for testing the truth in these cases comes from defining some substance *W* as being composed of another kind of thing, as water is composed of H2O, and then saying that some exemplification of *W* is composed of an alternative sort of thing, such as a hypothetical substance XYZ. This contradicts the original definition and is therefore necessarily false.

Epistemically, the concept of water is explicable and understood by reference to the concept of H2O molecules in the right amount and situation. *Ontologically*, all the "being" of water, its existence as such, is accounted for by a sufficiently large number of H2O molecules in a sufficient mass under the right conditions. There is nothing left unexplained, there is no "remainder", so the reduction can be counted as being completely successful.

In the realm of morality, however, *a posteriori* or metaphysical necessity also seems obviously to fail to apply. There appears to be no necessity of the kind that water is necessarily H2O as there is in saying that stealing is wrong. Stealing is not composed of little bits of wrongness, or vice versa. A posteriori necessity need not be compositional. For example, in identifying that the evening star is the same as the morning star, though this is not part/whole, the identity was discovered by close observation. But this is not how we discover moral truths, since moral properties are not observable.

Normative truths have concepts relevant to them and are not derivable from smaller constituent parts. Therefore, a posteriori necessity is not the source of necessary ethical truth.

(5.10) Synthetic Necessity

The last kind of absolute necessity that is to be examined here is the synthetic kind. Synthetic Necessity is defined as the necessity that happens when two or more things that are different *interact* in some way. When someone adds 5 and 7 together, then necessarily they have the sum of 12. Although this synthetic kind of necessity is real and important, it is difficult at first to see what relevance it has to the notion of deriving normative truths from non-normative ones. Prima facie, it is difficult to see how normativity can be a form of synthetic necessity. *And yet, some form of synthetic necessity seems to be required for ethical truths to be necessary, for natural concepts do not contain the concept of ethical necessity.*

For example, take utilitarianism. Assuming, for the sake of argument, that utilitarianism is necessarily true, there does not seem to be any way that the concepts involved in utilitarianism analytically include the concept of obligation. One can study the ideas of humanity, the most, happiness, and so on until one is blue in the face and not derive the concept of obligation.

The upshot of all this is that, given this example, any physical or psychological states are things by which normativity can be reduced to non-normative substances, properties, or events. This being the case, it seems that normativity is underivable from non-normativity, and thus cannot be reduced to the non-normative, by the very meaning of the terms involved.

This argument may seem to be a restatement of Moore's argument against naturalism.[46] There is a similarity, but the arguments are different. The essence of Moore's argument was that because one may always intelligibly ask of something if it is good, that goodness cannot be identical with that aspect of reality. For example, if one were a utilitarian, one would identify goodness with the maximal amount of happiness in the world. However, one can always intelligibly ask if happiness is good. By doing so, one shows that they are separate concepts.

The argument given here is different. It simply asks whence arises the necessity that is inherent in the concepts forming the basis for ethics. If one identifies moral goodness with happiness for everyone, it can be intelligibly asked *where the necessity arises*. Again, I have argued that at least some ethical propositions are necessarily true in the strong sense that they are true in all possible worlds. The basis for such necessity is

---

46. Moore, *Principia*.

the law of non-contradiction. But synthetic necessity by its very nature does not account for the contradiction to come directly from the moral concept at hand.

The only way that I can see that an ethical proposition can be necessarily true is because of a synthetic necessity, a necessity that is made true by external factors to the proposition itself. In this sense, ethical propositions resemble contingent propositions. However, what kind of factors could externally cause the necessity of a synthetically necessary proposition?

Synthetically necessary truths involve the concepts where the necessity is contained in *the intersection of more than one concept*. For example, Kant's famous example of $5 + 7 = 12$. This equation is a necessary truth, but the equation is not included in the concept of the number twelve. Alternatively, it is not in any other of the concepts involved, such as five, seven, addition, and equality. Because of this, these kinds of necessities are really "synthetic", because they do not flow from the nature of any one of the concepts involved, but rather, from their interaction.

A contradiction in synthetic necessities is thus not as straight forward as in the other kinds of necessity. The contradiction only arises with denying some essential property of the things involved. For example, blue paint when mixed with yellow paint (again, under normal circumstances and given the laws of nature) gives green paint. This fact is not analytically contained in any of the concepts of blue, yellow, green, or paint. One cannot have something colored blue with its properties and yellow with its properties, mix them, and not have green arise. The contradiction arises from the nature of the properties of the concepts involved and the laws of nature.

One might possibly argue that this law is only nomological, not logical, in its strength. In other words, there are possible worlds where the laws of nature are different from the actual world, and therein when one mixes blue and yellow together one gets purple. This may be the case. However, stating that the laws of nature are the same as they are in our world, then necessarily one will get green when one mixes blue and yellow. However, to reiterate, necessary ethical truths are ones that are true regardless of what set of the laws of nature would exist.

(5.11) Nomological Necessity

Nomological necessities are somewhat related to this. It seems to be true that, for example, the speed of light in a vacuum is about 186,282 miles per second. This is a fundamental constant of the universe. Yet it seems logically contingent. The explanation for both the necessity and the contingency lies outside of the realm of physics. That is, they are ultimately dependent upon the willing of God.

Whence, then, cometh the necessity for ethical truths?

What is needed for a strong or robust necessity in morality is some synthetic necessity that will somehow bestow necessity on the different requisite propositions of morality. The kind of necessity is absolute necessity, necessity that this is true in all possible worlds. This will be examined in the chapters below. To show the importance of this upcoming discussion, we will confirm that weak realist theories cannot do the job. In weak realism, what we have are metaethical theories that are based on some aspect of human reality. Because of this, many of them sound plausible. However, none of these theories are *necessary* in the sense that one is *ethically required* to choose any one of them. This makes the choice of any one moral system an amoral choice. To buy into any particular ethical system, one must choose apart from ethical values. They are thus based on *will*. Linda Zagzebski quotes Iris Murdoch on this point:

> The centre of this type of post-Kantian moral philosophy is the notion of the will as the creator of value. Values which were previously in some sense inscribed in the heavens and guaranteed by God collapse into the human will. There is no transcendental reality. The idea of the good remains indefinable and empty so that the human choice may fill it.[47]

My argument, thus, is that one can have a kind of realism, a weak realism with these theories, but all weak realist theories *depend upon an amoral act of will*. For a robust ethical realism, something needs to be added. So, it seems that only robust realism is acceptable. It is not only because we don't like a particular act, or society doesn't like it, or because we have contingently accepted some metaethical axiom that something is evil. Going into a school and shooting a bunch of children is evil, apart

---

47. Iris Murdoch, quoted in Linda Zagzebski, *Divine Motivation Theory*, 163.

from any theory we may hold. It is necessarily evil—evil in all possible worlds. It is evil even in those worlds where there are no sentient creatures that can kill or be killed, though, of course, there would be no one there who recognized the evil. Thus, only strong realism will fulfill the requirements for ethical propositions and values. These axioms are ones that are true in all possible worlds. Ethical values are a particular kind of value. Of all values, moral ones are most dependent upon persons. This point has important implications, as will be developed in the rest of the book.

CHAPTER 6

Antirealism

ANTIREALISM'S CATEGORIES

THE FOLLOWING TWO PROPOSITIONS are instances of antirealism.

- "[W]hen one reflects carefully on what it would take for an action to instantiate a property like *being morally forbidden,* one sees that too much is being asked of the world—there is simply nothing that is forbidden in the specifically moral sense of the word."[1]
- "To talk of intrinsic right and intrinsic wrong is absolutely nonsensical . . ."[2]

As we have seen, antirealist theories are divided into *cognitivism (subjectivism)* and *non-cognitivism,* both of which have subdivisions which are further divisible. The common foundational premise for all the different forms of *antirealism* is that, in the final analysis, *there are no objective ethical truths* as such. There are no ethical truths beyond all evaluative attitudes. There is nothing that is objectively right or wrong morally; all that ethics is, is an emotion, a prescription, or else simply a desire that people act in a certain manner; that things go a certain way, with nothing more fundamental than the individual's or the group's feeling that things would be (non-morally) best if certain strictures were accepted. Objective ethical propositions either do not exist, or else are mere inventions of human beings.

---

1. Joyce, *The Myth of Morality,* ix.
2. Nietzsche, *Geneology,* 49.

Introducing the Category of Cognitive Theories: Subjectivism (often labeled Relativism)

By way of review, the first subsection of antirealism is that of *cognitive theories*. These are those wherein *ethical statements express ethical truths*. They are listed above as *subjectivism* and *inter-subjectivism* (or *relativism*). As stated above, individual subjectivism is defined as what an *individual* thinks is morally right and wrong, while inter-subjectivism or relativism is just what a particular *group* thinks is morally right and wrong. Both hold that there are moral propositions that define moral reality. *Ethical truths are* therefore *relative to individuals or groups* and are learned in the same basic manner as other things are learned in society: via teaching and observation.

However, these are placed in antirealism because although they make statements thought to be ethical ones, really, they are nothing more than humanly sourced. Early in this book, ethical statements were defined as strongly realist if they are necessary and universal. With individual subjectivism and inter-subjectivism, neither necessity nor universality is met. Being that they are based on nothing more than human definitions, they are contingent and changeable. By reducing ethical propositions to non-ethical ones, they have gotten rid of the essence of what it is to be ethical. All forms of subjectivism are antirealist theories, for even weak realists think that ethics can, and in some sense must, be derived from some other aspect of contingent reality. Having said that, the line between antirealism and weak realism is gray and rather porous.

Introducing the Category of Noncognitive Theories: Reductionism and Eliminativism

Noncognitive theories espouse the *impossibility of evaluative ethical concepts*. All these theories have been much discussed, and in the end, all of them fail, falling to the fundamental problem that all antirealist theories are subject to—they all end up twisted into non-moral propositions. The essence of ethics, the morality, is lost.

Reductionism

This non-cognitive theory *reduces ethical statements to non-ethical ones.* The "ethicalness" of the statements is dismissed and eliminated by making these assertions about some other category of reality. As was explained above, non-cognitivism comes in three basic forms: *emotivism*, *prescriptivism*, and *expressivism*. The first, *emotivism*, holds that ethical statements are expressions of emotions or feelings. *Prescriptivism*, on the other hand, holds that ethical statements are prescriptions, recommendations, or commands for people to do or to refrain from doing. *Expressivism* is the view that in making ethical statements, what a person is doing is simply showing their attitude towards the statement. For example, if someone says that stealing is wrong, they are expressing their own personal negative view of stealing.

All these theories, among many other problems that they face, suffer from the obvious defect that when people make statements, they seem to be stating matters of fact, or what they believe to be matters of fact. This appears to be how most people interpret these ethical statements. To think that ethical statements are not really statements at all, seems to be obviously wrong. This problem has been called the Frege-Geach problem and has been considered a major challenge to non-cognitivism.[3]

Indeed, there are interesting issues involving non-cognitivism and the Frege-Geach problem. The basic criticism that will be leveled at non-cognitivism is that it is, in all its forms, essentially an antirealist ethical theory, which will be shown to be inadequate and unacceptable.

It should also be noted that proponents of antirealist moral theories have emotions, or feelings, or make commands based on what they *think* ought to be the case. A prescriptivist will make value prescriptions based on what he or she thinks would be good. Thus, these versions of

3. The Frege-Geach problem is explained by Mark Schroeder: "Theories in the noncognitivist tradition share the view that the distinctive meaning of moral words does not concern what they are about, and it either does not require or is not exhausted by any answer to what makes moral sentences true. For example, according to A. J. Ayer, the word 'wrong' works more like 'dammit' than like 'common', so that 'stealing money is wrong' means something more like, 'dammit, stealing money!' than like 'stealing money is common'. But standard ways of understanding the meanings of complex sentences, and of understanding the logical relationships between sentences, depend on an answer to what those sentences are about, or what would make them true. So noncognitivists need a different, nonstandard, answer to how the meanings of simple sentences give rise to the meanings of complex sentences. The problem of how to do so, and of whether it can even be done, has come to be known as the Frege–Geach problem." Schroeder, "Frege-Geach." 1.

antirealism may be founded on some version of weak realism, which will be discussed in the next chapter.

Eliminativism

Finally, we come to *eliminativist* theories. These are *nihilism* and *extreme nihilism*. With nihilism, moral propositions are thought to be assertions of ethics that correspond to nothing, for there is no category or aspect of reality that is ethical. Essentially, the category of ethics is eliminated. With extreme nihilism, the situation is even worse, for moral propositions are held to be literally meaningless. It is obvious that with both theories, the whole category of ethics is empty, so they both are extreme versions of antirealism. In these cases, it seems that for most people, ethics must be, in a sense, unlearned. That is, people come to think that ethical truths with which they were raised are not truths at all. Essentially, they are nothing.

ANTIREALIST COGNITIVISM

I have chosen the term *antirealist cognitivism* for this section because herein ethical propositions are held to be meaningful, therefore cognitive, but they end up as being arbitrary, based solely on beliefs.

As Michael Huemer writes,

> Anti-realists deny the existence of objective moral truths. If a moral statement is not objectively true, then there are just three possibilities: either it is non-objectively (subjectively) true, or it is false, or it is neither true nor false. Hence, we have the subjectivist, nihilist, and non-cognitivist positions, again.[4]

Huemer's definition of subjectivism here does not give all the detail I want to give. (It also includes theistic theories as subjective, which will be argued against below). What is meant by *objective moral truth* is ethical truths existing independently of what humans or other finite beings think or feel. I have split Huemer's third category, nihilism, into two because there is a meaningful difference between thinking that one is stating a truth about a category even when one is not and not saying anything intelligible at all.

---

4. Huemer, *Ethical Intuitionism*, 5.

Subjectivism—Individual and Inter-subjectivism

With *individual subjectivism*, the ethical system is chosen from an individual's own desires. If the subject thinks mostly of himself, he may decide to be an egoist. If the subject decides that he wants to help people and be altruistic, then he may decide to become a utilitarian.

Inter-subjectivism is subjectivism writ large, based on a *group's* desires, rather than on the wishes of an individual. The group as a whole has a set of ethical beliefs that is not based on anything beyond that which the particular group feels is right. Still, in individual subjectivist and inter-subjectivist theories, there *is* a belief that certain things are morally right or wrong, though these things are not considered to be from a different category than what is natural. They are a form of *natural judgment*.

What we will choose to do will be determined, to a certain extent, by the nature of the kind of creature that we are—in our case, human. Few people will choose to eat concrete, or have their skin entirely dyed green (though nowadays there may be some). Because we have the nature that we do have, our choices will be limited to a certain extent by humanity. In subjectivist or inter-subjectivist theories, therefore, what kind of ethical system is chosen is up to the desires of the individual or group that is making the choice. In subjectivism, ethics is reducible to the likes and dislikes of certain individuals and groups. Since likes and dislikes within this large scope of what human beings with their nature can and do have, this position ends up being nothing more than *subjective wants* and hence is a form of *antirealism*.[5]

Still, within the bounds of human nature, there is a very wide set of choices that may be made, and a vast number of ways of living that can be chosen, all consistent with human nature. In a subjectivist theory, what is chosen will be included within the bounds of what kind of creatures human beings are, but those bounds are quite wide.

Theological Voluntarism

There is one last antirealist metaethical theory to be explored here. This is *theological voluntarism*. Theological voluntarism holds that God's will is the basis for ethics. However, in contrast to other theistic metaethical theories, voluntarism purports that God makes rules that he could have

---

5. Hume, *Enquiry Concerning Morals*.

chosen to establish differently. For example, in the actual world God has decreed that kindness is good, while pointless cruelty is evil.[6] But, on an extreme version of theological voluntarism, God could have defined these in reverse, with kindness evil and cruelty good, though very few voluntarists would go this far.

ANTIREALIST NONCOGNITIVISM[7]

In Noncognitivist theories, ethics is reducible to either feeling or emotions, or else to commands and suggestions. The three main ethical theories that fall under this heading are *Emotivism*, *Prescriptivism*, and *Expressivism*.

Prescriptivism

In *prescriptivism* ethical statements are commands or suggestions about what the speaker wants done. Commands are neither true nor false. They are simply expressions of what one thinks should be done. In prescriptivism, to say that stealing is wrong is simply to assert that no one should steal. In this way, the rejection of stealing is *merely the speaker's opinion* about the matter.

Emotivism

In *emotivism*, moral statements are simply expressions of emotions or feelings. Thus, to the extent that they express anything about reality, they are about *the speaker's feelings*. In the case of the statement that stealing is wrong, what is really going on, in accordance with emotivism, is that the speaker is saying something like, "Stealing: Boo!" Again, emotions or expressions of approval or disapproval are not themselves true or false.

---

6. Given the right circumstances, of course. Dale Kratt has informed me that he knows of no contemporary theological voluntarists who actually hold to this—that God could have willed cruelty instead of kindness. However, it seems to be held by some Muslims. See Reilly, *Closing of the Muslim Mind*. See especially chapter 3.

7. A good introduction to noncognitivism is Schroeder, *Noncognitivism*. Noncognitivists include A.J. Ayer, R. M. Hare, and Simon Blackburn.

Expressivism

In *expressivism*, when someone makes an ethical statement, they are merely expressing what they think about a situation. Mark Schroeder defines expressivism in the following manner,

> For each sentence, 'P', an expressivist theory says what 'P' means by saying what it is to think that P. To think that grass is green, the expressivist will say, is to be in a state of mind with mind-to-world direction of fit—one which is like part of a map to the world we live in. But to think that stealing money is wrong, the expressivist will say, is to be in a different sort of state of mind—one with world-to-mind direction of fit, like the destination for which we are headed—pointing away from stealing money. Then a complete expressivist theory of meaning which follows Hare's suggestion will provide us with recipes which tell us how to determine, for complex sentences 'P', what it is to think that P, on the basis of what it is to think that Q, that R, and so on, for each of the parts of 'P'.[8]

Thus, what is meant by expressivism is that when one thinks that something is wrong, one is *thinking* that something is bad, that it *ought* not to be done. Therefore, if one thinks that "grass is green," then one has a state of mind that approves of the sentence that "grass is green." To think, "stealing is wrong," is to *think* that no one *should* steal money. They are thought to be non-cognitive because in them "moral thought is not cognitive or representational."[9]

The essence of what expressivists believe about morality is that rather than expressing external truths, that is, statements or propositions that describe objective, interpersonal reality—what they really do is something else. In these theories, a moral statement is not really a statement about the external world, but, rather, a statement about the mental and/or emotional state of the speaker who makes the moral statements.

To quote Michael Huemer again, "*Non-cognitivism* holds that evaluative predicates do not even purportedly refer to any sort of property, nor do evaluative statements assert propositions. Evaluative statements do not make claims about how the world is, not even about the part of the world that includes human observers."[10] To put the matter another

---

8. Schroeder, *Non-Cognitivism*, 159.
9. van Roojen, *Metaethics*, 295.
10. Huemer, *Ethical Intuitionism*, 4.

way, ethical statements are neither true nor false. Thus, concerns about the truth of ethical statements are beside the point.

It should be obvious that every one of these non-cognitive theories is itself antirealist in the sense that I have defined the term. That is not to say that the holders of them would deny that people might really command people to do things, or that they do not really have feelings or opinions about such things as stealing. It is simply that in both cases, ethical statements are about the person, rather than positing the existence of an *aspect of reality known as ethical* or moral, which is separate from individual feelings. There is for them, as for all antirealists, no necessarily existing truths about what is right and wrong.[11]

NIHILISM AND EXTREME NIHILISM

Numbers in Nothingness

The next antirealist position is *nihilism*, sometimes known as *error theory*. This is an extreme version of antirealist moral theory. It is analogous to the eliminative materialist theory in the mind-body problem. Here, all ethical statements are held to be necessarily false. Indeed, ethics is therefore considered a *false category*, applying to nothing that exists in extra-mental reality.

This can apply to other areas. Take, for example, a theory that numbers are fictional. Whatever Platonic abstract objects are, they are at least concepts, or combinations of concepts. We have the concepts of different numbers, so at least in that sense they exist. Whether they exist in some other manner may be debatable, but we must have a conceptual understanding of numbers, as they are necessary for us in doing highly abstract and technical forms of mathematics, as well as in ordinary life.

Therefore, even if numbers are fictional in some sense of the word, they are not in another sense of the word, for we can understand them and use them in various ways. However, even apart from these points, there is another. This is that mathematics is an actual aspect of reality. Even if numbers are fictions, there is a vast field of scholarship that uses them. This is because numbers and mathematical operations have well-defined terms and an infinite field of investigation with a frequent applicability to the physical universe. Because of this, it is difficult to understand why

---

11. Although in a sense there is, because given the truth of expressivism about morality, there are necessarily no moral truths.

anyone would question the existence of numbers—whether as Platonic abstract entities or as ideal objects in God's mind. Whether or not numbers exist in some other sense of the word, it seems that they obviously have at least a coherent conceptual existence.

Ethics in Nothingness

Having established the conceptual existence of numbers, we will move on to the question of ethics. Suppose it is true that all ethical propositions are, in fact, about *"nothing,"* as the nihilist claims. The whole category of ethics would be, in fact, an empty one, as this aspect of reality would not exist. This seems odd, as practically every day we use ethical terms, understand what they mean, and grasp the concepts involved which have a large impact on our lives. We reason about ethics, argue about morals, try to live our lives in accordance with the "shoulds" and "oughts", and even fight and kill over some related disputes. How often do we hear, "That's not fair!" or "That's wrong!"?

Even if in some sense numbers are fictional, their concepts undeniably exist and are understandable, and this is enough for mathematics to exist and be real, at least conceptually. Mathematics is still an actual aspect of reality. Similarly, the fact that ethical propositions exist, even if they are fictional in some sense of the word, their understandability shows that ethics is an actual part of reality, at least conceptually. The field of ethics is vast, and its various concepts fit together and have congruence with each other. In short, metaethics and ethics, in all their related matters, seem to be similar in these broad categorical aspects to mathematics.

Therefore, nihilism fails, for it posits that ethics is about nothing. Nihilism contradicts our experience that ethics *is* about something. One may thus think that in describing nihilism, one is describing a theory such as *phlogiston*. Phlogiston was a scientific theory regarding the nature of combustion. Put simply, it envisioned that heat was a kind of fluid named phlogiston. Phlogiston theory was popular over two hundred years ago, being replaced by the modern concept that heat is molecular motion.

So, one might think that given ethical nihilism, ethics is really a theory like phlogiston—something that was thought to exist but does not. However, nihilism is much more radical than getting rid of a false scientific theory, such as that of phlogiston's being the nature of heat.

The reason is clear. Phlogiston was an attempt to explain heat. Heat is a physical thing; it is the kind of thing that physicist's study. Phlogiston itself was supposed to be a physical substance of sorts. Though we no longer believe in phlogiston, its rejection does not remove an entire category of being. We have merely replaced one kind of postulated physical entity—phlogiston—with another kind, which is molecular motion. The existence of a kind of physical thing has been rejected, but certainly not the whole category of physical things, which are still very much around.

With ethical nihilism, the elimination is extreme. Here one is not just eliminating a particular kind of thing from existence, such as in the rejection of the existence of phlogiston, but one is rejecting an entire *category* of kinds of things. To give a better analogy than the rejection of phlogiston, one would have to reject the entire category of physical things—believing that they do not exist. Further, given the necessary nature of ethical truths in realism, rejection of the possible existence of all physical things would follow. This is far more radical than simply rejecting the existence of phlogiston.

Extreme Nihilism

As was mentioned above, there is a position that is even more radical than nihilism. This position will be called *extreme nihilism*. In nihilism, ethical propositions are not meaningful, but may sound like they are meaningful, though they are about an aspect of reality that does not and cannot exist. I am not certain that this even makes sense, which leads me to super nihilism. In extreme nihilism, *ethical propositions are literally meaningless and irreducible*. With extreme nihilism, people who speak of ethics are not really saying anything at all. Extreme nihilism is not emotivism but holds the position that ethical propositions are not only meaningless, they also cannot be reducible to anything else. Not only is the whole category of morality empty, but it also does not and even cannot exist. This is different from emotivism, where ethical statements are reduced to feelings. In extreme nihilism, these ethical thoughts are reduced to being totally unintelligible. Saying ethical propositions is like saying a bunch of nonsense words. It may not be the case that anyone holds this view, but it seems that it is possible to espouse, so it is included in the conversation for completeness's sake. This theory should, therefore, fall under non-cognitivism, as ethics is literally meaningless and irreducible.

This brings us to an interesting point. In nihilism, people understand ethical propositions, but claim they are literally about nothing. However, if they are understandable, they must fit into some category of reality. And if they fit into some category of reality, then must not that category of reality exist? It seems so. Therefore, there must exist an ethical category in reality. In what is a very important contradistinction, a nihilist will believe that no ethical statement is true and yet that this last statement is itself necessarily true.

ANTIREALISM IN SUMMARY

Antirealism in metaethics is therefore the idea that ethics is *invented*, not discovered or naturally derived from some other facet of the world—like rationality or human nature. Ethics here is simply something that we, groups or individuals, make up for various reasons, mainly to make our lives go better in some non-moral sense of "better." In antirealism, there is nothing *wrong* (in the normal ethical sense of the word) with stealing, or even torturing innocent people for fun. Rather, ethical statements do not even make claims about the truth or falsity of anything, because they are considered to be in an empty category.

ANTIREALIST ARGUMENTS

So here, we have a certain categorization of *antirealist theories*. Though different from each other, all of these theories *assert that there are no moral truths that exist apart from the will or feeling of finite minds*. In short, morality is a category of being or thought that was *invented* by human beings, rather than discovered or derived by them. The question then arises, what reasons have we for thinking that some version of antirealism is true? It is to this point that the investigation will now turn. How is acceptance of ethical antirealism to be justified? Writes Michael Ruse about this point,

> So how then do I justify my substantive ethical beliefs? I claim simply that there is no justification! I think the substantive ethics, claims like "love your neighbor as yourself," are simply psychological beliefs put in place by natural selection in order to

maintain and improve our reproductive fitness. There is nothing more to them than that. They have no ultimate backing.[12]

Antirealism is strongly counterintuitive to many people, including me. I cannot think that, for example, torturing people because you enjoy hearing them scream is not really a bad thing to do. By this, it is not just meant that it is impractical, tacky, or imprudent. Rather, in addition to these, there is an added factor—that it is wrong, immoral, unethical, and evil to do something like this. There is a whole other aspect of being involved, namely that of *morality*. It seems that most other people have the same intuition. Indeed, the very strong counter intuitiveness of antirealism is a major argument against it.[13]

How then can antirealists make a case for their position? There are three main arguments antirealists put forth for their stance. They are: 1) The argument from relativity; 2) The argument from queerness; and 3) The argument that there cannot be ethically evaluative propositions.

The Argument from Relativity

Different yokes for different folks

Antirealists have tried extensively to make their case. According to Andrew Fisher, there are three basic objections to any sort of realism in ethics.[14] The first argument for subjectivism is *the argument from relativity*. It is simply a matter of fact that different people, and different cultures, believe in different values. Although somewhat dated, J. L. Mackie will be used as an example of an antirealist. He covers all the bases. J. L. Mackie gives the basic version of the argument in this fashion:

> The argument from relativity has as its premises the well-known variation in moral codes from one society to another and from one period to another, and also the differences in moral beliefs between different groups and classes within a complex community . . . [I]t is not the mere occurrence of disagreements that tells against the objectivity of values. Disagreement on questions in history or biology or cosmology does not show that there are no objective issues in these fields for investigators to disagree about. But such scientific disagreement results from speculative

12. Ruse, "Naturalist Moral Nonrealism," 65.
13. See Lutz and Case, *Is Morality Real?*, 40–84.
14. Fisher, *Metaethics*, 39–53.

inferences or explanatory hypotheses based on inadequate evidence, and it is hardly plausible to interpret moral disagreement in the same way.[15]

The argument for relativism receives plausibility from the fact that different cultures have different—sometimes very different—ideas of what is moral and immoral. Westerners have usually supported monogamy, while Islamic cultures have accepted polygamy. We now think that slavery is one of the worst things that there could be, while throughout history most cultures have taken slavery for granted. Most cultures think of betraying someone as being one of the more immoral things that one can do, while the Sawi, a tribe in New Guinea, thought that getting someone in your confidence and then betraying them gave you great prestige.[16] The list can be greatly extended from these examples. Undoubtedly, differences between different societies can be very great indeed.

Further, not only do different cultures vary ethically from one another, but also within cultures there is often change over time in what is thought to be moral and immoral. Someone living in the United States through the last few decades can attest to the rapid change in American society's ideas of what behavior is ethically right and wrong. For example, decades ago abortion was held by most people to be morally wrong, and at least shameful. Nowadays, many people think that there is nothing wrong with it. In fact, now the pendulum has swung to the opposite side, with many considering a view against abortion to be morally untenable.

From examples like these, some argue that because there is no agreement on many ethical issues, there is not one "correct" standard of right and wrong. Different cultures and groups, with variations over time, and even individuals at different points of their lives, can have dissimilar, and sometimes greatly disparate ideas of what constitutes right and wrong.

An obvious rebuttal to relativism is to simply point out that it is quite possible for cultures to be wrong on ethical matters. In the ancient world, apparently most people thought that the world was flat. Now we know that the world is spherical. Many people believed in astrology in ancient, medieval, and early modern times. For that matter, many people still do, though educated people tend to think of it as a mere superstition. The ancient Babylonians seemed to think that one could tell the future

---

15. Mackie, *Ethics*, 36. Other books that defend fictionalism are Joyce, *The Myth of Morality*; and Olson, *Moral Error Theory*.

16. Richardson, *Peace Child*. The Sawi thought Judas was the ultimate hero for betraying Jesus with a kiss.

by looking at sheep livers, but few believe that now.[17] The point is that people, even whole civilizations, can be wrong about things. Therefore, the realist can respond to the argument from ethical relativity by simply pointing out that disagreement can be a sign that people have false beliefs about some matter, not that there is no truth to the matter.

Mackie's response to this is that disagreements about scientific matters can be settled by empirical evidence. The reason that people have false beliefs about scientific and related matters is often that there isn't enough evidence available to tell the correct solution. The ancient and medieval eras simply didn't have the information available to know the truth about the real nature of our solar system, for example. When the information did become available, beliefs about the nature of the solar system changed.

The problem is that, as Mackie points out, we cannot interpret moral disagreement in the same way. Whether slavery is very wrong, as we now think, or acceptable, as most people of the past thought, the question of slavery's rightness or wrongness cannot be settled empirically the same way that the disagreement about geocentrism versus heliocentrism was eventually settled by empirical scientific evidence. That kind of evidence is just not available to settle ethical disputes.

Responses to the Argument from Relativity

What can be said in response to this? First, just because there may be no way to settle a disagreement in ethics by empirical investigation does not disprove the point that cultures can still be wrong. It may just mean that the truth about ethics is harder to find than the truths of natural science (though those certainly are not always easy to discover), or that certain cultures are ignoring morality for other reasons.

Still, it must be admitted that the lack of any direct way to discern what real ethical truths are seems to be a problem for realism. Later, it will be argued that in some cases, there are ways. For now, I will show that the argument is not as strong as Mackie thinks that it is.

Ethical systems may not be as varied as is sometimes asserted. C. S. Lewis (along with many others) argued for a great deal of similarity between many different cultures regarding ethics.[18] Though there are,

17. Barfield, *Why the Bible Is Number 1*, 21–23.
18. Lewis, *Abolition of Man*.

unquestionably, differences, there is also a great deal of similarity. This leads to the following point.

Real ethical roots must produce real flourishing, but we don't always see that

Second, it seems plausible a priori that if there were a true ethical system, it would generally lead to flourishing—human and otherwise. That is, it seems quite plausible that an ethic that led many people in society to have short and unhappy lives would not be the correct one. One does not have to believe that ethics is that which promotes human flourishing to think that the "real ethical system" (if there is one) would promote flourishing. It seems perverse to think that if everyone acted ethically all the time, then everyone would be miserable. That doing the right thing can make one miserable at times seems to be undeniably true, but that such an effect would always exist systematically for everyone and for all places just seems wrong. Therefore, it appears that a test of a true ethical system is that it would promote human happiness. This test need not be infallible, but it would still have weight.

Ethical systems depend on Worldviews

A third point in response to the argument from relativity is to give an explanation as to why different people and societies hold to different ethical systems. They base their ethics on what worldview they hold. Both worldviews and the ethical systems influence each other. We already briefly visited worldviews above, but here we will investigate further the relationship between worldviews and ethics.

If, for example, one believes that there is a happy place where people may go after death where only the best and bravest go, one may think that warrior virtues are things to be developed, and that war may be basically a good thing rather than a bad one. There were ancient cultures that seem to have held this kind of belief.

If, on the other hand, one believes that there is no afterlife, that whatever goodness one will ever have is in the here and now, then one may be caused to think that hedonism is the worldview and ethical system that ought to be adopted. Thus, though this conclusion does not follow with demonstrative force from the premise, it nonetheless seems to be a rational response. Many people have accepted it.

However, the main point here is that the notion of worldview gives us an insight into *why* different ethical systems from different cultures (or from different individuals, for that matter) have the forms that they do. Taking the virtually universal notion that there are things that ought to be, or not be, done, the idea is developed in a variety of ways, which is largely determined by the nature of the whole worldview.

It seems to be the case that human beings recognize the ethical sphere. They understand, as part of their nature, that there are things that ought to be done or not be done. That is, they understand the ethical aspect of reality. However, the ethical aspect is merely one part of our understanding, one part of our beliefs about the nature of reality. What else people believe about the general overall nature of reality becomes a bed upon which the various aspects of reality, including the ethical ones, are fitted. Because of this, it soon becomes apparent why the genre of ethics is so different from empirically definable categories.

For whatever the ethical unit—the culture, sub-group within the culture, or the individual—belief makes a difference. For example, belief in God or gods strongly influences the group's morality, as often they think that their God has something to say about what *ought* to be done. Similarly, whether the above units believe in an afterlife will have something to do with what ethics are held. Believers in an afterlife will extrapolate about what behaviors should (or should not) be attempted. For example, those with a belief that a good afterlife is possible, but must be attained by acting in some manner, will have a reason for acting in that way. In this case, the afterlife can be considered delayed gratification that will influence one's behavior here on earth.

The point about beliefs in God or gods is a very important one, though the point is partly psychological. Theists, especially modern monotheists, think that God is the most important part of reality. This is why theists will automatically link ethics and God. They have a difficult time understanding that God cannot be connected in some way to ethics, because God is necessarily connected to everything.

On the other hand, non-theists, and especially atheists of a militant breed, think that belief in God is absurd or at least unwarranted, and therefore reject any dependence of ethics on God. For example, antirealist Richard Joyce writes, "Plato cannot resist appealing to a supernatural supplement to the main argument . . . This is no better than Hesiod's magical hypothesis of an anthropomorphized Justice who runs weeping to Zeus."[19]

Even apart from religious concepts such as God or an afterlife, the ethics involved is dependent upon how the rest of reality is conceived to be. A collectivist vision of humankind, such as in Marxism, will think that a certain set of things ought to be done. An individualist vision of how things are, as in Ayn Rand's Objectivism, will think that a different set of things, perhaps radically different, ought to be done.[20]

The list can be extended ad nauseum, but the point should already be made. Ethical systems differ from one another partly because the nature of the worldview may differ radically. It is important to emphasize this major point on these issues. Just because the fact that worldviews differ radically from one another does not mean that there is no finally correct worldview. Indeed, by the nature of things, *there must be a finally correct worldview, as there can only be one description of reality that is totally correct.*

So, just because there is disagreement in ethics between different groups and individuals, and it cannot be easily shown who is correct and who is not, this does not at all imply that there is no "correct" answer. One could say the same thing about worldviews. It is necessarily the case that one worldview is correct, and the others, to the extent that they disagree with this one, are wrong. Yet, there are many different worldviews in existence, and it is not easy to determine which is the correct one, as often people ardently disagree about them. There is no consensus. Indeed, there is more agreement in morality than there is in worldviews. Almost everyone will believe that pouring gasoline on babies and setting them on fire because one likes hearing them scream is grossly evil. This belief seems to me to be more strongly established than many beliefs about empirical objects. Therefore, this argument of relativity for antirealism fails, or at least is not nearly as strong as it might at first seem to be.

The Argument from Queerness

The second argument for antirealism is the argument from queerness. This argument, made by J. L. Mackie and others, asserts that ethical

---

19. Joyce, *Myth of Morality*, 33.
20. See also Peikoff, *Objectivism*. For a defense of Objectivist ethics, see Smith, *Viable Values*.

truths do not exist outside of the human mind, because if they did, they would be too queer, and so, they don't fit in with the rest of reality, which is entirely describable by non-evaluative statements. Mackie expounds upon the argument from queerness thusly:

> Even more important [than the argument from relativity], however, and certainly more generally applicable, is the argument from queerness. This has two parts, one metaphysical, the other epistemological. If there were objective values, then they would be entities or qualities or relations of a very strange sort, utterly different from anything else in the universe. Correspondingly, if we were aware of them, it would have to be by some special faculty of moral perception or intuition, utterly different from our ordinary ways of knowing everything else.[21]

The Epistemological Argument from Queerness

This argument basically states that given that ethical propositions are so different from propositions about physical things, for example, there seems to be no way that we could know them. Therefore, it is reasoned, if there are these ethical propositions existing as abstract entities, then it seems impossible for us to grasp them. But, there's a hole in this argument. This only applies to certain kinds of abstract entities. For example, numbers seemingly do not depend upon any existing thing in our universe. Other kinds of abstract entities, like the equator, do depend upon things existing in the universe and hence can be measured. But for Platonists, the first kind of abstract entities, like numbers, supposedly exist in "Plato's heaven" as aspatial, atemporal, and causally inert. How then can we physical creatures access them? This question will be further examined in the chapters on abstract entities and theistic conceptualism.

The Metaphysical argument from queerness

To put the metaphysical argument more specifically, other true statements about reality are about the *physical* universe. They include statements about size, shape, mass, and motion, and hence are quite unlike evaluative statements. Other true statements about reality include *psychological*

---

21. Mackie, *Ethics*, 38. A similar argument is made in Olson, *Moral Error Theory*, 116–38.

ones, about what people are thinking, and about what they are capable of thinking. Now let us revisit proposition *T*, which is, "It is wrong to torture anything for fun." Mackie is arguing that ethical statements, like statement *T*, are so different from all the other objects that exist in our world, that it is hard to see how they could exist. Hence, the "queerness" concept.

Still, it can be argued that we do make statements about other things than just physical objects, properties, and relations in our universe. Other statements are about abstract entities. These would include truths about mathematics, the relations of universals to one another, and many others. What does Mackie say in response to this? He writes,

> Indeed, the best move for the moral objectivist is not to evade this issue [of queerness], but to look for companions in guilt. For example, Richard Price argues that it is not moral knowledge alone that such an empiricism as those of Locke and Hume is unable to account for, but also our knowledge and even our ideas of essence, number, identity, diversity, solidity, inertia, substance, the necessary existence and infinite extension of time and space, necessity and possibility in general, power, and causation.[22]

Mackie's response to this line of argument is to allege that all the items in the above are explicable empirically, that is, by means of sense perception. In other words, knowledge of the items in the list can be known by the same means by which we come to knowledge of physical things. Further, Mackie writes, "If some supposed metaphysical necessities or essences resist such treatment, then they too should be included, along with objective values, among the targets of the argument from queerness."[23]

In response, this argument presupposes the truth of empiricism, philosophical naturalism, and physicalism—that the physical world is the whole of reality and that the only way we learn is through sensation. With these theories, fundamental concrete reality is thought to be of non-conscious physical entities, and everything else that exists is derived from these.[24] Empiricism alone is incapable of explaining much of our knowledge. We know about universals, propositions, and numbers. Their

---

22. Mackie, *Ethics*, 39.

23. Mackie, *Ethics*, 39.

24. I am not certain if Mackie rules out the existence of abstract entities, but judging from what he wrote, he seems to.

existence may be deduced from physical objects, but there is much more to it than only through sensation. Pure reason is necessary for knowledge of these things.[25] In naturalism, what is believed to be true is that reality's ultimate nature is impersonal. It is a mystery how, in naturalism, any knowledge is possible. In naturalism, minds appear by accident out of mindless "stuff." This stance is very hard to comprehend by itself. In a mindless universe, how can minds understand anything?

The Argument Against Ethically Evaluative Propositions

If all that exists is physical things, then it does seem difficult to see how and why ethical statements would be part of reality, let alone deemed to be true. Propositions about physical things would seem to be able to cover all the states of affairs in the universe. A green or round object would make the proposition about said green or round object to be true (or false, depending upon the statement made). Propositions about physical objects, properties, and events would seem to cover everything that has existences.

If one is not a physicalist, then this problem is not nearly as large. The rejection of physicalism and naturalism greatly reduces or eliminates the problem that Mackie raises here. In short, rejecting Mackie's starting points undercuts his argument against knowledge of abstract objects, as they are based on his *presuppositions*.

We thus seem to have come to something of an impasse. Mackie was an empiricist, accepting that all knowledge comes from sensation, and that any alleged knowledge of other concepts, if they cannot pass the test of empiricism, should be dismissed outright. In a simple response to this, empiricism, especially of the strong variety that Mackie espoused, is not without serious difficulties. As noted above, to examine empiricism and its rivals in the nature of knowledge and justification would easily take a whole book to cover adequately.[26] Suffice it to say that since Mackie's underlying premise of empiricism is on rickety standing, so too, arguments based thereon would be iffy.

Regarding the existence of platonic abstract entities, even nominalists and antirealists usually do not deny that two plus two will always

---

25. The investigation of the theory of empiricism as the sole basis for knowledge would be a very long one for which there is no space here. I will simply say that I think that it is false. For a refutation of Empiricism, see BonJour, *In Defense of Pure Reason*.

26. For another critique of empiricism, see McGinn, *Inborn Knowledge*.

equal four, that red is a color rather than a number, and that everything is identical with itself. These descriptive assertions seem to be propositions that are all present in reality and true, and necessarily so. Even given the views from empiricism and antirealism about abstracta-like propositions, the mere fact that ethical statements are not reducible to physical objects does not rule out their existence, if they are *about* physical things. However, the problem for *ethical* statements to the antirealists, unlike the other kinds of statements mentioned, is that ethical statements are *evaluative* rather than merely descriptive.

Ethical propositions are evaluative insofar as they say that some things are right and others wrong, and that certain things ought to be done and others not. And the *ought* has a very strong sense. One should not do some things no matter what.

The other statements are non-evaluative. They describe how things are, or how they might possibly be. They do not say how things *ought* to be in an ethical sense. One may then ask how ethical evaluative statements could be true. They would be radically different from all other statements, even ones about abstract entities, and are, therefore, queer. This gives the basic argument that Mackie employs.

Here, a point made above will be expanded on. Not only is ultimate reality physical, given naturalism and materialism, but also, reality is ultimately impersonal. That is, ultimate reality is held to be made of things that are unconscious, not subjective, non-rational, and without intentionality. Persons, to the extent that they are held to exist, are just an odd, unplanned occurrence of evolution, which itself is held to be completely unplanned.[27] Exactly how and why consciousness appeared in a completely physical world has never really been given a satisfactory explanation by naturalists and physicalists.[28]

However, given theism, this problem disappears, or at least is greatly reduced. In theism, God, who is ultimate reality, exists personally with consciousness, subjectivity, rationality, and intentionality. There are therefore, in this view, things that are deeper than the physical. In theism, the limitations on what ought to exist are significantly reduced. If

---

27. By "exist", I mean as conscious beings. Eliminative materialism denies this, as in the writings of Paul and Patricia Churchland. See for example Churchland, *Neurophilosophy*.

28. Parrish, *Knower and the Known*.

abstract entities can be thought of as ideal objects, or simply as divine ideas, they can all really exist in the mind of God.[29]

In fact, Mackie agrees with this. In the last part of his book, he agrees that *if* God exists, then there is a solution as to how an objective ethics could exist, and the problem of queerness could be avoided. However, Mackie was an atheist, thinking that the problem of evil and the advance of science removed any grounds for belief in a God of such a nature. There are significant responses to these basic arguments against God, but adequately answering these atheistic assumptions would take us too far afield to evaluate here.[30]

The Argument Against Normativity

Another related argument against realism in ethics is the whole notion that normativity is false. Realism in ethics holds to normative statements such as, "We ought to be kind." However, a few philosophers have taken the assault on normativity broadly, thinking that absolute standards do not exist in any area. For example, some say that there are not, and cannot be, any reasons why we should believe anything. This position is extremely implausible.[31] How can we believe that we shouldn't believe anything? This is self-contradictory. It seems obvious that there is normativity in reality in many different areas, and hence normativity in ethics cannot be ruled out.

ONE MORE PROBLEM FOR ANTIREALISM

One argument against antirealism has already been mentioned, the fact that it is strongly counter intuitive. In chapter 8, more challenges will be given to refute antirealism. However, with all antirealist theories, there is also a pragmatic problem for many people, including me. One quote will

---

29. For an interesting take on this, see Rasmussen, "Argument for Supreme Foundation."

30. In the last few decades, the literature on arguments for and against the existence of God has grown immensely. For one recent entry see Walls and Dougherty, *Two Dozen Arguments*. For a long time after Hume and Kant, most philosophers believed that there are no strong arguments for God's existence. This view is changing, but naturalist atheism is still deeply entrenched in much of academia.

31. I will defer the reader to the discussion in Lutz and Case, *Is Morality Real?*, 85–116.

dramatically exemplify what this is. Ted Bundy, an infamous serial killer, stated the following:

> Then I learned that all moral judgements are "value judgements," that all value judgements are subjective, and that none can be proved to be either "right" or "wrong." ... I discovered that to become truly free, truly unfettered, I had to become truly uninhibited ... Surely, you would not, in this age of scientific enlightenment, declare that God or nature has marked some pleasures as "moral" or "good" and others as "immoral" or "bad"? In any case, let me assure you, my dear young lady, that there is absolutely no comparison between the pleasure I might take in eating ham and the pleasure I anticipate raping and murdering you. That is the honest conclusion to which my education has led me ... [32]

I think that behind much opposition to any form of antirealism is the thought, and the fear, that were antirealism true, it would reduce the inhibitions on destructive behavior that morality provides. I am not saying that antirealists are bad people, but that holding to antirealism opens a door that may lead to very bad things. Most people aren't like Ted Bundy, but reduction in the inhibitions that hold back individually and socially destructive behavior is bad for almost everyone. This is a practical problem, not a theoretical one, but of such importance that it is entered here into the discussion. Just because a theory has disturbing implications may not automatically mean that it is false. However, if some theory entails a terrible consequence in the world, we have good reason to examine it to see if the theory is true or deeply flawed.

Since antirealism is the position that there is nothing that is *really* morally evil or good, it removes a major barrier or deterrent on people's negative behaviors. We should try to avoid this conclusion if we honestly can. Given that it is also very counter-intuitive to most people, this gives us reasons to *put a burden of proof on antirealists*. Indeed, one may say that the burden is already there because our pre-reflective "folk morality" is already morally realist in its commitments, as David Enoch has argued.[33]

---

32. Quoted in Christensen, *What about Evil?*, 62–63. I think that much contemporary antirealism ultimately derives from scientism, which is the theory that all knowledge comes from science, or at least scientific knowledge is superior to any other kind. See Williams and Robinson, *Scientism*.

33. Enoch, *Taking Morality Seriously*, 50–84.

We are often so used to living in a society that accepts certain values, such as human beings' having intrinsic value, that it is easy to forget that many societies have not believed this. Deeming aggressive war, torture, or slavery as bad is an assumption that we now think is self-evidently true, though in earlier cultures their acceptability was often taken for granted. But if one does not believe that human beings have intrinsic worth and therefore should be treated with dignity, these values are undercut. Recently several books have been published that argue that this valuing of human lives comes from Christianity.[34] It seems to me that by embracing antirealism, and yes, also by discarding Christianity, we are cutting off the branches upon which our most distinctive and important values are based. People often only act well because they think that they are supposed to. By removing Christianity's ethos, the hold that important values have on us weakens, including that of the sanctity of human life.

David Brog quotes the Roman writer Tacitus, who wrote, "Among the Jews all things are profane that we hold sacred, in the other hand they regard as permissible what seems to be immoral."[35] Brog goes on to quote Tacitus as saying that something the Jews did was "sinister and revolting" to the Romans, writing that among the Jews, "[I]t is a deadly sin to kill an unwanted child."[36]

The main reason that later western civilization took the Jewish and Christian perspective is the biblical teaching that human beings are made in the image of God.[37] However, though there were many failures in upholding this standard, it was always there and has worked tremendous good in the world. With the fading of Christianity, we have moved back to killing unwanted babies in abortion.[38]

Attempts to abolish aggressive warfare, torture, and slavery were built on the belief that human beings are created in the image of God and hence have intrinsic worth. Those who think that we can get rid of God and an absolute ethic yet still hold on to the value of human life, have lost any secure basis for their stance. Inevitably, therefore, any moral code

---

34. Scrivener, *The Air We Breathe*; and Holland, *Dominion*.
35. Brog, *In Defense of Faith*, 2.
36. Brog, *In Defense of Faith*, 2.
37. Gen 1:27.
38. According to Philip Rieff abortion is one of main death works today that are poisoning our civilization. For more on the decline of our culture see also his book, Rieff, *The Triumph of the Therapeutic*, as well as Paul C. Vitz's, *Psychology As Religion*.

is built on nothing.[39] The stance that human beings' having a "natural" or "normal" belief in ethics, apart from God, goes against history. It was mainly Christianity and biblical teaching that established an understanding of human worth. Critics who are non-theists, and especially antirealists, who hold to the intrinsic moral value of human beings, falsely think that these values are obvious. As Brog writes, "Growing up in the heart of a Judeo-Christian society, such critics begin life on a high moral summit and believe that they have scaled a mountain."[40] Attempts to explain this belief in the *intrinsic* value of human beings based on some weak realist theory (or on abstract entities as do non-theistic strong realists) will fail. Antirealists have only their desires to preserve a moral code, and this is entirely inadequate.

If one is an antirealist, and believes that there are no moral truths, then what is left to base a system of rules to govern life is merely desire. And if desire is all that there is, with no necessary standard by which to judge the different desires, the result is *moral anarchy*. Stephen L. Gardner, referencing Philip Rief's analysis of Freud writes, "In the end, though, even the lucidity and intellectual self-reliance of Freud's 'analytic attitude' reflects a resigned admission that modern desire is a lost cause, yet still cannot be abandoned. For the psychoanalyst, it is all there is."[41] If antirealism were true, then this is true not only for psychoanalysts, but for everyone.

---

39. Some philosophers are attempting to provide a strong ethical basis without God by appealing to Platonism. This will be examined and rebutted in chapter 9.

40. Brog, *In Defense of Faith*, 4.

41. In Rieff, *Triumph*.

CHAPTER 7

Weak Realism[1]

ONE WAY OF THINKING about the nature of the different metaethical theories is the division between *realist* theses, where ethics is thought to exist, expressible in true propositions, and *antirealist* notions, which deny ethics.

James Drier, in describing realists, writes,

> Realists, by contrast, think the phenomenology of moral thought is that of "fact-finding," that our moral judgments at least purport to be (and sometimes really are) about the moral facts themselves, that the truth of the matter transcends the attitudes we bring to the table, that there is such a thing as getting it right or wrong.[2]

However, there is a major distinction between robust or strong realist theories, and weak ones. As explained above, in *strong realism, moral truths are discovered*, in *weak realism, they are derived*, and in *antirealism, they are invented*.

WEAK REALISM AS DERIVED ETHICS

Simply put, all weak realist theories are dependent upon non-necessary *axioms*. For example, utilitarian theories begin with a choice of an axiom, or fundamental principle, upon which all the rest of the theory is

---

1. Examples of weak realist systems include Bloomfield, *Moral Reality*; Foot, *Natural Goodness*; and Sinnott-Armstrong, *Morality Without God?*
2. Dreier, *Contemporary Debates*, xix.

derivable.[3] However, why choose this standard? There is no contradiction in not choosing it. There are other axioms that one may choose, such as one that is the support of egoism, that personal happiness is the highest good. In weak realism, choosing one axiom instead of any others, or even just ignoring the whole question of morality, does not land one in absurdity. There is no necessity in choosing any one of them. People have many different *reasons* for choosing one over others.

Constructivism[4]

As stated above, in weak realism, ethical propositions are *derived* from other things. One version of weak realism is *constructivism*, though it seems to me that in a very real sense, all weak realisms are forms of constructivism. Writes Bagnoli,

> Constructivism comes in several varieties, some of which claim a place within metaethics while others claim no place within it at all. In fact, constructivism is sometimes defended as a *normative* theory about the justification of moral principles. Normative constructivism is the view that the moral principles we ought to accept are the ones that agents would agree to or endorse were they to engage in a hypothetical or idealized process of rational deliberation.[5]

In constructivist naturalism, human nature is sometimes appealed to. That is, human beings have a specific nature, which though it contains a certain amount of variability, it also has a large amount of definiteness. In other words, human beings, in the manner that they are "constructed," need and want certain things, and do not need or want other things. People need food and drink. They need protection from the elements. They need sex for humanity to continue, and so on. They also have mental and social needs. Almost all people want friends and companionship, for

---

3. I have been advised to use terms such as "fundamental moral principle" rather than axiom, as most moral philosophers do not use the word axiom, so I shall sometimes do so. However, I think that axiom is a good term, for it brings out in some way the resemblance of metaethics to the foundations of mathematics. Also, it shows that there are starting points that may be taken as foundational to different philosophers and as so, cannot be proved. These foundational principles or axioms may appear obvious to some, but not to others.

4. Constructivism is about much more than just metaethics. For a critique see, Smith, *Exposing the Roots*.

5. Bagnoli, *Constructivism in Metaethics*, 1.

example. Human beings are also curious creatures who try to understand the world around them. Human beings seek *happiness* (with varying impressions on what they may construe happiness to be, or what it might entail). But the beliefs of what constitutes *flourishing* vary considerably more in different people.[6]

Human beings also have a sense of their own identity, which they seek to preserve, and for most people this is very important. For example, Christine Korsgaard writes,

> A normative moral theory must be one that allows us to act in the full light of knowledge of what morality is and why we are susceptible to its influences, and at the same time to believe that our actions are justified and make sense ... I believe that the answer must appeal, in a deep way, to our sense of who we are, to our sense of identity.[7]

David Copp has developed a constructivist theory, which he entitles a "society-centered" theory. He writes,

> We live in societies, and we need to live in societies. We order our lives partly on the basis of norms we share, where our sharing them facilitates beneficial cooperation and coordination among us. To the extent that the currency of these norms actually functions as well as can be, to make things go well in society, the norms are justified, and corresponding moral judgments are true."[8]

---

6. This appeal to human nature can be made in more than one way. In natural law theory, God is usually appealed to in explanation of what human nature is, and what should be derived from it. However, since the Enlightenment, man is often portrayed as being on his own. This is quite problematic. Andreas Kinneging writes, "Conservatives have never tired of pointing out the huge paradox inherent in this Enlightenment doctrine. On the one hand, it elevates man to the Lord of Creation, to a veritable Prometheus who gradually robs nature of its secrets and molds the world ever more to his will, thereby ridding himself of disease, pain, poverty, coercion, and oppression. On the other hand, the Enlightenment doctrine rejects the inner battlefield—and with it, inner freedom and responsibility—reducing man to a creature that reacts quasi-mechanically to external incentives and thus does not fundamentally differ from an animal, or even inanimate nature. *Voila* the Enlightenment's image of man: cognitively, man is a demigod, but on the conative level he is a centaur. In both respects, the conservative believes, the Enlightenment doctrine clearly misunderstands what it means to be human." Kinneging, *Geography of Good and Evil*, 24.

7. Korsgaard, *The Sources of Normativity*, 17. However, this establishes no single morality, as one may change one's mind as to who we are. In addition, one may have a horrible sense of who one is, like Ted Bundy quoted above.

8. Copp, "A Skeptical Challenge," 274.

There is much truth in the above quote, but what it does in the final analysis is to reduce morality to prudence. There is no necessity in accepting the view that Copp holds. So, torturing people or animals for fun is not wrong in itself, but merely it makes living in an ordered community more difficult. Since there is no necessity, no one need buy into the theory. The criterion for truth becomes our *endorsement*. Social contract theories have the same problem.

Rationalism

This is an ethical system based on the nature of rationality itself. It is, of course, the case that human beings are rational, at least to a certain extent, and at least intermittently. To be rational is therefore a part of human nature. However, even though reason is a necessary part of any ethical theory, theories that are not based on the nature of reason itself are not considered rationalist theories.

Animals are creatures but they cannot reason in the human sense of the word and are therefore non-ethical. Animals cannot act immorally, because they have no understanding. To be a being that is moral entails that the being understands the concept of morality. This means that the being must also understand statements—in other words, have language of some sort. If some being without language, without a fully developed rationality, felt bad every time that it did some immoral action, that being would not have ethics. Rather, it would be like an animal who is conditioned to feel fear or shame when it does something that its owner considers wrong.

As we can see, rationality *is* a necessary part of being an ethical being. Because of this, some have attempted to base ethics on the nature of rationality. That is, rationality is believed to be, in some sense, the standard by which what is ethically right and wrong is determined, because it is a necessary precondition for being an ethical being.

It will be argued below that although both constructivism and rationalism provide objective ethics in some sense of the word, they are only forms of weak realism because they fail to provide a *necessary* basis for ethical truths. This is because they are based on *contingent* aspects of reality.

The "Ideal Observer" Theory

There is one form of rationalism that bases itself on the concept that ethics is what an ideal observer would think is the right thing to do.[9] In a way, this may be considered to be an attempt to combine naturalism and rationalism.

The general idea is that if we were to posit the existence of an ideal observer, an observer who was completely rational and knew all the relevant facts, then what the observer would decide was morally correct would indeed be what was morally right.[10] Here this is being taken as a weak realist position, though it is compatible with strong realism. This is because the ideal observer theory grounds morality and ethics on what such a morality-determiner would choose, not on the existence of necessarily existing moral truths. Of course, if the ideal observer "knows" what the moral truths are, then it is really a realist theory and does depend on moral truth.

If some forms of robust realism were true, then the observer, knowing all the relevant facts and being perfectly rational, would know that this theory was indeed true with all its implications, and accept that. *However, if either antirealism or weak realism were true*, then the observer would know that also. Would the observer then be able to say what the best or true ethical theory is?

It seems not. The reason for this is that if there were no robustly real ethical theory, then on what basis would the observer make the choice as to the best one? What seems to me to be the case is that whichever theory the Observer would choose would best contribute to the ultimate goals that the Observer has. For example, if the Observer valued the maximal happiness for humanity, and maybe animals too, then some version of utilitarianism would be chosen. If, on the other hand, the Observer valued his or her own happiness the most, then some version of egoism would be chosen. Similarly, if the Observer valued some form of behavior or virtue most, then some form of deontological ethics would be chosen. And so on.

So, the Observer would choose the metaethical theory that would best support what ultimate aim the Observer had. However, how would the Observer choose the ultimate aim? It is here that a major problem for

---

9. For more on this concept see the discussion in chapter 3. A defense of Ideal Observer Theory from an atheist's perspective can be found in Martin, *Atheism, Morality*.

10. Jollimore, "Impartiality."

the Ideal Observer theory arises. For, if no version of strong realism is true, then there is no *ultimate value* that the Observer would necessarily take. What the Observer would choose would be based on the worldview that the Observer has. At the beginning of the book, I mentioned that if ethics is what most people normally think of it as, then ethical statements are necessarily true, universal, and absolutely binding on people. However, from the argument that is given here, there is no one metaethical system that the hypothesized Ideal Observer would follow, which *removes the necessity and universality*. What this means is that Ideal Observer theory can only give a form of weak realism, just like the others. Because of this, there is no reason to think that the whole concept of an Ideal Observer is coherent, except if the Ideal Observer is God.

Parfit's Theory

Some brief attention must be made here to Derek Parfit's work. Parfit rejects Platonism,[11] naturalism,[12] and non-cognitivism, about which I agree. Where the difference between us lies is that I purport that ethical truths exist in the mind of God, whereas Parfit does not. Yet he seems to have thought that ethical truths are necessarily true. How is this possible?

Parfit's answer to this seems to be that though it is true that human beings did not have to exist in the manner that they do, there will be propositions that they should recognize as being necessarily good ones. That is, if creatures like us are to exist, then necessarily we should recognize certain propositions as being moral truths. However, this seems to me to still be a form of weak realism, for two reasons. First, these propositions would not necessarily be moral truths for all sentient creatures, as some could potentially exist with very different natures than the one we have. Second, though creatures like us might think, upon a full reflection of the matter, that these *are* truths, there is still no logical contradiction in not following them.[13]

There are many forms of weak realism. However, are they really forms of realism, or do they ultimately fall into some version of antirealism? It seems that ultimately, they must collapse into antirealism.

11. Parfit, *What Matters*, 2:486.
12. Parfit, *What Matters*, 2:263–378, and 3:41–162.
13. In essence then, these truths would only be de dicto rather than de re. That is, they would have to be *with our thinking of the truths*, rather than *with the truths themselves*.

The case here is simple. Each of the forms of weak realism is based on a set of fundamental moral principles or axioms, which is held to be the foundation of what is right and wrong morally. However, since the acceptance of one of these principles is not necessary, none of them can provide the *basis* for a strong realist theory of ethics. Accepting any of the principles must occur prior to choosing ethics that are based on the principle and hence is an *amoral choice*. Therefore, given this view of morality, there is nothing morally wrong in not choosing any one of them, or any of them at all, because they are *prior* to morality. They may be realist in a sense, as they are based on something real regarding human nature or reason, but they are antirealist in the sense that they are chosen for non-moral reasons. *In both weak realism and antirealism, morality is based on the non-moral.*

FOUNDATIONAL ETHICAL PRINCIPLES OR AXIOMS

One more critical issue is the use of foundational ethical principles or axioms in ethical theorizing. Axioms are important, especially in weak realist theories, though both antirealism and strong realism may also have them. This is because *weak realist theories* as defined *start with an axiom* that cannot be morally justified within the system. That is to say, the moral propositions in a particular theory depend upon the axiom, but to choose the axiom itself is an amoral choice.

The use of the word *axiom* is unusual in ethical thinking, but the basic concept is used, and bears resemblance to other areas of scholarship.[14]

Axioms are Starting Points, Foundational Principles

Axioms are important concepts in several areas of scholarship. Every proof needs a place to begin; starting places cannot be dispensed with. Without a starting place, the proof cannot even begin. Any other attempted proof would have some other starting point, and then that axiom would be the relevant axiom. This is not to say that the choice

---

14. There is arguably a closer similarity between ethics and mathematics. Justin Clarke-Doane writes that the truth of most mathematical axioms is debatable. Some of them might be necessarily true or false, while others are simply choices to do mathematics in a certain way. This last category is similar to what is done in ethical axioms, insofar as there is no necessity accepting the axioms. Clarke-Doane, *Morality and Math*.

of these principles is necessarily arbitrary. Though an axiom may be the foundational proposition for a theory, that does not mean that one must adopt it with a blank mind. One may carefully investigate different foundational principles to see what they lead to and evaluate the coherence and explanatory power that follows.

Axioms or foundational principles are usually adopted because 1) they are considered *self-evident*, or 2) they are considered *well-established* principles, or 3) they are *assumed true* for the sake of argument. One of these areas where axioms may be used, and indeed, often is used, is in metaethics. Looking at the many different metaethical systems, one can argue that the various fundamental statements of the different systems may be considered axioms at least in the sense that they are assumed to be true. From these axioms the rest of the system is deduced or derived.

Therefore, there are many different ethical systems which all have basic principles of *metaethical foundations*. These principles may be considered axioms in their respective systems. It is also the case that axioms cannot stand alone; they need auxiliary factors in order to be "fleshed out." However, the axioms or foundational principles of a particular ethical system are often quite radically different from maxims of other systems. For example,

> (7.1) *Bentham's and Mill's utilitarianism* is founded on the axiom that morality is based on promoting the greatest amount of good. Usually this is understood as pleasure or happiness in the world—the greatest happiness for the greatest number.[15] This can be interpreted in a variety of ways, and hence there really may be more than one utilitarian axiom, though they are all similar to each other. They all aim for the *greatest good for the greatest number*.

> (7.2) *Kant's deontological system* of metaethics is founded on the axiom of the *categorical imperative*—that one should only will those things that one could consistently will to be a universal law. Another axiom that Kant might use is that one should never use a person merely as a means nor as an end. Of course, to be made serviceable, these axioms naturally need to be developed in order to deal with different situations.

---

15. For one of the main presentations of utilitarianism, see Mill, *Utilitarianism*. See also Sidgwick and Rawls, *Methods*. For a modern defense, see for example Brandt, *Good and Right*.

(7.3) *Naturalist systems* of ethics are founded on different axioms, but all of them are founded on the general principle that morality is based on certain aspects of *human nature*. For example, since human beings are creatures that have a certain nature, being ethical means acting in such a way as to promote the flourishing of that nature. What is considered flourishing might be differently defined, depending on how human nature is conceived to be. What exactly is defined by human nature and what is caused by the culture one lives in is not always easy to say.

(7.4) *Rationalists* think that morality involves striving for the best outcome in whatever moral situation one finds oneself. How one defines what is the *best outcome* is itself defined in terms of various factors. Here again, the axiom must be fleshed out from different concepts of what is the "best outcome." Nonetheless, the driving force of the system is the concept that what is ethical is that which rationally produces the best outcome, which is conceived to be different from utilitarianism.[16]

(7.5) In *egoism*, the axiom is that what is morally good is *that which serves each individual's best self-interest*. This is the basic starting point, and everything else is derived from this. The most popular exponent of egoism in the twentieth century was Ayn Rand, who has had quite a bit of influence among general readers, though philosophers usually look down upon her and her theories.[17]

The list could be extended, as there are many different ethical systems. However, what is listed above shows that the different metaethical theories are based on different foundational principles that are here labeled "axioms", because they function much the same as axioms do in logic and mathematics. However, there are also several differences, which match the differences between the subjects of mathematics and metaethics.

Differences in Axioms between Math and Ethics

First, in mathematics, the fundamental axioms, such as some of the geometrical ones of Euclid, are seemingly self-evident. To deny them entails

16. Parfit, *What Matters*, Vol. 1–3.
17. Rand, *Virtue of Selfishness*.

a contradiction. A person considering a geometrical axiom can often see its necessity. This is true even if he or she cannot derive a contradiction from a denial of the axiom involved. How we have this ability is an interesting question, but it seems undeniable that we do.

Interestingly, one of Euclid's axioms is considered to not be self-evident. This is the parallel postulate, which is now known to be unprovable, and is now the basis for non-Euclidean geometry. Still, the other four axioms of Euclid are universally considered necessary, and from them much can be rigorously proven in the subject.

The main problem in comparing axioms of math and metaethics is that though different metaethical axioms or moral principles may appear to be self-evident to different people, they do not, unlike most of Euclid's geometrical axioms, seem self-evident to every qualified individual. Indeed, ethical axioms can appear to be self-evidently true to some people and self-evidently false to others. Again, this is not to deny that certain ethical truths seem self-evident to certain people. However, the denial of these metaethical axioms does not immediately lead to contradiction, and this is something that the normal person will intuitively see.

For example, take the utilitarian axiom, "What is morally correct is that which promotes the most happiness in the world." To deny this foundational principle, one merely must assert that what is morally correct is *not* that which promotes the most happiness in the world. The two propositions contradict each other, but there is no other apparent contradiction. It is not logically absurd to say that what is morally correct is not promoting the greatest amount of happiness in the world, but something else, or perhaps there is nothing ethical at all.

This shows that the claims of self-evidence in geometry and mathematics on the one hand, and metaethics on the other, are quite different from each other. What is true is that the *scope* of mathematical and geometrical axioms seems to be that of logical or *absolute necessity*. Our knowledge of them seems therefore to be *based on intuitive reason*, wherein human beings have the ability, at least in some limited situations, to grasp the necessity of the truths.

It is plausible to think that human beings have built into them the notion of what ethics is—that we are born with the ability to understand the concept of what morality is. However, the filling out of what morality consists of is dependent upon a number of factors. Which ethical system one will accept will depend partly upon the nature of the individual, and partly upon the nature of the culture in which the individual lives.

Differences in Axioms by Contingency or Necessity

Because of this, *intuitions about moral right and wrong will vary* much more widely than in the case of intuitive reason regarding mathematical, geometrical, and other truths. The ability to intuitively grasp and understand these verities seems built into human nature. However, which ethical truths one will be conditioned to hold seems to be dependent upon other sources.

Whether or not this entails that ethical truths are only contingently true is another question. Just because it is the case that a particular proposition does not *seem* necessarily true to us, that there is no way to directly prove it does not mean that it is only contingently true. Similarly, the fact that a proposition seems obviously true does not automatically mean that it is a necessary truth. To think otherwise is to confuse certainty with necessity.

Therefore, in weak systems moral propositions are *contingently* true. This is the case wherein the moral propositions are derived in some manner from contingent other propositions. Strong realist theories deny that all moral propositions are only contingently true.

Differences in Axioms because of Differences in Worldviews

There may be difficulties even with this concept, however. As we have seen in previous discussions on the nature of worldviews, an ethical system is part of the worldview held by different groups or individuals. These varying worldviews contain ethical statements. The question then becomes, how do the axioms fit into the worldview? Or to put it another way, why is some axiom (or axioms) part of that worldview? Are the metaethical axioms somehow entailed by the worldview, in which case they should be derivable from deeper axioms, or are they merely ad hoc additions? Either way, it seems that there are vexations.

If the former, then the axioms must be derived from some deeper metaethical axiom. The reason for this is the "is-ought" issue, which is the problem of how to derive ethical *ought* statements from purely descriptive statements. To derive a proposition Y from another proposition X, means that whatever concepts exist in Y, also in some sense exist in X.

For example, given proposition X, that a person has two cats, then the proposition Y, that this person has at least one cat, follows. If one claims that red, blue, and yellow are colors, it follows by necessity that yellow is a color. The point is that if the truth of Y is deducible from X, then the concepts in Y must also be analytically contained in X. If they cannot be deducted or derived, then the concepts in the axiom must be from somewhere else.

Therefore, if metaethical axioms analytically contain the concept of being required—of having an "oughtness" in them—then either that exists of its own inner necessity, or else is derivable from somewhere else. If derived from some other proposition or some other state of affairs, the same analysis is applicable to this deeper proposition or situation.

How metaethical axioms fit into a worldview

There is, therefore, the problem of *how* metaethical axioms fit into a worldview. The three options seem to be that (7.6) they are derivable from the nature of the worldview, or (7.7) they are consistent with it but not strictly derivable, or else (7.8) they are inconsistent with it. Here all three options are examined.

(7.6) That ethical axioms are *derivable* from the worldview.

First, what does it mean that a metaethical axiom is derivable from the worldview as a whole? Take for example some versions of theism. Given the God of perfect being theology, it seems that a certain metaethical axiom is naturally derivable. If God is understood as being perfectly good, then he will endorse certain ethical propositions and deny others. E.g., kindness is good, while pointless cruelty is bad. If this God necessarily exists and has this nature necessarily, such that goodness is a necessary part of his nature, and that the good ought to be followed, then one can see how the axiom of obedience to God is an axiom of metaethics and that "oughts" of kindness and goodness logically follow from God's nature. It would be necessarily true.

(7.7) That ethical axioms are *consistent but not derivable* from the worldview.

In contrast, assume that some version of philosophical naturalism is the case. In other words, the only concrete beings that exist are physical ones that are found in the natural universe, which do not depend for their existence upon anything more fundamental. Does this entail any particular metaethical axiom as being necessarily true?

It does not seem to me that it does. Take for example Utilitarianism and Egoism. Both theories are *consequentialist*—with the former in favor of humanity and the latter benefiting the individual. Both are compatible with naturalism. In fact, it seems that several metaethical theories are compatible with naturalism.[18]

(7.8) Those ethical axioms are *inconsistent* with the worldview.

Therefore, some versions of naturalism by themselves do not determine any particular metaethical theory to be true. These versions of naturalism do not have a Platonic view of abstract entities—the physical world is held to be all that exists. They would be *compatible* with several metaethical theories, which means that naturalism by itself is neutral between them. This is an important consequence, for if naturalism does not entail the truth of any individual metaethical theory, then naturalism in and of itself cannot provide the *necessity* that seems to be a part of any strong or robust metaethical theory. Therefore, the normativity or "oughtness" of an ethical theory seems to be incompatible with strict naturalism, in the sense that naturalist worldviews do not entail any form of strong realism in metaethics.

WEAK REALIST THEORIES ADDED UP

What does this add up to? It means that weak realist theories ultimately *depend upon making an amoral choice*. This means that though the choice might be reasonable to some extent, it is not *necessary*, nor would it be *universal*. In other words, to have morality, one must first make an amoral choice as to what system to accept. For, if one did not have a moral system, the choice is necessarily amoral. There is sort of a chicken and egg problem here.

Weak realist theories, though they seem plausible in some sense of the word, are not necessary, because the choice of them is dependent upon whatever *values* are *already held*, and these values are ultimately amoral, because they are before whatever moral theory is accepted. In short, *in this sense* weak realist theories are all like antirealism, as they

---

18. One exception to this is if the naturalist is also a Platonist regarding morality. In Platonism, there are abstract entities that exist apart from the natural universe. It is debatable whether naturalism is compatible with Platonism, but since many naturalists think that it is, I will accept that one may be both a naturalist and a Platonist.

are both based on an amoral choice. This is not to deny that there are significant differences between the two positions.

One last point should be mentioned. It could be said here that my account presupposes *foundationalism*, which is, of course, controversial. However, it does seem that some of the most popular metaethical theories, like utilitarianism or Kantianism, are foundational in the sense that they begin with a certain axiom. But, trying to justify the acceptance of these theories might not depend upon foundationalism. That is, one might argue for the truth of utilitarianism forming a *coherentist* point of view.

Whatever their virtues, weak realist theories depend upon contingent things and hence they are contingent themselves. To accept one is an amoral choice. *Because these "truths" are contingent, no one is obligated to accept them, or be considered immoral if one does not accept them.*

For this reason, it seems that weak realist theories are reduced to antirealist ones, though there does remain a difference between them and other antirealist theories. For as has been shown, weak realist theories take as their starting point some aspect of reality that seems self-evidently good. They may be considered more objective than strict antirealist theories, but they are basically the same in the final analysis as they are normative only if they are chosen, only if one opts in.

There is one more thing to add. In a society where there are only weak realist theories, wherein there is no necessity in accepting any of them, what is moral for each individual depends only on an amoral choice. As Carl R. Trueman writes, "This death of metaphysics also connects to Alasdair MacIntyre's claim that moral discourse today is so fruitless because it lacks any commonly accepted basis on which moral differences can be discussed and assessed."[19] This leads to "today's moral anarchy."[20] With no commonly accepted moral agreement, matters will be of necessity settled by force. Thus, weak realism opens the door to incessant struggles among the holders of the different theories. In this manner, weak realism is akin to antirealism.

---

19. Trueman and Dreher, *The Rise and Triumph*, 195.
20. Trueman and Dreher, *The Rise and Triumph*, 195.

CHAPTER 8

Strong Realism

THE ABOVE TWO CHAPTERS discussed anti and weak realism. The last of the three fundamental categories of metaethical theories is strong realism. To investigate *strong realism*, some terms must be delineated. The first of these concerns the notions of *hypothetical* and *categorical imperatives*.

HYPOTHETICAL AND CATEGORICAL IMPERATIVES

In his work on metaethics, Immanuel Kant made the distinction between hypothetical and categorical imperatives.[1] It is here that the necessary nature of ethical truths given realism is most clearly shown. When fully explicated, this relationship will help delineate the essential differences that exist between strong realisms, weak realisms, and antirealisms. *Categorical Imperatives* will be written as *CI* and *Hypothetical Imperatives* as *HI*.

I should clarify here that Kant's definition of "categorical" refers to something you are *obligated to do, regardless of your desires*. This is not to be confused with simply establishing a category of issues. Categorical is used here in the sense of absolute, such as the statement, "This is categorically the greatest show on earth!"

An *HI*, put simply, is a situation where, if one wants to obtain *Y*, then one should first do *X*. If one wants to get a good grade in a class,

---

1. See also his Kant, *Religion within the Bounds*.

then one ought to study. If one wants to keep one's job, then one should probably not show up for work drunk. If one wants to be a good chess player, then one ought to learn the rules of the game, practice a lot, and so on. An endless number of *HIs* can be generated, and indeed, they are an integral part of ordinary, everyday life for human beings, and for that matter, for animals.

A *CI*, in contrast, is a concept that is fundamentally different. Here, anyone in some situation *S* has an *obligation* to do *X*, whether one wants to or not. Or, on the forbidden side of the equation, one *must not* do Y, even if one craves to do so. For example, one ought not to torture people or animals for fun, no matter how much one enjoys it. One's desires in the matter are irrelevant, due to the nature of the categorical imperative, for they are binding on us regardless of what we wish. Indeed, it is morally wrong even to want to do these and similar things.

The fundamental difference between these two imperatives is that an *HI depends upon the desires* of the person or persons (or animals) to whom the imperative is directed. Whereas a *CI* is directed at every personal being in the relevant situation and *does not depend upon their desires*. Assuming for the sake of argument that weak realism is the true situation about ethics, ethics then falls under the rubric of the *Hypothetical Imperative*. In *HI*, the rightness of an action depends upon a *choice*. On the other hand, given any sort of strong realism, ethics is about what one *ought* to do, rather than what one wants to do. What one desires to do is irrelevant; indeed, one may very much not want to do what the *CI* requires.

Normative Propositions

The matter of ethical propositions' being normative propositions should be clarified. Ethical statements are prima facie normative statements. A normative statement is basically one wherein something is *required*. But, obviously, not all normative propositions are ethical ones. If one wants to add correctly, then one *must follow the rules* of addition. If one wants to communicate, then one *must* speak or write according to certain standards of communication.

In these matters of speaking or adding, it is possible to opt out. One can choose not to add, not to communicate, or even not to live. Granted, opting out of many of these different realms often carries a very high price—including one's life, or many other things that most people consider to be valuable. Nevertheless, there is no *logical necessity* in entering these realms of reality—that is, there is no contradiction entailed. They are, in this sense, optional, just as wanting to be a good chess player is optional.

Do Categorical Imperatives exist?

The question is, do moral *CIs* also exist in reality? Further, if they do exist, why and how do they exist? That is, how can they exist, wherein people have an obligation to do something even if they have no desire to do it, or even if they have a strong desire not to fulfill the requirement that is given by a particular categorical imperative? Where does the strong or robust "*oughtness*" that is an essential part of their nature come from? *It is this difference of categorical imperatives from the normal hypothetical imperatives that is a major motive for antirealists to deny the existence of moral absolutes.*

Comparing Ethical Categorical Imperatives with the Laws of Nature

For rational humans, a *CI* is something that cannot be evaded in a normal life. One cannot choose to opt out of it, in the sense that if one does opt out of being ethical, then one is doing something wrong, something that one ought not to do. In this respect, moral *CIs* resemble the laws of nature. One cannot choose to opt out of the law of gravity for instance. If one tries to ignore the laws of nature like gravity, one may pay a heavy price. For example, if one wants to fly by flapping one's arms and jumps off a high cliff, one will immediately discover the impact of consequences showing that disobeying the law of gravity is not a safe or wise option.

On the other hand, the ethical laws in robust realism are not like the laws of nature. If one somehow disobeys the laws of morality, one may not pay an immediate price in the way that trying to avoid the law of gravity would entail. One may conceivably murder, rape, and steal, and not necessarily pay a price for doing so.[2] Nonetheless, given realism, one has done something wrong, and almost inevitably, someone will pay a price of some sort.

---

2. At least in this life. Given an afterlife, one could conceivably necessarily pay a price.

STRONG REALISM 131

Another difference between the laws of nature and a *CI* is that the laws of nature seem to be contingent. It is conceivable that there are worlds wherein there are different laws of nature than the ones in our universe, or even none at all. Therefore, the laws of nature did not have to exist or have the strength that they do, but any *CIs* that exist are necessary, existing in all possible worlds. Even in worlds where there are no sentient creatures, any categorical imperatives would still exist, even though there was no one to understand and follow them, just as the laws of fundamental arithmetic are necessary and true in all worlds, even in worlds where there are no creatures to do any counting, subtracting, or multiplication.

In effect then, the laws of nature and the ethical laws, given a robust realism, are opposite from each other. The laws of nature are contingent, while moral laws are necessary. However, the laws of nature may not be broken, while ethical laws are broken every time someone does something morally wrong.

Comparing Ethical Categorical Imperatives with Mathematics

Are there any other areas of reality besides ethics where a *CI* exists? It is arguable that one area is basic mathematics. Mathematics is full of *necessary truths*. Two plus two necessarily equal four, and not just if one wants them to equal four. This necessity would seem to be intrinsic to the notion of addition and other mathematical activities. Further, external reality in the form of laws of nature behaves according to the laws of mathematics. Natural laws are describable by different mathematical formulas.

Compare the laws of math with the laws of chess. The laws of chess are contingent. One may alter the rules of chess in countless ways. In fact, there are many other forms of chess besides western chess, including Chinese chess, Korean chess, Japanese chess, Burmese chess, Malay chess, Thai chess, Turkish chess, and even Martian chess.[3] It is an interesting question of how far the rules of chess can be changed and still legitimately be considered a variation of chess, but we need not go into this matter. Here, as in so many issues, there are gray areas.

Mathematics, on the other hand, cannot be changed and still remain legitimate. To be sure, there are different mathematics rules in some different theories. For example, there are different geometries—those of

---

3. About one game that may be called a kind of Martian Chess, also known as Jetan, see Burroughs, *Chessmen of Mars*, vol. 5. There are other games known as Martian chess besides Jetan.

Euclid, Riemann, and Lobachevsky. In higher mathematics, there are many different theories. Nonetheless, many of the fundamental laws of mathematics are necessarily true because they are based on logic. Where there are differences, it is because different axioms have been chosen, and the rules follow necessarily from the axioms.[4] The same basic point is true with higher logic, and any other discipline that deals with purportedly necessary truths.

However, if one does not want to operate mentally in a realm like mathematics or logic, then one does not have to. Even if one wants to do mathematics or logic correctly and one's thoughts and actions are necessarily circumscribed, there is no absolute necessity to buying into either math or logic in the first place. Their most basic laws are necessarily true, but a decision to abide by them is contingent. One could choose to be insane, though even that choice would depend upon the laws of logic.

By being the kind of creature that human beings are, *one must use logic*. Even if one decides to act in an illogical manner, one must use logical thinking to understand the situation and act accordingly. In essence, one must use logic to be illogical. Again, however, this is analogous to necessarily being subject to the law of gravity if one is a material being. Material beings have no choice but to obey the law of gravity, at least in this universe.

Desires are Irrelevant in Categorical Imperatives.

In contradistinction to all the above, given strong realism in ethics, one is *obligated* to follow the rules whether one wants to or not. One is doing something wrong if one does not attempt to act in an ethical manner, whether one wants to or not. *Ethics is by its very nature binding on people in a manner that the other aspects of reality mentioned are not.* In a sense, this is the crucial difference: what one wants to do is irrelevant in the face of a *CI*. However, there is more to the matter.

ARGUMENTS FOR STRONG ETHICAL REALISM

Here are given three arguments *for* ethical realism.

---

4. Clarke-Doane, *Morality and Math*.

First: Intuition

In antirealism, there is absolutely nothing morally wrong with any action, no matter how awful it seems to us. There would be nothing immoral about pouring gasoline on babies and setting them afire simply because you like hearing them scream. This would be an action most of us would find appalling and egregious, but there would be nothing intrinsically wrong with it because there is nothing morally wrong with anything, were antirealism true. This is all *very* counter-intuitive, and hence this gives us a reason to think that moral truths exist.

Second: Common Sense Morality—Cuneo, Huemer, Enoch, Landau-Shaffer, Wielenberg, Kulp, etc.

The second argument shall simply be stated here, instead of being developed at length, because this line of reasoning has already been explicated extensively by robust realists such as Terence Cuneo,[5] Michael Huemer,[6] David Enoch,[7] Russ Landau-Shaffer,[8] Eric Wielenberg,[9] and Christopher Kulp among others.[10] Many of these are atheists, which shows that the widespread contemporary acceptance of strong realism is not limited to theists.

This argument may be stated thusly: speech *about morality by its very nature assumes a form of robust realism*. This morality, which Kulp correctly calls *common sense morality*, is what people think they are saying when they are speaking of moral issues.[11] Almost everyone whose mind has not been warped by the study of philosophy assumes this. Common sense morality takes for granted that there are ethical truths in the robust sense. People agree, disagree, and argue about what is ethically right and wrong. What this shows is that theories such as emotivism, prescriptivism, expressionism, nihilism, and extreme nihilism are radically at variance with normal human conversations about ethics.

---

5. Cuneo, *Speech and Morality*.
6. Huemer, *Ethical Intuitionism*, 99–250.
7. Enoch, *Taking Morality Seriously*, 16–84.
8. Shafer-Landau, *Moral Realism*.
9. Wielenberg, *Robust Ethics*.
10. Kulp, *Metaphysics of Morality*, 189–232.
11. Kulp, *Metaphysics of Morality*, 10.

Other antirealisms, like subjectivism and relativism, as well as weak realist theories such as naturalism, rationalism, and voluntarism, do not as quickly show that common sense morality is wrong. However, since all these theories are either forms of antirealism, or else ultimately collapse into antirealism, or something close to it, then, ultimately, they too are at variance with common sense morality, which is also the robust kind.

Third: Ethics is understandable

The third argument may be stated simply like this: Ethics is an understandable mode of being. *Human beings understand morality as an aspect of reality*. When we can understand an aspect of reality as it is, we have good reason to think that this aspect of reality actually exists. Therefore, ethics as an aspect of reality exists. Put more formally, the argument therefore goes something like this:

(8.1) Ethics is an understandable, irreducible, aspect of our thought.

(8.2) Whatever is an understandable, irreducible, aspect of thought must exist in reality apart from human invention.

(8.3) Therefore, ethics is an actual aspect of reality, which exists apart from human invention.

One must be careful here about what is meant by the term "aspect of thought." Obviously, what is not meant are things like a particular kind of animal, for example. One can easily conceive of a kind of animal that does not exist—a unicorn for example—and the fact that we can imagine it hardly means that unicorns exist in the external world. However, unicorns are not a separate category of being; what we have is the *concept* of a unicorn—an animal that could have existed but does not.

What is meant by this is that ethics is an aspect of reality, such as physical phenomena, mathematics, logic, beauty, and others. Morality by its very nature fits into this kind of thing. It is an existing aspect of reality. This being the case, the existence of this moral *category* is as much a part of reality as chemistry and mathematics are. The question then becomes, "How do we account for its existence, and what kind of worldview would accommodate its existence?"

ETHICAL PROPOSITIONS AND REALISM

Granting all this, the question at hand remains as to how ethical statements conceived in a robustly realist sense fit in with the rest of reality. One response to this is to deny robust realism. However, even for philosophers who accept morally robust realism, there is the necessity of giving an answer to the question of *why* some propositions are robustly normative statements.

Looking at *T*, one can discern at least three different attributes that *T* has, and that any ethical statement construed in a robust realist fashion would have. These three attributes are:

(8.4) *T* is a necessary proposition.

(8.5) *T* is a universal proposition.

(8.6) *T* is necessarily a person related proposition.

I will examine these three attributes one by one. Whatever else is true about ethical statements, granting some form of robust realism, these at least seem to be necessarily true.

The First Property—Necessity

Necessity (8.4) is an obvious correlation of any robust realism. If there are ethical truths of this type, then it seems that they exist, and have their intrinsic properties necessarily, as do many other abstract or ideal objects. It is not true, for example, that 2 + 2 just happens to equal four, or that it might just as easily have equaled 17. No, 2 + 2 necessarily = 4, in virtue of the nature of the numbers involved. Necessarily existing abstract entities have their intrinsic properties necessarily.[12] If universals, propositions, or numbers really exist, for example, then it seems clear that they must exist in all possible worlds.[13] Even if they don't, as in the case of nominalist theories, they still exist as necessarily existing objects that may be thought. I will mention again that not all ethical statements

---

12. These do not include, for example, properties of the number three being Rebekah's favorite number.

13. There is an exception to this in the theory of Absolute Creationism, wherein abstract objects are created by God, but only in some possible worlds. E.g., in worlds where there are no creatures with eyesight, God would not create orangeness. However, even here, these abstracta must still exist in the mind of God. For a critique of this, see Parrish, "Defending Theistic Conceptualism."

are necessarily true, but the paradigm cases are. Non-necessary ethical statements will be discussed below.

It is also true that the instantiation of some of the different abstract objects in different worlds is itself contingent. For example, the Earth's equator and the orbit of Mars are abstractions, as they do not exist necessarily, and indeed neither the earth nor Mars exist necessarily. However as was argued above, even in possible worlds where Mars does not exist, the orbit of Mars in the real world has a certain shape—some sort of elliptical orbit. The shape of that orbit as an abstract entity exists necessarily.[14]

Again, if numbers, colors, and propositions exist, they necessarily exist. This is because it is a necessary part of the nature of reality that phenomenal colors can exist, that things can be numbered, and that there are states of affairs that can be described by propositions. Necessarily if X, then possibly P, and necessarily possibly P. It is metaphysically or absolutely necessary that phenomenal redness exists as a possibility, even if never instantiated in the actual world. Although the existence of phenomenal red does not come from logic alone, nevertheless, to deny its necessary existence is to commit a contradiction. Anything that possibly exists necessarily exists as a possibility, given standard S5 modal logic.[15]

In this manner, possibility, necessity, and impossibility flow from the nature or essence of the concept at hand along with the law of non-contradiction. This twofold dependence upon essence and the law of non-contradiction determines what is, and what is not possibly existent.[16] An example already given is that six-sided dice necessarily, as part of their *essence*, have eight corners. Is the *essence* of something possible?[17] Then it is necessarily possible. This is basically the Brouwer axiom of modal logic. Therefore, ethical propositions are necessarily true ones. That it is immoral to torture anyone for fun does not just happen to be true; it could not have been false.

---

14. For a classic defense of this theory, see Husserl and Dummett, *Logical Investigations*, vol. 1.

15. Rasmussen, *Correspondence Theory*.

16. However, one could just as easily use the Law of Identity in place of the Law of Non-contradiction.

17. For a short discussion of essences, refer to chapter 1.

The Second Property—Universality

The second property, being *universal* (8.5), also seems to be intuitively obvious. If P is true in a strong realist sense, then it applies everywhere and always. It is not the case that P is binding on women, but not on men, or vice versa; nor can it be the case that it is true in Michigan but not in Ohio, or vice versa; or that it is true on weekdays but not on weekends, but not vice versa. If strong realism is true, then it is true always, everywhere, and for everyone. It would even be true for Klingons, Wookies, Hobbits, Tharks, or any other kind of sentient creature that could exist. Weak realisms, on the other hand, do not necessarily have this property of universality, because they are dependent upon the existence and nature of contingent things, and on particular invented axioms or theories.

It might be said that it is unnecessary to bring this second property out, as it really flows naturally from the first one. That is, if something is necessarily true, then it is always true for everyone and all places. Similarly, $2 + 2 = 4$, is a necessary truth, and therefore is valid everywhere and at every time. So, the same may be thought of regarding ethical propositions. They are universally true because they are necessary.

This is indeed the case, but I include it to emphasize that ethical statements, if they are real, *apply to everyone, always, and in all places.* It should be noted that some non-ethical statements may be necessarily true, but not applicable everywhere and at every time to everyone. Most basic mathematical statements are necessarily true, but do not apply to everyone. Not every person in the world finds calculus relevant. Red is necessarily a color rather than a number, but in places like black holes, where there is no redness, this is rather irrelevant. On the other hand, if realism about ethical statements is true, then these truths are binding on every human being able to understand them, and on any other rational beings that might exist. Moral propositions therefore have a universal scope.

The Third Property—Person Relatedness

The third property, (8.6) is that of *person relatedness*. In other words, ethical truths are knowable only by persons and are only binding on persons. Of course, they affect other things. For example, it is obviously wrong to torture animals, even though animals do not understand ethics. Nonetheless, only a person, a being with the capacity for reason and language, can understand ethics. It may be the case that one can be a person and can have no conception of what ethics is. Perhaps it is possible that persons can be born with an ethical deformation—the part of the mind that can recognize ethics is missing or broken. However, unquestionably only a person—a conscious being that can use rational thought linguistically and can both understand ethical propositions and what kind of category they are—can be ethical.

Phenomenal colors such as red necessarily exist and are irreducible to another part of reality. Nonetheless, they depend for their existence upon the prior existence of consciousness. Which is to say, without phenomenal consciousness, there is no phenomenal color. Yet, it is also true that color is not the only aspect of phenomenal consciousness, for we consciously entertain things other than color—sounds, feelings of pleasure and pain, and thoughts about mathematics. It is also true that each phenomenal color is irreducible to anything else. Hence, being able to visualize the existence of red, by itself, shows the existence, and indeed necessary existence, of the color red, and that redness is irreducible to anything else.

Non-persons cannot act ethically (or unethically). A rock is not acting immorally if it hits you on the head. A transmission that breaks down and costs an arm and a leg to repair is not being wicked in doing so (though you may feel at the time that it is). A computer that refuses to obey the commands that one is giving it is not doing so out of spite, no matter how much one may believe it. If a dog bites a person who has done nothing wrong, the dog is acting badly, but the dog is not being evil, for it has no ethical comprehension.

If there were animals that had ethical understanding, which would necessarily go along with other properties of being a person, say dolphins or chimpanzees for example, then they would have to be accounted as being persons. It also follows that if there are beings with reason, the ability to use language, and an understanding of ethical concepts, then they would be "persons", even if they were in other ways quite different from human beings.

Though these three characteristics are not the only relevant properties that one may rightly attribute to moral statements, they are crucial ones when trying to understand the nature of morality.

Having delineated these three points, we are now able to judge what they entail. In contrast to some other abstracta, numbers for example, ethical truths are relevant only to persons. I don't mean just that only persons can understand the nature of ethical truths, but also that, unlike numbers or shapes, ethical truths in their primary sense of being applicable, are binding only on persons. The physical universe in its behavior is describable by various mathematical formulas, but ethical truths in themselves have no bearing on the universe's behavior. Ethics, given realism, seems to be a necessary, but limited, part of reality.

The question now is how ethical statements can be true, considering their nature? The antirealist will deny that they are true, and some have even denied that they are meaningful.

NECESSARY AND CONTINGENT ETHICAL TRUTHS

One more distinction will be drawn here. Above, it was said that many ethical propositions are necessarily true (or false). Let's assume that there are, in fact, necessarily true ethical truths—truths which are true in every possible world. Take for example, T, which states that it is morally wrong to torture anything for fun. If this is true, then it is necessarily true, and therefore any ethical axiom and the system derived from it that conflict with T are themselves necessarily false. Further, it seems that any metaethical theory that cannot account for this necessity must itself be false.

The problem here is that some ethical statements seem to have exceptions. There are other statements, which, though they are not conflicting with necessarily true ethical statements such as T, seem only to be contingently true. However, if there are necessarily true ethical statements, then it seems that any ethical truths that are derivable from them must be necessary. How can contingent truths be deduced from necessary ones? This seems to be impossible.

For example, almost all ethical systems will say that normally, stealing is ethically wrong, but many would make exceptions to the rule. For example, if one's family is starving, there is no other food available, then stealing food from someone who would not miss it or who could easily replace it, is permissible. This contrasts with T. It is never permissible to torture innocent people for fun. Why the difference? In addition, how can contingent truths be deduced from necessary ones? (There is also the definition of what stealing is. What is theft in some cultures may not be considered theft in another.)

There are implications for ethics from the different theories of the nature of ultimate reality. By ultimate reality, what is meant is that portion of reality that does not depend upon anything else for its existence, but upon which all other things in reality depend for their existence.[18] The major rival theories in the West today are *theism*, where God is ultimate reality, and *philosophical naturalism*, where the physical universe is considered the ultimate concrete reality.[19]

If some version of robust realism is true, then it seems that what we have is a choice between *Platonism* and one of the two theistic theories, *conceptualism* or *absolute creationism*. It is this issue that the next two chapters will cover.

---

18. Clouser, *Myth of Religious Neutrality*.

19. There are also pantheistic theories. However, if the pantheistic God is considered to be impersonal, then the same problems that arise with naturalism also afflict it.

CHAPTER 9

Some Strong Realist Theories

HAVING OUTLINED THE BASIC positions and the nature of the category of ethics, I will now look at *Platonism*. Platonism is a strong realist theory of ethical truths. There are three basic realist positions: *Platonism, absolute creationism* (where abstracta exist but are created), and *theistic conceptualism* (where abstract entities exist as ideal objects in God's mind). All three will be briefly described and their relevance examined, but only Platonism will be addressed in detail in this chapter. Absolute creationism and theistic conceptualism will be discussed in the next chapter.

INTRODUCTION TO REALIST THEORIES

(9.1) Platonism

Here ethical truths exist eternally and necessarily from their own nature, uncaused by anything else. They are a necessary and fundamental part of the furniture of reality, for in some manner concrete entities participate in their nature, vague though that thought may be. Given Platonism, abstract entities exist in a "third realm," and are unlike physical or conscious entities, existing necessarily and eternally without change. Trope theory holds that there are no independently existing "forms" or universals, for they only exist when they are instantiated in either physical things or consciousness. Although different from Platonism, abstract entities are still things that are *eternally instantiable*. For example, if all red things disappeared from the universe, redness would still exist as a permanent possibility of instantiation.

If one is an atheist and a robust realist, then one should embrace some sort of Platonism. After all, if God does not exist, and yet there are necessary ethical truths that we discover rather than invent or derive, they must exist in some manner, necessarily and eternally. And this is Platonism.

However, it should also be noted that one can be a theist and be a Platonist.[1] The problem here is that accepting this stance means that there are entities—Platonic objects—that were not created by God. Many theists, including me, have a problem with this concept.

(9.2) Absolute Creationism

In this option ethical truths exist, perhaps eternally and necessarily, but are caused to exist by something else (presumably God). Some versions of this might be called voluntarism, because according to voluntarism, God voluntarily created certain ethical truths but did not have to. Here, ethical truths are not required to be necessary truths, as God could have created other ethical objects, or none. That is, in some worlds, such as W, God would endorse some ethical propositions; in others, such as W', he would endorse different propositions, even including ones that are contradictory to any that he endorsed in W. In this theory, God's will is what determines what is ethical and what is not. There could be a variation to this as some absolute creationists might think that God will always cause the same ethical propositions to exist. This theory is, in a way, a theistic version of Platonism, with the exception that in Absolute Creationism, God creates the Platonic entities. However, since they were created, they are not literally Platonic entities. Which shows how confusing this topic is. Because it is in some ways similar to atheistic Platonism, some of the criticisms of Platonism also can be used against Absolute Creationism. More shall be said on this topic in the next chapter.

(9.3) Theistic or Divine Conceptualism

According to this option, ethical truths are ideas in the mind of God, where they exist eternally and necessarily, because they are, in some

1. Yandell, "God and Propositions," 21–35.

sense, a necessary part of God's very being. In this case, abstract objects are concrete to God, for they exist as ideas in God's mind but are abstract to us. Here one might also propose "the Absolute of absolute idealism" as a substitute for God, as F. H. Bradley purports.[2] However, since the absolute of idealism seems to be unknowable, theism is a stronger and much better option, since we at least have some idea of what we are talking about. At any rate, the whole concept of explaining something by referring to an unknowable being seems pointless.

Theistic conceptualism will be discussed in detail in the next chapter. It is listed here to show the range of strongly realist theories of ethics.

ULTIMATE REALITY

In Theism

As we saw before, there are many different concepts of God. The one being used here is Perfect Being Theism, wherein God is considered to be a perfect being, and nothing greater can be conceived.[3] For example, on this account, God is omniscient, omnipotent, and omnibenevolent. This contrasts with various theistic theories wherein God is limited or finite in certain ways.

In Naturalism

In contradistinction to theism, there is naturalism. Naturalism is fundamentally the theory that the physical universe is all that exists, or at least that it exists independently of anything else. A consistent naturalist may countenance the existence of other physical universes but must deny that any non-physical concrete reality external to the universe (or the multiverse) such as God exists.[4] The universe is therefore considered to be ultimate reality in that it does not depend upon anything else for its existence, whereas everything else that does exist, such as atoms, rocks, cats, planets, and galaxies, depends for its existence upon the universe and the physical "stuff" of which it is composed.

---

2. Bradley, *Appearance and Reality*.
3. Anne Jeffrey argues that only a "thick" view of God, which has more than just a minimal theism, can serve as the basis of ethical truths. See Jeffrey, *God and Morality*.
4. It is possible to be a naturalist and not a physicalist.

In Panpsychism

One other position that should be mentioned is *panpsychism*. This view holds that material entities, such as electrons and quarks, are conscious, though these two examples would have very low levels of consciousness. Panpsychism has become more popular in recent years. It may become a serious rival to physicalist naturalism.[5] This point of view does seem to have attracted some notice in contemporary philosophy, but it will not be examined in more detail here.[6]

REALITY—PERSONAL OR IMPERSONAL

In Theism

In theism, *reality is ultimately personal*. This is a major point. In direct contrast, in naturalism *reality is ultimately impersonal*.[7] This difference is a very important one in all areas of philosophy, but especially in issues such as metaethics.

The main reason for the importance of this issue is the existence of persons in the world. In a theistic context, the existence of persons is not surprising, because in theism, God is the ultimate reality, and God is a personal being.[8] Since God is personal, it is not at all surprising that persons are among the things that God created. In theism, human (and any other) persons are finite imitations of God, so to speak, and share some of his attributes, including knowledge, power, and values, though God's are infinite and ours are not.

---

5. I should point out though, that some panpsychist theories are compatible with theism.

6. On this, see for example, Goff, *Galileo's Error*; and Goff, *Consciousness and Fundamental Reality*.

7. A debate on theistic personalism versus atheistic impersonalism is in Rasmussen and Leon, *Is God the Best*. See especially 101–83.

8. Some would say that God is a person, but in orthodox Christianity, God is three persons. See chapter 12.

In Naturalism

In naturalism, on the other hand, persons are rather odd interlopers into what is fundamentally an impersonal, physical reality.

WHY THE UNIVERSE EXISTS AS IT DOES

In Theism

Think of it this way, in theism this possible world is actualized because God, for reasons known only to himself, chose to actualize it rather than any other of the infinite number of possible worlds that are imaginable. Why this universe exists is because God knew it and created it for a purpose.

In Naturalism

In naturalism, there are two different accounts of how and why the universe exists in the manner that it does. They are *necessity* and *chance*. That is, either this world is necessarily the only possible world, or else there is an infinite number of possible worlds and the one we have happened only by chance.

Account One in Naturalism: By Necessity

In the first account, this world exists of *necessity*. It is logically, metaphysically, or absolutely necessary that this world be instantiated. For this not to be the case would entail a contradiction, in the same sense of 2 + 2 equaling 5 or 137.5, or red's not being a color, or a cube's not having eight corners is contradictory. Everything in the world had to be the way that it is on pain of logical contradiction. This is very difficult to believe. That my cat must necessarily have exactly the number of hairs on her body that she does (because if she did not there would be a contradiction) seems obviously false. It seems impossible that *everything* in the universe is the way that it is because if it were not it would entail a contradiction.

Revisiting necessity: There are many kinds of necessity that have been described or alleged to exist. These include logical necessity, metaphysical necessity, broadly logical necessity (which might be the same as metaphysical necessity), causal necessity, nomological necessity, and others. To reiterate the discussion in chapter 4,[9] the kind of necessity of interest here is *necessity in all possible worlds*. The term "absolute necessity" is used to describe it.[10] I have argued elsewhere that this notion of absolute necessity depends upon the law of non-contradiction.[11] To put things briefly and broadly: something is true with absolute necessity if and only if it is true in all possible worlds, and the reason why it is declared true is that its denial in some way entails a logical contradiction. Possible worlds are worlds that contain no contradictions. Impossible worlds are ones that do contain logical contradictions. Therefore, the basis for necessary truths or beings or states of affairs is that to deny their existence entails a contradiction, which is the strongest kind of reason that there is for accepting this absolute necessity.

The only way that one could plausibly think that everything in existence is necessary—that this world is the only possible world—is to put the necessity somewhere else. By this, what is meant is that God exists necessarily, and that this is the only world that he would instantiate. The necessity is thus located in God's values and desires, which would be necessary and unobservable by us. God *could* actualize some other world. He has the power to, but he would never want to do so. Perhaps the biggest objection to this God-centered scenario is that it is hard to believe that this existing world is so great that God would never want to create any other.

Because of this, most naturalist philosophers believe that this is not the only world that could have been actualized, that in fact an infinite number of others could have been actualized, though of course this world is the one that was actualized. Therefore, the concept that this world is actualized of necessity seems to be wrong.

Account Two in naturalism: By chance, Brutely

What this entails is that this world was actualized instead of any other, however, this world is actualized by *chance*, which is to say, *for no reason*. The account is as follows: some world had to exist, even if it were a world

---

9. Melnyk, *A Physicalist Manifesto*, 69.
10. I got this from Hale, *Necessary Beings*.
11. Parrish, *God and Necessity*, 1–21.

totally devoid of concrete objects. However, given naturalism, there is no God to choose which world is the one to be actualized. This means that which world is actualized is totally by chance, or for no reason at all. One world had to exist, and this one is the one that got lucky, so to speak. There was a cosmic lottery with an infinite number of tickets and only one winner, our world, by chance, was the one that came up.

This by itself raises some difficult issues for naturalism. There are vastly, perhaps infinitely, more worlds that are chaotic than those worlds with a set of consistent natural laws, such as ours. Chaos is much more likely by chance than happenstance organization. Any parent of a teenager will confirm this. Further, since this world exists by chance, there seems to be no reason why, by chance, the universe in which we dwell could not "go chaotic" or go to another law order at any moment. Given the long history we have of order in this world, it seems to be absurd to consider that with the ultimacy of chance, there is no good reason why this world would not be in utter chaos.[12]

Given philosophical naturalism the reason why human beings and any other persons exist is, therefore, by chance, or "brutely", without a reason. Since chance is impersonal, because in a sense it is really nothing at all, persons in all their many capacities are strictly creatures that come to be, without thought or purpose. It all just happened by an infinitesimal chance. An unplanned universe somehow was born out of nothing, to be composed of physical things, and of persons with all their capacities for phenomenal consciousness, reason, subjectivity, ethics and intentionality, among other traits. None of these qualities existed before the coming into being of firstly conscious animals, and then personal beings such as humans. Therefore, given naturalism, persons are just a strange quirk of nature.

So, it might seem that all atheists might be antirealists or weak realists. That would, however, be mistaken. In fact, there is a strong movement among atheist philosophers (or at least non-theistic philosophers) to advance a non-theistic form of robust realism. To do so, they appeal to a kind of Platonist theory of ethical truths. Some of the philosophers who have done this are Michael Huemer,[13] David Enoch,[14] Russ Landau-

---

12. See Parrish, *God and Necessity*.
13. Huemer, *Ethical Intuitionism*.
14. Enoch, *Taking Morality Seriously*.

Schaeffer,[15] Erik Wielenberg,[16] and Christopher Kulp.[17] This leads us to secular strong or robust realism. For a critique of this point of view, see Kratt.[18]

Recently, as mentioned above, some philosophers have put forth a theory of "Brute Necessity," which is that some things are both brute and necessary. This is an oxymoron, at least within the definitions of the terms. This concept will be addressed in detail later.

PLATONISM

Platonism Detailed

Abstract objects in Platonism[19]

Platonism will now be further evaluated in view of abstracta and how that impacts ethics. Platonist theories hold that *abstract objects exist as ontologically independent*. They just exist out of their own necessity, uncaused by anything else. Therefore, Platonism is compatible with some forms of naturalism. Some philosophers believe that Platonism is also compatible with theism, while others disagree.[20]

Platonism is an ancient theory and versions of it are still held to by many philosophers and mathematicians. One reason for this is because,

---

15. Shafer-Landau, *Moral Realism*.
16. Wielenberg, *Robust Ethics*.
17. Kulp, *Knowing Moral Truth*; and Kulp, *Metaphysics of Morality*. Interestingly, they all seem to posit the existence of such norms without any real explanation as to *why* they would exist.
18. Kratt, "Secular Moral Nonnaturalism."
19. There is more than one kind of Platonism. For example, there are "heavyweight" and "lightweight" Platonisms. The difference is that in asserting the existence of heavyweight abstract entities, one is making a statement of existential quantification. This means that there are things that exist. Lightweight Platonism does not make that claim. I find the notion of lightweight Platonism obscure, so will concentrate on the heavyweight version. For extended reading on this matter see van Inwagen and Craig, *Do Numbers Exist?*
20. For a defense of Platonism by a theist, see Yandell, "God and Propositions," 21–35. For a response, see Gould, *Beyond the Control*, 36–45. For a debate on the subject, see van Inwagen and Craig, *Do Numbers Exist?*

in the case of mathematics for example,[21] mathematicians have intuition, backed by experience, that we are still discovering truths that are already "out there." "The number three squared is nine" is a proposition that is true, and necessarily true, whether anyone discovered it or not. It is not something we make up. Therefore, Platonism seemingly has a strong argument here against any fictionalist type of theories, though this is a matter of dispute.

Propositions in Platonism

However, there is a problem in Platonism which arises when we come to propositions. If propositions exist, then we have abstract objects that are by their nature *intentional*. That is, they are *about something*, if that something can be clearly delineated. Therefore, propositions about ethics must be about moral rights and wrongs. How do these righteous statements exist in Platonism? How do they exist in an abstract "heaven" apart from minds? It seems absurd to say that mind-correlative entities, ones that have mental characteristics, exist independently of minds. Even more preposterous is the thought that there are intrinsically *impersonal* entities that apply to persons.

With most necessarily true propositions, propositions that are true in all possible worlds, the truth is *internally* decidable, by means of the logical laws of identity and non-contradiction. That is to say, a proposition such as two plus two equal four is true because of the meaning of the concepts involved, when adjudicated by the fundamental laws of logic. What is important here then is the *nature* of the concepts involved. Because of this, the truth of most necessary propositions is decided *internally*—that is, *by content meaning*.

However, this brings us at last to the problem of ethical propositions, such as *T*, where one may claim that it is indeed wrong to torture people for fun. As stated above, the problem is that there is no apparent contradiction to denying propositions such as *T*. *T* is deniable without generating a contradiction. How then can it be necessarily true? It seems unquestionably true that it is necessarily morally wrong to torture innocent people for fun. How can something be necessarily true if its denial

---

21. For a deep defense of realism involving abstract entities see Williamson, *Modal Logic*. For a critique of Platonism, see Craig, *God Over All*.

does not entail a contradiction? This is the biggest problem with a Platonic account of ethical truths.

It is vain to imagine another account of T's absolute truth, as we are dealing with matters of necessity here. Suppose that one posited a sort of factor to explain why some ethical propositions are true while others are false. Say that true ones had some sort of non-ethical property associated with them, while false ones did not. But being non-ethical, it would do nothing to explain why true ones have this property and false ones do not, and necessarily so. Non-ethical factors by themselves cannot explain a strong or robust ethical truth.

It seems obvious that the external factors would have to be necessary themselves. If they were not, then they would be contingent, and need not apply to every one of the necessary propositions. Only something necessary can "make" something else necessary. The fact that all prime numbers except for the number two are odd is a necessary fact about prime numbers. However, the fact that a number is odd does not entail by itself that that number will be prime. Thus, the oddness of a prime number is a necessary precondition for that number's being prime, but oddness is not identical with being prime.

Therefore, the factors that make for the necessity of ethical propositions, granting realism, must themselves be necessary. Could the factors that synthetically cause the necessity of ethical propositions themselves be abstract entities of some sort or another? That is, could something like numbers or universals be the cause of the necessity of ethical propositions? It is exceedingly difficult to see how this could be the case. Most abstract entities, granting their existence, are self-contained entities. They refer to nothing outside themselves, though they do have necessary implications.

The same is true about universals, like the color blue. Blue has the implication that if something is colored blue, then it has both spatial and temporal extension—a blue colored thing cannot exist outside of space and time. It certainly does not directly imply anything about ethical propositions, as its essential nature is non-ethical.

Therefore, in Platonism, propositions, and it seems other abstracta, cannot justify the existence of realism regarding ethics. What can then? This brings up another aspect of ethical propositions that is a real difficulty for impersonal theories.

Persons required

As noted above, ethical truths themselves seem to be necessarily involved with persons. Only persons have minds that can understand ethical propositions. This fact rules out any impersonal origin of ethical propositions. These moral revelations apply only to persons, can come only from a person, and they create a framework of mutual accountability—a scaffolding for society (persons), like the laws of logic.

Take for example, an ethical rule like *T*, that one ought not to torture people or animals for fun. If any ethical propositions are true, then it seems that *T* would certainly be one of them. This rule, unlike necessary truths about mathematics or physical objects, is inherently person related. The question arises, even given *T*'s necessary truth, *why* is it true? Why is it ethically required that one does not torture innocent creatures for fun, no matter how much one enjoys hearing them scream? Do abstract principles really care about these kinds of things?

It seems that *T* is relatable to deeper ethical principles. That is, *T* seems to be part of a larger ethical truth that one ought never to mistreat people or animals. That the person is reckoned innocent adds to the overall ethical nature of the proposition involved. Indeed, the whole notion of innocence is itself an ethical concept and adds complexity to the problem. Not only are there necessary ethical truths, but there is also, given the concept of innocence, the notion of how human beings relate to these truths.

The basic point being made here is that *ethical propositions do not just stand on their own*, apart from anything else, including other ethical propositions. Rather, they seem to stand together in a web of interrelated propositions, which entail each other, or at least are congruent with each other in a systematic set of relations. Further, they are in a society made up of persons who exist and interact with each other in various ways. For example, torture only is relevant to sentient beings, as are murder and rape. Stealing only makes sense in a society with the notion of property. Abstract objects by themselves are blissfully unaware of all this.

This must be accounted as a major difficulty for Platonism. Platonic abstract entities are impersonal objects. They know nothing, and they care about nothing. In Platonism, ethical propositions necessarily exist on their own, apart from whether the objects that they refer to exist or not. Why is torturing innocent people for fun wrong while not torturing them is right? What about the propositions in and of themselves determines that? Nothing about the propositions per se can explain the difference. Thus, Platonism seems to be unable to account for either the existence of ethics or the necessary truth of its statements.

Why would Platonism or Naturalism have Moral Rules?

The question then becomes, why are there necessary truths regarding the behavior of persons, as Platonism holds? What are some fundamental moral rules regarding such things as torture, murder, theft, rape, and related matters. Why would an impersonal reality, constituted by abstract entities, which exist by a) their own inner necessity on the one hand, or b) an unconscious physical universe existing brutely, by chance, on the other hand, have rules against doing such things? Since personal beings to whom ethics apply are unplanned additions to the universe, why are there laws governing their behavior? Why would either the universe or the collection of abstract objects care about such things?

Some atheistic philosophers have attempted to give answers to such questions. Erik J. Wielenberg's book on metaethics, *Robust Ethics*, has received a good deal of attention, and deservedly so.[22] For example, in an issue of *Philosophia Christi*, Adam Lloyd Johnson,[23] William Lane Craig, Tyler Dalton McNab, and Mark C. Murphy all criticize the book, with Wielenberg's giving a response to each of his critics.[24] Though he addresses many interesting and significant points in the book, in this section only one will be discussed. This is what might be called his *atheistic ethical Platonism*.

---

22. Wielenberg is far from the first to deny theism a place in ethics. For an introductory example, see Wielenberg, *Value and Virtue*. For an examination of this theophobia in ethics, see Rist, *On Inoculating Moral Philosophy*. See also Rist, *Real Ethics*.

23. Adam Lloyd Johnson also edits the book Craig and Wielenberg, *Debate on God*. For other debates on the relationship of God and morality between theists and atheists see Garcia and King, *Is Goodness Without God*; and Loftin, *God & Morality*.

24. Johnson, "On Eric Wielenberg's Robust Ethics"; Craig, "Eric Wielenberg's Metaphysics"; McNabb, "The Perils of Godless Ethics"; Johnson, "Fortifying the Petard"; Wielenberg, "Reply to Craig, Murphy, McNabb, and Johnson"; and Murphy, "No Creaturely Intrinsic Value."

Wielenberg's Atheistic Ethical Platonism examined—Brute Necessity

In *Robust Ethics*, Wielenberg endorses a model of metaethics wherein ethical truths exist and exist necessarily apart from God. I have several criticisms of this position. The first criticism of Wielenberg's book is that his position implies the existence of ethical propositions that exist both *necessarily* and *brutely*.

Brute = by chance.

The concept of *brute fact* is one for which there is no explanation. In other word, it exists by pure chance.[25] There are thought to be two kinds of brute facts: epistemic and ontological. *Epistemic* "brute facts" are ones that have no explanation of which we are aware, though there may be an explanation. In my view, epistemic brute facts should not be called that. For, if there is an explanation, then it is not "brute." There may be facts that are forever beyond our finite ability to discover the reason for their existence. But God knows. *Ontological* brute facts are ones for which there really are no reasons or explanations as to why they exist or exist in the manner in which they do. They just are.[26]

The concept of things whose existence is *brute*, but is also *necessary* is a strange notion, but one that has been appealed to in several different contexts. Eric Wielenberg appeals to *brute necessity* to explain his version of robust realism.[27] Brian Rieiro uses brute necessity to explain the existence of beauty.[28] Joseph C. Schmidt argues that existential inertia is explained by brute necessity.[29] Graham Oppy also seems to have adopted a version of it.[30] However, the whole notion of "brute necessity" is inconsistent, at least in its relevant formulation.

25. Philip Rieff writes, "Chance is a third culture pseudoprimordiality, an empty god-term." Rieff and Hunter, *My Life Among the Deathworks*, 19.

26. Bruno Whittle defends the concept of brute necessity. However, his definition is different than mine is. For him, a sentence is metaphysically brute if "(i) it is metaphysically necessary; (ii) it is purely non-referential; and (iii) it cannot be transformed into a logical truth via metaphysical analysis." Whittle, "There Are Brute Necessities," 4. However, as he uses a different definition than I do, it is not strictly relevant to my thesis.

27. Wielenberg, *Robust Ethics*, 37.

28. Ribeiro, "Argument from Beauty," 172.

29. Schmid, "Existential Inertia and the Aristotelian Proof."

30 Graham Oppy has appealed to the notion of brute necessity without specifically

In response, I will start with the basic nature of Wielenberg's theory. He writes, "This account entails the existence of certain *objective* ethical facts."[31] He uses the example of a professor who sees a student on fire, as an *objective*, normative reason to put the fire out. "Regardless of the attitudes of any actual or hypothetical observers, the fact that the student is in pain is a decisive normative reason for me to douse the flames."[32] What are these normative reasons? According to Wielenberg, they are a kind of Platonic entity. Being non-natural, they nonetheless supervene on the physical world in different states of affairs. He writes, "I argue that it is at least as plausible [as founding ethical truths on God] to construe objective moral truth as not needing an external foundation at all."[33]

Wielenberg is partly correct in this estimate of basic *ethical truths*. They exist, they exist necessarily, and they are binding on us. This part of Wielenberg's thesis is therefore true and very important in this white-washed age of ethical antirealism. He should be thanked for defending the robust reality of ethics. The problem with his thesis is that it seems to be unsustainable given his *impersonalist* atheism.

Let's review the must-have characteristics of ethical truths and see how Wielenberg deals with each.

- First, they are non-natural objects. Which is to say, they are *irreducible* to anything else. For Wielenberg, this includes both being non-natural and non-supernatural. That is, they are based on nothing in this physical universe, and they are also not based on God, or on any other purported supernatural entity (like "Q" of Star Trek The Next Generation fame).[34]

---

naming it. He wrote, "(1) [A]ll worlds share an initial causal history with the actual world and diverge from it only as a result of the outplaying of objective chance; (2) all worlds share the same causal laws." Here Oppy seemingly rejects the notion that this world exists of necessity, as is shown by his mention of other worlds, and of objective chance. Yet at the same time, he thinks that the natural, causal laws of nature are necessary, in that all worlds share them. By necessary, I mean what is sometimes called broadly logically, metaphysically, or absolutely necessary. This has some strange results, as for example, the strength of gravity cannot be other than it is, yet the strength that it has does not seem at all to be reducible to the laws of logic. That its strength is what it is, must be brute, and yet could not be other than it is. The other laws of nature are in the same boat. Thus, what Oppy seemingly is appealing to are brute necessities. Oppy, "Naturalistic Axiology," 137.

31. See also his earlier work, Wielenberg, *Value and Virtue*.
32. Wielenberg, *Robust Ethics*, 8.
33. Wielenberg, *Robust Ethics*, x.
34. If God exists, he is certainly not nothing, even if we were to accept the concept

- Second, since they are irreducible, it follows that these ethical entities must be *necessarily existent*. Take some basic ethical proposition like T. It seems obvious that T must be necessarily true. In contrast, the number of blades of grass in my lawn is not necessarily established. One may easily imagine that my lawn could have one more blade of grass than it has, as the number of blades in my lawn is contingent and could have been different.

  As argued above, it seems absurd to think that our ethical proposition T just happens by chance (i.e., is brute) to be necessarily true, when it could have been false. That it is a mere contingent fact that it is wrong to torture people or animals for fun and might just as well have been false would undercut the realism that Wielenberg is defending, and indeed any sort of robust realism at all. Any robustly true ethical proposition must therefore be *necessarily true*, and thus true in all possible worlds. It would even be true in worlds where there were no sentient creatures to whom it would apply.

- Third, it seems that in Wielenberg's theory at least some ethical propositions must ultimately be *ontologically independent*. What is meant by this is that some ethical propositions may be deducible from others, but that some must not be. For example, T might be derivable from some more basic proposition, such as that it is always wrong to be unnecessarily cruel to anyone (or anything). If this is the case, it must still be true that the more fundamental propositions are not based on anything else. This is one of Wielenberg's points: that making ethical propositions dependent upon anything else robs them of their specific identity as ethical statements, which is a reason he does not think that ethical truths should be based on God.[35]

In response to Wielenberg, David Baggett and Jerry Walls write about Wielenberg's stopping point.

> It is a dubious insistence that says, since explanations must come to an end, stopping where Wielenberg does is just as good a place as any. It is true that explanations have to come to an end, but the final explanation needs to be adequate to the task. It is

---

of the existence of God as brute.

35. Wielenberg, *Robust Ethics*, 80–84.

not at all clear what explanatory work is done by saying that an act of deliberate cruelty simply makes something wrong.[36]

Mark Belauger makes a similar point. If some Platonic propositions about ethics are necessarily true, and their denials necessarily false, the question remains, "What makes this the case?" Being facetious, Belauger writes,

> I want to consider one more way in which you might think that platonistic facts are relevant to the what-is-wrongness question. You might think that one of the wrong-like properties is "glowing" somehow in platonic heaven. In other words, you might think that in addition to the kinds of platonistic facts I've been talking about, there are other kinds of platonistic facts that privilege certain abstract objects.[37]

As he goes on to write, "There are multiple problems with this view."[38] Besides the absurdity of abstract objects "glowing," or something similar, what could these different platonistic facts be, if all that exists are the propositions themselves? If the extra facts are non-normative, then the problem of how they themselves cause "oughtness" is unsolved. If they are normative then the question merely moves to explaining how they can be normative. In either case, the problem remains as difficult as it was before.

A related point is this: given that there are Platonic metaethical objects, why is it the case that some are necessarily true and others necessarily false? For example, take T, that it is wrong to torture anything for fun. That is a Platonic abstract proposition that is necessarily true, according to the atheist robust realists. However, there is another abstract proposition, say $\sim T$, that it is morally acceptable to torture people or animals for fun. These are both equally abstract propositions. So, given that they are independent entities, why is one necessarily true and the other necessarily false? At the level of the existence of Platonic abstracta like these, there is no answer to be seen.

Though Wielenberg can conjecture that there are Platonic objects that exist in all possible worlds, he cannot account for ethical propositions being necessarily true in all possible worlds. Therefore, there would

---

36. Baggett and Walls have written extensively on the relationship between God and ethics. See also, Baggett and Baggett, *Morals of the Story*.

37. Balaguer, "Moral Folkism," 305.

38. Balaguer, "Moral Folkism," 305.

be worlds wherein it is acceptable to torture people and animals for fun, and worlds where it is not right to torture anything for fun. On the other hand, more basically, the whole category of morality is empty, and arguably it is neither moral nor immoral to torture anything for fun, or to do anything that is considered to be ethically right or wrong. In other words, there must be something more than merely the existence of the proposition that makes it true or not.

Responding to Wielenberg. How do ethical truths fit into naturalism and physicalism?

Brute and Necessary?

The concept of ultimate ethical propositions *must be either* brute *or* necessary but not both. They are not necessary in themselves, so without theism, their existence must be brute—by pure happenstance. However, *brute necessities* are a logical impossibility. Brute and necessity are oxymorons. Therefore, Wielenberg's theory fails.

Wielenberg's argument is that theists, in thinking that God exists necessarily but brutely, are in the same situation that he is. The naturalist and physicalist (or materialist) views of the nature of reality are the mainstream views today. How do ethical truths, if there are any, fit into a naturalist and physicalist ontology? This is where a problem arises. At this point, the *nature of realism in ethics* must be addressed—to show how it fits in with naturalism, and why it is impossible for the naturalist to be a realist in the sense that has been defined. The specific conundrum is, given the nature of naturalism and physicalism, how can we understand ethical truths as existing as abstract entities?

The existence of abstract entities is not incompatible with every version of naturalism and physicalism.[39] However, for naturalists to accept the existence of abstract entities as "necessarily existing non-physical objects that are not located in space and time", they would have to accept some version of Platonism. In Platonism, abstract entities exist ontologically independent of anything else. Since, by definition, the naturalist is not a theist, he or she cannot accept the notion that abstracta are ideal objects existing in the mind of God. Therefore, *the naturalist who is also*

---

39. On this see Melnyk, *A Physicalist Manifesto*, 11.

a realist about abstract entities will necessarily accept some version of Platonism.

So, the argument against Wielenberg here is that *the whole notion of a brute necessity is contradictory.* Wielenberg writes that many theists think that God's existence is both brute and necessary.[40] While it is true that some theists think that God's existence is brute, and some think that God's existence is necessary, one cannot consistently hold that God's existence is both brute and necessary.

To be brute, something must exist ultimately for no reason. As Wielenberg writes, "Some states of affairs that obtain are what we may call *brute facts*; their obtaining is not explained by the obtaining of other states of affairs."[41] What he seems to mean is that a brute fact or brute state of affairs just is. There are no reasons or explanations as to why it exists. Given this, it seems obvious that a brute fact state of affairs did not have to be. The world could have existed differently than it is and could have not included the brute fact. All of this seems to flow conceptually from what it means to be a brute fact. A brute fact just is, with no prior reason or cause.[42] Wielenberg goes on to write,

> The claim here appears to be that part of the *meaning* of the word "God" is "a being worthy of worship." From this it follows that the central brute fact of traditional monotheism—that God exists—*includes* the fact that there is a being worthy of worship, thereby rendering this fact brute as well. But that there is a being *worthy* of worship is an ethical fact; in the passage just quoted, Craig thus commits himself once more to the existence of substantive, metaphysically necessary brute ethical facts.[43]

In contradistinction to this, an ontologically necessary fact, or being, or situation, is one that must be absolutely necessary.[44] Absolutely necessary truths simply must be. They are true in every possible world. As was argued in chapter 1, take a basic truth from mathematics like $2 + 2 = 4$. Since $2 + 2$ can be broken down into $1 + 1 + 1 + 1$, and the same may be done to 4, this gives reason for the necessity. They are thus tautologous

---

40. Wielenberg, *Robust Ethics*, 37.
41. Wielenberg, *Robust Ethics*, 37.
42. On the concept of brute fact see, Wielenberg, *Robust Ethics*, 8.
43. Wielenberg, *Robust Ethics*, 55.
44. See the discussions in chapter 4 on various kinds of necessity.

and therefore this mathematical fact is true in every possible world. In other words, they are necessary because of the basic laws of logic.

Ergo, with "brute necessity", we have two concepts which seem to be the opposite of each other: brute fact, which is for no reason, and necessary fact, which is the strongest kind of reason. Something cannot be both necessary and brute. As I stated above, to think so entails a contradiction and therefore is itself necessarily false.[45]

Since this is an important point, let me put the matter formally.

(9.4) An ontological brute entity will exist, and in the manner that it does, for no reason, simply by chance.

(9.5) An ontologically necessary entity will exist by logical necessity applied to its nature. It could not fail to exist.[46]

(9.6) An entity cannot both exist for no reason and exist out of logical necessity.

(9.7) So an entity cannot exist both brutely and necessarily.

Regarding God, as Wielenberg notes, some theists think of God's existence as brutely necessary. They are wrong about this, and rather, God's existence is analytically necessary, a position that is argued for at length elsewhere.[47] But why would God have necessary existence? The answer is an Anselmian one: that God's necessary existence is analytically contained in the notion of God as thought of in perfect being theology—God is the greatest possible or conceivable being. His existence is therefore self-explanatory, and the opposite of brute.[48] The fact that we can imagine the non-existence of God is not a strong argument against God's absolute necessary existence, because we cannot fully conceive of

---

45. To quote Brand Blanshard about this, "Now it seems to me that the notion of a contingent necessity is a half-way house in which we cannot rest." Blanshard, *Reason and Analysis*, 469.

46. There is an issue that is not addressed here. Could a being exist necessarily and yet not in precisely the same manner in all possible worlds? E.g., could God exist necessarily but have actualized a different universe in different possible worlds? If so, then God's knowledge would be different in those other worlds.

47. Parrish, *God and Necessity*, 23–119.

48. See Parrish, *God and Necessity*. Jeff Speaks's criticisms of the attempts to show God as the Greatest Possible Being fail. I already answered Speaks's arguments in *God and Necessity*. James Van Cleve writes of autonomous necessities. Autonomous necessities are ones that come from the nature of the entity itself. This is true. Specifically, God's necessity is autonomous, as it depends upon nothing else. Van Cleve, "Brute Necessity."

God's being.[49] Because of human limitations, it is possible for us to conceptualize that some necessary truths are false, and vice versa.

Can ethical propositions likewise be necessary on their own? It is difficult to see how. Ethical propositions, if they are considered to be Platonic entities, exist necessarily in all possible worlds. So, would all other propositions. However, even if all propositions were to *exist* necessarily in all worlds, they would not all be *true* in all worlds. A proposition may be true in many worlds, and false in others.

Only necessarily true propositions are true in all worlds. What makes a proposition true is either that it is intentional to some actual or possible state of affairs, or else, in the case of necessarily true propositions, that its denial entails a contradiction. In the case of Platonism, neither condition holds. There is, in non-naturalism, no state of affairs that by itself is ethical or not. Ethical propositions themselves are not analytically true. In short, some synthetic necessity is needed. From where, then, does the necessity of this and other ethical propositions come? If it cannot come from the nature of the proposition itself, then it must come from some other source. But, given Wielenberg's atheism, and his concept of ethical propositions as being ontologically independent, there is no other source from which the necessity could be derived. Given atheistic Platonism, synthetic necessities are not available to him at this point.

It should be noted that when I mention logical contradictions, they are not limited to strict, narrow, logical contradictions. There are contradictions that are not strict logical ones. The theory being presented here is God's nature contradicts his willing certain things, because they contradict his nature.[50] It is unquestionably true that red is a color and not a number, but the contradiction here is not of the strict, narrow, logical kind.[51] There are contradictions that we cannot manage to put in strict, narrow, logical form, but not all contradictions need be in this precise form.

---

49. Similarly, given the question of whether there are four 7's somewhere in a row in the decimal expansion of pi, the answer is that we do not know, because we cannot see the whole expansion. We can conceive of the answer as being yes or no, but whether there is or not is a necessary truth. Thus, we can conceive, and even firmly come to believe for some reason, something that is necessarily false.

50. On this matter see Hale, *Necessary Beings*. Note especially chapter 6.

51. Plantinga calls this broadly logical necessity. Plantinga, *Nature of Necessity*. Others may call it metaphysical necessity.

Theistic Response

The theistic response is, or should be, that God, as a necessary being, knows all propositions and affirms the truth of all true propositions, because of his nature. God is essentially and necessarily good and loving, and ethics ultimately flow from this. In the case of necessary propositions, God affirms them all, in all possible worlds. Therefore, the necessity of T and related propositions comes from God's affirmation. Further, because God is a necessary being, with a necessary nature, he would affirm propositions that accord with his nature, and hence all necessary propositions are *necessarily* necessary.

My criticism here of Wielenberg's view is that even granting that propositions exist as Platonic entities, his atheism prevents any plausible concept of why and how propositions such as T can be true. Atheistic naturalism, even when combined with Platonism, is still an impersonal view of the nature of reality. What is ultimate are, on one level, abstract objects, and on another level, physical concrete entities. Abstract objects exist necessarily, while physical objects, in most views, exist ultimately by chance.

So, what is ultimate in a Platonic atheism is both chance *and* necessity. This is itself rather odd, because the two concepts are opposites of each other. It is also difficult to understand how, given the atemporal, aspatial, and acausal nature of abstracta, they can somehow be instantiated in concrete entities that themselves exist by chance. However, besides these considerations, there are several things that can be said to extend these thoughts.

As argued above, although it might be considered at least initially plausible that some kinds of abstract objects, such as numbers or some universals like geometric shapes, may exist without a mind, the existence of propositions seems dubious. Propositions are, by their very nature, things that can be grasped by minds. However, in atheism, minds are rather bizarre things that arose by chance by a process of blind evolution of material things. So, why, given impersonalism, is a necessarily existing part of reality—a proposition—tied by its very nature to something like a conscious, rational mind? These minds, given naturalism, exist by chance, and given any version of naturalist physicalism, are rather strange entities that are difficult to explain physically.[52]

---

52. Wielenberg attempts to answer this in Wielenberg, *Robust Ethics*. While I think that he makes the evolutionary hypothesis as plausible as possible, that we can intuit

This may not be an absolutely decisive argument, but it seems apparent that theism can explain the existence of propositions more plausibly that atheism can. In theism, propositions can be considered as ideas in the mind of God. They thus can be easily explained in a theistic worldview but cannot be accounted for in a naturalistic atheist one.

Further, the whole idea of moral propositions' being true or false, indeed necessarily true or false, in an atheist universe seems quite odd. This may be thought of as a revised argument from a queerness objection. Given atheism, that sentient beings exist at all is a rather queer feature of a physical universe that itself exists by chance—that is, ultimately for no reason. Why should propositions like T be true in such a universe? Chance and abstract necessity have no regard for right and wrong.

Propositions, if they exist as abstracta, all exist necessarily, but their truth value is, except for necessary truths, dependent upon the existence, in some manner, of concrete objects. We have already seen that given atheistic Platonism, ethical propositions like T do not have their necessity intrinsically. It is also apparent that they cannot receive necessity, or even just truth, from the physical world where they are instantiated. Given atheism then, there is nothing from which to make them true, let alone necessarily true.

A similar case may be shown regarding the laws of nature: that is *nomological necessity*.[53] The laws of nature seem to be nomologically necessary. With gravity one can be certain that if a book is dropped, it will fall, until something impedes its falling. This seems to always be true everywhere and at all times.

Yet, it also seems that the laws of nature are not logically, metaphysically, or absolutely necessary. It is easy to non-contradictorily conceive of universes wherein the force of gravity is half or twice what it is in our universe, or where there is no such thing as gravity at all. The force of gravity and most, if not all, other laws and constants of nature can be denied without entailing a logical contradiction. They are, therefore, logically contingent.

---

ethical truths still does not flow as easily from naturalism as it does from theism, with God as a personal being who in some manner creates other personal beings. At an even deeper level, there is a problem for atheists in that given evolutionary physicalism, there is really no answer as to why humans have consciousness in the first place. See Parrish, *Knower and the Known*; and Dale Kratt, "Necessity."

53. See chapter 4.

Nevertheless, they hold universally in our universe. Why is this the case? In theism, it is because God creates and sustains objects with certain natures, from which the laws of nature are derived. In clear contrast, I do not see any plausible answer to this within naturalist atheism.[54] In this case, the laws of nature and ethical propositions are similar as inexplicable conundrums.

To close the case here, ethical propositions like *T* seem to be necessarily true—I emphatically agree with Wielenberg on this point. However, while a theist can justify this, an atheistic Platonist cannot. What this means is that Wielenberg, like Huemer, and Enoch, and others, have failed to show how a Platonic theory of ethical abstract objects is possible. To state the matter again, why in an ultimately impersonal reality are there necessary ethical truths, such as that cruelty is wrong? There cannot be necessary ethical truths in a world that is ultimately impersonal. The non-theistic Platonists believe that there are ethical laws without a lawgiver, and these laws are for persons, in an impersonal world where the very existence of human persons is some sort of quirk.

Wielenberg not only defended a Platonic theory of ethical truths, but he also attacked theistic theories. One attack he makes is that theists, no less than atheists, depend upon brute facts. In short, Wielenberg again appeals to the notion that theists and atheists are in the same boat, so to speak, when it comes to the existence of what is ultimate in their systems, and specifically what is ethically true. Both, he claims, are ultimately dependent upon brute facts. Wielenberg goes on to write, "On both types of views, [theistic and atheistic] the bottom floor of objective morality rests ultimately on nothing."[55] But does it sound at all plausible that in this vast, extraordinarily complex universe, in the end, everything depends upon *nothing* for its existence over time and space?

Wielenberg makes the case for an atheistic strong realism as well as anyone can. However, I maintain that the existence of ethical truths is not brute, but flows from the very nature of a necessarily existing and necessarily good God. This will be expounded upon in the next chapter.

---

54. I have never seen what seems to me a theory that explains how universal natural laws come from either brute fact or logical truths, as well as the category of morality. On this, see my book *God and Necessity*.

55. Wielenberg, *Robust Ethics*, 55.

What's left?

In this chapter, atheistic Platonism is mainly discussed. Absolute creationism is a theistic Platonist theory and avoids the major criticisms that have been leveled here against atheistic Platonism. It is, therefore, a theory that theists can accept. However, it seems that theistic conceptualism is superior, and the reasons why should become clear in the next chapter.

As the Platonistic realist views of metaethics discussed in this chapter fail, we come to Theistic theories. However, for this deliberation, I will first have to explore in detail the concept of God.

CHAPTER 10

Theistic Antirealism, Absolute Creationism, and Theistic Conceptualism

HAVING EXAMINED PLATONISM ABOUT abstract entities, problems with the nature of abstract entities from the Theistic angle, especially regarding their existence and nature, will now be investigated. To do so three theistic theories regarding the nature of abstract objects will be explored. The first is *Theistic Antirealism*, wherein there are no abstract objects.[1] Second is *Absolute Creationism*, wherein God creates abstract objects. The last is *Theistic Conceptualism*, according to which abstract objects are actually ideal objects in the mind of God. The difference between the last two is subtle, as will be shown while defending theistic conceptualism and examining and critiquing Craig's theistic antirealism.

THE NATURE OF ABSTRACTA ON THREE THEISTIC THEORIES

Theistic Antirealism

Antirealism has been defended by William Lane Craig, though he prefers to be called an anti-Platonist.[2] I will not examine theistic antirealism itself in this book, but rather examine it in contrast to theistic conceptualism, which will be defended. Craig makes an extended critique of theistic conceptualism, and in doing so, he brings out several issues that, in my

---

1. This theistic antirealism has been defended of late by William Lane Craig. See Craig, *God and Abstract Objects*.

2. Craig, *God Over All*.

opinion, really show the superiority of theistic conceptualism to both Platonism and Absolute Creationism on the one hand, and antirealism on the other. Absolute Creationism will also be critiqued by comparing it to Theistic Conceptualism.

Briefly summarizing, Antirealists think that abstract entities do not exist but are fictional in some way.

In contradistinction to antirealism there is realism. Realism is, of course, the view that abstract objects really do exist *in some manner*. Platonism is a realist theory, as is Absolute Creationism. So, in a sense, is theistic conceptualism, though in this theory the objects are concrete rather than abstract. Why accept some form of realism instead of antirealism? Put simply, abstract entities can be thought of. If one thinks of the number three, and you are thinking of the number three, and God is also thinking that, then we are all thinking of the same thing. The number three necessarily exists at least as an eternally existing concept that is either a thought or something which can be thought. The essential properties of three are also necessarily contained in the concept of three. The same can be said for all other abstract or conceptual entities. This is realism. So, at least conceptually, we are all thinking of the same things when we think of concepts. This leads into the conceptualism defended below.

Theistic Conceptualism—Introductory Thoughts

Theistic Conceptualism has been defended by Greg Welty,[3] James Orr,[4] and me,[5] among many others. Indeed, this has been the traditional view of most Christian philosophers and theologians. This theory will be examined in this chapter and the following two chapters. Basically, theistic conceptualists conclude that abstract objects or entities are ideal objects, or which less philosophically might be called "ideas", ideas in God's mind. So, instead of the number four's existing in some third realm of abstract objects, it is, rather, in the mind of God, who eternally and necessarily thinks it. Thus, the theistic conceptualist believes that "abstract objects do not exist," but their equivalents do, but not abstractly, as the Platonist or Absolute Creationist thinks, but rather as concepts in God. On this

3. Welty, "Theistic Conceptual Realism."
4. Orr, *The Mind of God and the Works of Nature*.
5. Parrish, *Knower and the Known*.

theory, God has created the universe according to the concepts that he has.[6]

To quote James Orr,

> [T]he strategy at the heart of this scheme involves replacing the lawmaking universals commonly invoked by naturalists and platonists with *divine ideas*—that is, those ingredients in God's mental life informing the creative decisions that provide the ultimate explanatory ground for the lawful regularities that order physical reality.[7]

This viewpoint has been strongly challenged. In his review of my book *The Knower and the Known*, R. Scott Smith makes several criticisms of my defense of theistic conceptualism. The first is that I do not carefully distinguish the difference between *nominalist* and *realist* theories of abstracta. That is, I call universals on both nominalist and realist theories "abstract entities." But, given nominalism, abstract objects do not exist, and what they are referred to instead are *particulars* that can be treated "in an *epistemically abstract* manner." These are metaphysically "not sharable," unlike what abstract entities would be like.[8] This is the only criticism that Smith makes that I think may have some merit, though the problem here is terminological, rather than conceptual.

Just as elsewhere, the terminology can be confusing. The reason is that abstracta are paradigmatically considered atemporal, aspatial, and acausal, and, in Platonism, they are thought to be ontologically independent. In absolute creationism, they do not exist independently or even necessarily. In any other theory of what abstract objects are, such as in nominalism and theistic conceptualism, they are not literally abstract objects in the Platonic sense of the word. In *The Knower and the Known*, universals of both nominalism and realism were being treated in a functionalist manner, as to how they function.

Because of this, for clarification, alternative theories to the existence of abstract entities are not the abstract entities themselves, but rather some alternate theory as to the *existence* and *nature* of them. That is, they are something other than abstract entities but fill many of the same roles. Still, if there is any doubt when dealing with these alternatives to abstract

---

6. A book that defends the necessary use of concepts to understand reality is Porter, *Restoring the Foundations*. A work that to me shows how concepts are used in the nature of the objects in the world is Inman, *Substance and the Familiar*.

7. Orr, *The Mind of God*, 7.

8. Smith, "Book Review: The Knower and the Known," 518–22.

objects, let it be thought that what is being done is writing about abstract objects and their functional equivalents, whatever the nature of these equivalents might be.

The concept of God being used here is that of *Perfect Being Theism*. God is a being who is perfect in every relevant respect. He is the Greatest Possible Being (GPB), which means that he is not only the greatest being in this world, but in every possible world. It is impossible that God be greater or better in any way. I somewhat prefer Greatest Possible Being to Greatest Conceivable Being, which is how Anselm puts the concept,[9] because it is more objective, depending upon the nature of the entities rather than depending on what can be conceived. What God *is* does not depend upon our powers of conception.

As was noted above, one property that God has is omniscience. That is, he knows the truth of every proposition.[10] The point is that God is not only omniscient, but in lieu of the fact that God is the GPB, he is *essentially* omniscient. He not only knows everything, but he knows every possibility in every possible world. God's knowledge is coextensive with all potentialities. Indeed, in a sense, God's knowledge is of all possibilities; it contains everything that is or that could be.

Therefore, the knowing of the truth of all propositions and facts is a necessary part of the nature of God. It is an opinion among philosophers that either there is one possible world, or there are many.[11] If there were only one possible world, then God would know everything in that world, and in all the impossible worlds. If there are more possible worlds, then God knows everything in each of those worlds, as well as in the impossible ones. Indeed, God knows why they are impossible. If God exists in all possible worlds, God will be omniscient in every world, but his knowledge of what he created will be different in each world.

Because of this, if God had actualized world *A*, then he knows that everything in that world is the case, while if, on the other hand, God had actualized World *B*, then he would know everything that is the case in that world. Since *A* and *B* differ, God's knowledge as to what was actual would also differ, but in both worlds, God would know the existence and truth-value of every proposition. Therefore, a proposition that is true in *A* might be false in *B* and vice versa.

---

9. Anselm, "Proslogium," 1–33.
10. Ignoring the issues with the concept of indexicality and other issues.
11. Which may not be true, given theism.

Of course, given Perfect Being Theism, God knows in every possible world what would be the case in any world, if that world were actualized. Further, God knows all necessary truths, and being necessary, these truths therefore do not vary from world to world. Included in necessary truths would be an exhaustive knowledge of all possibilities.

Does God therefore create abstract entities, conceived as existing aspatially, atemporally, and acausally? It depends upon what one means by created. In the theory outlined here, because God is essentially omniscient, he does not create abstract entities in the sense that God created the universe. In some other sense of the word *create*, God does create them, for without God's existing and thinking, they could not and would not exist. They depend upon God for their being. To attempt to keep things clear, what God thinks are *not literally abstract objects*, but ideal objects or ideas, which are themselves concepts and propositions. These ideal objects are dependent upon God for their existence, but they also exist necessarily, for God exists necessarily, and God is necessarily omniscient. So, while being thought of by God is necessary for the object's existence, the ideal object's existence is also necessary for God, in that God, being essentially omniscient and therefore knowing the ideal object and everything about it, is part of God's necessary nature. In other words, ideal objects or ideas, must exist in God's mind for him to be omniscient.

Further, some of these ideal objects are propositions that are about one or more concepts. Alternatively, to put it another way, they are about the things that either exist in our world or could exist in other possible worlds.

Some philosophers and theologians have a problem with the concept of God's being dependent upon anything, even the concepts in his mind. They say that it makes God dependent upon other things, which is bad. However, if we conceive of God as having concepts as part of his being, then the problem disappears.[12] In other words, concepts such as the phenomenal red or numbers or moral propositions, are part of God, not something external to him. This *might* be a problem for God if God is conceived of as being absolutely simple, but in that case, absolute simplicity should be denied. The alternative is to think of God as not knowing anything, and that must be utterly rejected in any concept of God.[13] Fur-

---

12. For a version of this theory, see Ward, *Divine Ideas*.
13. For a defense of God's Absolute Simplicity see Dolezal, *God without Parts*. For a critique, see Hinlicky, *Divine Simplicity*.

ther, there are other versions of simplicity which may be more plausible than the absolute version. This will be discussed in the next two chapters.

Absolute Creationism

There is another position, *Absolute Creationism*, wherein abstract objects are thought to exist outside of the mind of God but are created by God. Their existence is contingent at least in the sense that they depend upon something else for their existence, i.e., God. Therefore, they are quite like ideal objects in all ways except in their "location." Ideal objects are *inside* the mind of God, while abstract objects in absolute creationism are *outside* of his mind.

Objects

What does it really mean to say that an abstract object is an object? One may easily (or at least relatively easily—for philosophers have a way of making commonplace notions difficult) understand how a physical object, a ball, a car, or a cat, for example, can be an object. A ball is an object in the sense that it is physically separate from other physical things. It may move around as a single thing, while every other object stays still. One may consider it as an individual thing that has properties, that it, and it alone, has—such as occupying a particular space at a particular time.

Of course, as mentioned above, things are not that simple.[14] On the one hand, one may seriously doubt that the ball may be considered a lone item. For it can easily be taken apart, and its individual parts then can be objects themselves. As an example of this, two men may shake hands, and in one sense therefore their combined hands could be considered a single object, yet the bond between them is merely temporary, and is easily broken. Therefore, the fact that a physical object has parts that are bound together does not by itself make it a single object.[15]

On the other hand, some philosophers have argued that widely disparate things can legitimately be considered one object. For example, the Eiffel Tower, my cat Squirt, Donald Trump's left ear, and the dwarf planet Pluto may be thought to be a single object. If this is true, then the

---

14. In philosophy they never are.
15. van Inwagen, *Material Beings*.

dividing line between objects and non-objects becomes very difficult to draw. Almost anything may be considered an object in this sense.

Perhaps one way of simply defining an object could be that an object is a substance, which may possess properties but which itself cannot be the property of something else. In this case, the ball that was mentioned above would be an object because, though it may have properties, such as being colored, or being a specific size, it cannot be a property of anything else. A child may hold the ball, in which case in some way the child-ball may be considered a composite object. But neither as a single thing nor as separable things may the child and/or the ball be thought to be the property of something else.

Abstract Objects

Which brings us to abstract and ideal objects. How can they be thought of as objects in the light of the above discussion? Take for example some abstract entity, such as the shape of roundness, or the color orange. Can they be thought of as substances? At first glance no, for if objects are substances, then they cannot be properties of something else, and some objects, such as a ball, may both be round and colored orange. On this criterion, it seems that abstract and ideal objects cannot legitimately be objects, confusing though that sounds.

However, things are even more complicated than that. For while it is true that a physical object such as a ball may be round and colored orange, and that therefore being round and colored orange are properties, it is not the case that roundness and orangeness are properties of the ball. That is, a ball may be round, and roundness is therefore a property of the ball, while at the same time, the abstract object of roundness is not a property of the ball. If it were, then no other physical object could be round; there could be no other round balls, which is clearly false. There is ambiguity between property instances and property universals, between being round and roundness itself.

A related question is, can God create abstract entities in the sense that absolute creationism postulates? Since God is essentially omnipotent as well as omniscient, it might seem that he can. However, even God cannot do intrinsically impossible things. God cannot make red to be a number rather than a color, or 5 + 7 to equal 93, or triangles that have 46.319 sides, or any infinite number of other impossible things. Different concepts have different essences, ways that they must be. Creating a triangle is necessary in creating something with three sides. Even God cannot make nonsensical things to exist just by sheer power or cleverness—or by any other way for that matter.

This brings us to another point that Smith makes. He writes the following in criticizing my position:

> The concern that drives these problems is Parrish's wise move to be sure abstracta are dependent upon God's mind. But a different solution could achieve that same end. J. P. Moreland has suggested that one can modify Platonism such that God created abstracta (that is, sustains them in existence eternally), so that they are dependent upon Him.[16]

This kind of thinking is echoed by Paul M. Gould and Richard Brian Davis when they write the following:

> In what follows, we shall argue two things. First, it is plausible to think that conceptualism [the concept that all abstract entities are really ideas in the mind of God] holds with respect to propositions; in any event, it does a much better job than its closest competitors (platonism and nominalism) in accounting for the truthbearing nature of propositions. Secondly, it is wholly implausible (so we say) to take the added step and equate properties and relations with divine concepts.[17]

I will make one point immediately regarding the idea that properties and relations are not divine concepts. This is certainly true in a sense. The property of my cat weighing as much as she does is not in itself a divine concept. Neither is the relation of my distance to the Eiffel Tower a divine concept. However, God does have concepts *about* these, and all other relations and properties. In short, God comprehends them all, and this is all that one needs to be a coherent theistic conceptualist.

As was stated, in opposition to theistic or divine conceptualism on the one hand, and Platonism on the other, *absolute creationism* holds that while propositions are ideas in the mind of God, others—such as properties and relations—are not. Rather, God causes abstract objects to exist and these abstracta are different from the ideas that exist in God's mind.

---

16. Smith is referring to Parrish, *The Knower and the Known*. In spite of my criticism of Smith, Gould, Davis and Craig, I greatly appreciate the work they have done. I especially appreciate Smith for his help in reviewing the book and for calling one of my moves "wise."

17. Gould and Davis, "Modified Theistic Activism," 52.

Because God is essentially omniscient, theistic conceptualism would argue that ideal objects in his mind necessarily exist. In contrast, in absolute creationism, God creates abstract objects, and there may be possible worlds where they do not exist (depending upon whether God would have created a world where these properties and relations do not exist, or possibly created nothing—that is, a world where only God exists).

To examine this point brings up the question as to whether God *can* create abstract entities. Given the definition that Platonism gives, the answer is no. Abstract objects given Platonism are ontologically independent, and if God has caused them to be, then they are not ontologically independent. Hence, according to the standard definition of abstract objects, ideal objects in God's mind are not really abstract objects, though they function as such, at least to us. So, we must stipulate that in modified theistic activism, abstract objects as Platonically conceived do not exist. What we have instead are quasi-abstract objects of some sort. These do have the other characteristics of abstract objects, save for the two properties of 1) having been created, and thus 2) being ontologically dependent.

One problem with this proposal is the following. Can abstract entities, supposedly created in the manner that absolute creationism holds, *actually* be created? One might think that it would be easier for God to instantiate some orange thing (like an orange) than to create orangeness. Of course, for an omnipotent being, all things are equally easy. God, by being omnipotent, causes things to exist merely by willing them. Still, it is *relatively* easy to see how God could will concrete objects to exist; it is not at all easy to see how God could will these quasi-abstract objects into existence. For God to create something, he must have the concept of that thing first.

It could be asked, "Why is it easier to imagine that God could create something with substance versus a concept?" Or "Wouldn't creating dirt be just as hard as, if not more difficult than, creating a concept of dirtiness?" In response, abstract objects according to Platonists and Absolute Creationists are not just concepts, but objects in themselves. It is difficult to think of an object that is spaceless, atemporal, and acausal if it is *not* considered to just be a concept.

I can understand (at least to an extent) how God can create orange objects. Nevertheless, how can even God create orangeness itself? What would orangeness be like, and how could it be created? How would this abstract entity of orangeness cause the world in which it exists to have the ability to create orange things? It is aspatial and acausal and hence, by definition, really does not *do* anything. This does not seem to make sense, and it is doubtful that anyone has any real understanding of any of this. Why does God have to create orangeness to be able to create orange objects? We simply do not know enough about the nature of the things involved.

Suppose God wants to actualize a world, and two worlds in particular are the leading candidates for divine actualization. One of the worlds contains orange objects, while the other does not. Presumably, on Absolute Creationism, to be able to create orange physical objects, God needs to create the quasi-abstract entity of orangeness. If he does not need such an object, it is difficult to see what the point would be in creating quasi-abstract entities at all.

Therefore, if God decides to create the world with orange physical objects in it, then he will need to create the quasi-abstract entity of orangeness. How can he do so? Well again, by the standard definition of God as a perfect being, God is omniscient and therefore knows all about how to create orangeness—otherwise he could not create it, and by proviso, then could opt not to create any orange physical objects.

However, there seems to be a problem here. If God knows how to create orangeness, to create orange physical objects, there seems to be no reason why he would need to create orangeness as a quasi-abstract entity. Think of it this way: God is essentially omniscient and therefore understands orangeness and orange things exhaustively. Given God's exhaustive knowledge of orange (and everything else), why does he need orangeness to create orange things?

All the information, all the knowledge, that is in orangeness, so to speak, already exists in God's mind as ideas. Why not eliminate the middleman and just create orange physical objects based on what he knows? Everything that is in orangeness already exists in the mind of God, which makes the whole notion of the quasi-abstract entity orangeness suspect, at best. The same may be said for almost any other universal that one may think of. An omniscient God already necessarily has exhaustive knowledge of every item in his mind. Of what use are these quasi-abstract objects then, given the existence of an essentially omniscient God? God, being a creative agent, can use the concept of orange that he already has as an ideal object in his mind to be able to create orange things. It seems that he would not need a separate abstract entity to create orange things.

Another issue is this: some universals, like phenomenal colors, seem to be intrinsically conscious concepts. That is, seeing colors like phenomenal orange is a mental event. Since this is intrinsically a conscious event, and therefore can exist only in a mind, it is difficult to see how a universal like phenomenal orange could exist outside of a mind. Therefore, how could a universal such as the orangeness that theistic activists think exists as created by God, but that exists external to his mind, really exist? If phenomenal color is essentially an aspect of consciousness, then there could be no abstract object of orangeness or any other color. This is not a problem for the theistic conceptualist; for he or she holds that ideal objects like phenomenal colors exist eternally and necessarily in God's mind.

The whole notion of created abstracta therefore seems rather pointless in allowing the theist to be able to explain the existence of orange things and other concrete universals. Why then have able theistic philosophers rejected the theistic conceptualism and advocated in its place the theory of the existence of abstract entities conceived in the manner of absolute creationism?

Concepts

One reason for this is because of the thought that if abstract objects are actually just ideal objects, and ideal objects are just concepts, then there is a problem in ascribing the objects to non-mental things. In other words, if concepts were intrinsically mental events, then to say that they exist in physical objects would be to say that physical objects, in instantiating concepts, are mental events, which is absurd. Writes Smith on this point,

> On Parrish's TC, [theistic conceptualism] all properties that can be predicated of objects are concepts. Concepts are properties appropriate for minds, due to their natures. But they seem inappropriate for being predicated of other kinds of things, like physical objects, due to their natures. Moreover, on TC, it means that as a property of concepts, intentionality would be predicated of physical objects. But this seems mistaken; how can a physical object be of or about something else?[18]

I think that there is an ambiguity here. Suppose that one understands the notion of a blue ball (to give a change from orange so that the discussion does not become too monotonous). One understands both the concept of ball and the concept of blue. Given this, one thus understands

18. Smith, "Book Review: The Knower and the Known," 521–22.

the two relevant concepts here. The concepts of being a ball and of being colored blue therefore both exist in my mind.

They also exist in some manner in the ball. Need the ball thus have mental objects, and hence be conscious and intentional in its nature? Is the blueness of the ball actually the ball thinking about what color it is? To solve this puzzle, it seems to me that what we have here are two different meanings in the word "concept." In one meaning of a concept, a person, either a human being, or angel, an alien, or God or even something else like an animal, has the concept in mind if he or she is thinking about it, or arguably, has the concept somehow stored in the mind even if not currently thinking about it. With the other meaning, the concept is instantiated in a physical object.

What about the concept in the ball, for example? In this case, the concept is physically instantiated. It is a concept instantiated in a physical thing. The ball is not conscious (or at least we would be extremely surprised if it were),[19] but it is something that can be an object of thought. A concept is one of the things that one uses in understanding something. That I have the concepts of both blueness and sphericity enables me to understand what the ball is.

Of course, the concepts of being colored blue and of being spherical are both predicated on and can *only* be predicated on a physical object. So, the concept of being a blue ball (which necessarily, analytically contains other concepts within it), is the concept of something physical. So, the move is from the properties the object is represented as having to an object that has those properties. Or, as Angus Menuge writes, "So, as I understand it, the ball does not exemplify the concept qua intentional entity but rather exemplifies what the concept is of. And as you can say, we can think of non-mental objects. So, the move is from the properties the object is represented as having, to an object that has those properties."[20]

In other words, concepts are concepts of something. When directed at an object with an understanding of the object, the mind knows what the object is and what some of the concepts describing it are. This brings us to the crux of the matter. Concepts can be of various things: of substances, properties, and events, for example. If truly known, therefore, the subject's understanding an object will know what properties it has. Some of the concepts will be of the properties that the object has. Therefore,

---

19. Although in some versions of panpsychism the ball might be.
20. A personal note to me from Menuge.

the object itself does not contain concepts; concepts are how things like properties can be understood.

The properties instantiated in an object like a blue ball are not literally mental concepts; concepts are things that minds use in understanding the world. However, they *match* the world in various ways. Therefore, the allegation that this theory of universals and individuals leads to the absurd conclusion that physical objects must have some sort of mentality to contain the properties that the concepts are of fails. All concepts that are *contained in the blue object*, though, are contained in it in quite a different fashion than when *contained in the mind*.

In short, the physical world is the instantiation of ideal objects. The world is modeled on, created in the image of, the ideal objects that exist in the mind of God. Therefore, we can genuinely know the world as it is (with some caveats of course. We do not always experience the world exactly as it is. E.g., physical objects look solid to us but are composed of atoms that are widely separated). Thus, mind and world match each other. This is a form of realism, because we, via the concepts that are in our minds, match the world as it is.

Idealism

Is this also a form of *idealism*? Idealism in philosophy has several different meanings, but if by idealism one means that reality is most fundamentally mental, then it may fairly be called a version of idealism. For perfect being theism, God is a personal being (and for that matter, is so considered in other versions of theism). If God is a personal being, then ultimately, God is a mind.[21] God is ultimate reality and essentially a conscious being, and everything else that exists is created and sustained by God, based on the knowledge that he essentially, in himself, has. It follows that everything else that exists is a copy of God's thoughts, an instantiation of some of the things that exist in his mind. There is nowhere else for them to come from.

This should not be surprising, because on a theistic understanding of reality, everything that is or could have been, exists first as an idea in the mind of God. God creates what he first knows. Physical objects are in some sense *conceptual actualizations* of what God has in his mind. God does not just have propositions in his mind. He also has phenomenal

---

21. Or minds in relational trinitarianism, see chapter 12.

ideas like orange, blue, and sphericity. Concepts are ideal objects, and physical objects are thus instantiations of different ideas or concepts that eternally exist in the mind of God.

The Bootstrapping problem

The bootstrapping problem needs to be briefly addressed here. This challenge is that if properties are things that God must instantiate, then does he not have any properties intrinsically? In other words, if God must create his own omnipotence, how could he, for he would be without power to begin with. My answer is that God necessarily and essentially has all the properties contained in the concept of his being the Perfect Being God. Other properties, like blueness or circularity, exist as ideal objects in his mind.

On perfect being theism, God has exhaustive knowledge of all possible worlds. They are ideal objects in his mind. They are concepts. God's thoughts about these concepts are God's thinking. However, they, the ideal objects of possible worlds, are *not themselves conscious*. So why should knowledge of existing physical things include thinking of them as conscious?

This is the reason, for example, physical objects are not just ideas or concepts—they are ideas *willed by God into having extra-mental existence* of material substance. It also explains why we can use our concepts to understand external reality, such as the physical universe. If the external world matches the concepts in God's mind, and we have some of the same concepts as God, then our concepts match the external world. Essentially, it is mind to mind, with the route going through the created things in the world.

It is possible to have consciousness without concepts. One can experience something without yet having a concept of it. Babies, when they are born, have no concepts, yet they can experience the world to an extent. However, because our minds are made to understand the world, they begin to obtain concepts, have conceptualization, and gain the ability to use language. A newborn baby lacks concepts but can experience things phenomenally. Again, the baby will develop concepts of things experienced to have greater understanding of the world in the future—concepts permit a much greater understanding of the world, because, among other things, they enable us to use language.

Consider, also, the case of Mary, the woman who for her entire life was locked in a room which contained only the colors white and black, including of her own body.[22] However, she knows all the scientific facts about color, so she has concepts about the wavelengths of orange and blue, the ways that brains perceive them, etc. When she eventually escapes the room, and then sees colors like orange or blue, though not having the concept of what phenomenal orange or blue look like, she will still be able to see and distinguish the colors. When experienced, the concepts of what orange and blue are like phenomenally will come after she has seen them.

The point is not that human beings have concepts for everything that they experience, but that there are concepts for everything. God has the concepts for everything, even if no one else does. What is being proposed here, therefore, is that everything that exists is intelligible, and thereby in some manner understandable by means of conceptualization, even if we do not possess the concepts, and indeed even if the concepts involved are beyond the human capacity to understand. Unlike God, our minds are finite and formed to understand only some things. Numbers, and other mathematical objects exist as thinkable things, with certain definite properties. The properties that are analytically contained in the concept of the number four, are necessary, and exist independently of human thinking.

For example, take some fantastical number N, which is a huge number that has never been thought of by any finite mind, and multiply it by some other monstrously huge number M, that has also never been thought of by any finite mind. The result of the multiplication will be some even more preposterously large number P. The relevant point here is that the result will be necessary. It will be P, and by necessity not some other number. Therefore, whether or not there are any such numbers as M, N, and P, they are all determinate thoughts that have necessary properties that are analytically contained in their concepts. They are necessarily thinkable things with necessary properties. Some extremely complex geometrical figure—say some object with ten thousand sides and ten thousand angles, each of them with different lengths and degrees—will necessarily have the exact relationships between the sides and the angles that it does, even though no finite mind will ever know this. Yet every

22. Poor Mary—fated to be locked in a room of only black and white for decades. This references a standard philosophical scenario commonly used for exploring issues such as the mind-body problem.

one of the relationships between lengths and angles in this object will be necessary.

To sum up, considering universals like colors and shapes, or else mathematical objects like numbers, what we have are necessarily thinkable things that at least could be possibly thought of. This being the case, what the "objects" in mind then consist of are eternal and necessary ways to think about things. They are not that different from propositions, though ideal objects such as orangeness or numbers are essentially concepts, not propositions. However, propositions are themselves formed from concepts. This, of course, includes ethical ones. Though finite creatures like we are may never think of them, God does. God thinks everything and thus has all concepts in his mind. This is essentially what Theistic Conceptualism is.

God can create by actualizing copies of ideal objects that already exist in his mind. This involves making to exist *externally* what already exists *internally* in God's mind. A concept of something like a rock or a car is essentially and necessarily a concept of something that is itself not conscious and therefore cannot be a conscious concept—something being thought of by the object that possesses that concept.

Summary of Absolute Creationism vs Theistic Conceptualism

Therefore, I do not see that any of the criticisms directed by absolute creationists at theistic conceptualism succeed in disproving it. In fact, investigation seems to show the opposite, that theistic conceptualism has resources that absolute creationism does not have. The point to emphasize here is that *concepts can be instantiated*, so that what exists in the mind of the knower is also that which is outside the mind and has many of the same properties that the concept has when purely imagined. At any rate, Absolute Creationism is a theistic theory, and therefore, if true, is not a problem for theists.

Theistic Conceptualism

Abstract Objects

So, given theistic conceptualism based on perfect being theology, do abstract objects exist? With a broad enough definition of what it is to be an abstract object, the answer is yes, they exist, as there are objects upon which the things of this world *are conceptually created and instantiated*. Given a narrower, standard definition, they do not, but functional equivalents for them exist conceptually, created eternally and necessarily as thoughts in God's mind. Any number of the requisite kinds of minds can think of a concept, and if the concept is instantiable, then there is no limit to how many instantiations of said concept there may be.

Ethical Propositions

Coming back to metaethics, the point made here is that ethical propositions are, like all other concepts, *concepts in the mind of God*. However, God only affirms some of them, like T, and rejects others, like $\sim T$. The basis of why some are affirmed, and some are rejected will be further discussed in the next chapter. Ethical concepts exist as abstract objects in the mind of God, and necessarily so. This is where the point that was made earlier about synthetic necessity is relevant. Moral propositions do not have necessity within themselves, but when combined with the necessary will of a necessary GPB, they obtain it. The necessity is therefore of a synthetic kind. With this established, I will now move on to analyze some other metaphysical issues.

The ideas discussed above are not the only issues in determining the correct theistic theory of abstract entities. Other points will also be examined here.

Ethics is an Interrelated System

It seems that ethical propositions do not stand alone but are part of a system. What we have is 1) *an inter-related system* of ethical propositions, that are 2) intrinsically *person related*, and 3) *seemingly necessary*—but which neither considered individually nor collectively seem to be necessary in the sense that their denial entails a contradiction. The necessity must come from something that 1) itself has necessary existence, and 2) is itself necessarily person related. The only plausible candidate for this position seems to be God.

How does God know propositions?

Granting perfect being theism (henceforth just referred to as theism), there is, in fact, someone thinking all the propositions in every possible world, in at least one sense. This would have to be, of course, God, who exists in all worlds, and is omniscient in all worlds. Since God is therefore essentially omniscient, all propositions exist necessarily in God's mind. Therefore, God eternally thinks, as part of his nature, that Cleveland is in Ohio, but judges this proposition true or false based on whether or not, in that world, Cleveland and Ohio really exist, and Cleveland really is in Ohio. However, other beings can also think the same thought. Indeed, an indefinite number of beings can think the same thought, because it exists as a permanent part of the nature of possibility.

The difference between theism and Platonism would thus be that in theism the propositions have a place to live, a home, while in Platonism there are countless propositions that no one ever thinks of.

Of course, there are issues with this point of view. In the case of Cleveland's being in Ohio, for example, both Cleveland and Ohio are vague objects. If Ohio had quite different borders than the ones that it does, would it still be Ohio? Alternatively, suppose that Cleveland were located in a slightly different place, had been founded at a different time, in a different country (suppose that Canada had decisively won the War of 1812 and had annexed Ohio), and had completely different people living in it. Would it still be Cleveland?

While not denying in the slightest that there are gray areas (wherein it is not clear if we are speaking of the same thing), if the terms are precisely defined, then the propositions exactly refer to them.

Indexicals

Another issue is that of indexicals. "An indexical is, roughly speaking, a linguistic expression whose reference can shift from context to context."[23] If God is outside of space, that is, has no spatial location, how can he know propositions like, "It is raining here." If he is outside of time (which is a far more controversial position than God's having no spatial location), that is, has no temporal setting, how can God know that "It is

---

23. Braun, "Indexicals."

raining now"? Alternatively, how could God know propositions when other individuals think of them?

Take the proposition, "I am the poorest poker player in Plymouth," when being thought of by Paul. Paul could think this easily enough, for example, after losing his 413th game in a row. However, how can others, such as God, know it? God could, of course, know that Paul is the poorest poker player in Plymouth, but it seems by the very nature of things that God could not know, "I am the poorest poker player in Plymouth," simply because God is not, and cannot be, the worst player. For one thing, God does not play poker in Plymouth, and if he did, then he would necessarily be the best poker player in Plymouth.

My answer to this is that God has a different mode of access to propositions than we do. God cannot know, "I am the poorest poker player in Plymouth," but he can know that Paul is, and that Paul could truly, and quite reasonably, think of himself as being the poorest player.

The point is that on the theistic view being presenting here, propositions are not things, not abstract entities, but rather are possible *thoughts* that one could have, and indeed that God has. However, even God does not literally think every possible proposition, such as in the case above about poker. Rather, he knows every possible thought from his own mode of access.

Therefore, God does not believe in every proposition. Countless propositions are false, and many of these are necessarily false. Further, as in the case of indexicals, even true ones, God does not always affirm their truth. In the case of the unfortunate Paul and his woeful lack of skill in playing poker, God knows the proposition that Paul may sadly think of himself, but only indirectly affirms it. That is, God knows that Paul is the poorest poker player in Plymouth and affirms its truth. Or perhaps God knows that Pauline has lost 414 games in Plymouth, so Paul's thought is false. Regarding the proposition, "I am the poorest poker player in Plymouth," when applied to God, or less skilled poker players than Paul, God affirms its falsity. When thinking of the proposition as being thought of by Paul, God affirms its truth, knows how Paul thinks it, and thus indirectly affirms its truth.[24]

What is the point of all of this? Simply, it is to say that in theism, *God knows all propositions*, whether directly or indirectly, *and affirms their truth or falsity*. God knows all the numbers, even pi. God knows the true

24. Kvanvig, *Possibility*.

location of Cleveland. God even knows how many quarks there are on Pluto at this moment. God not only knows all propositions, but also each of their truth values. The truth or falsity of a proposition is therefore determined, in the case of contingent propositions (which are propositions about contingent things), by whether or not the referents exist and stand in the relation that the proposition affirms. So, in contingent propositions, the truth is made true externally, that is, by factors external to the proposition itself. Metaethics, like virtually every other issue in philosophy, can become very complicated.[25]

Theistic Antirealist Objections to Theistic Conceptualism

Objections from Craig

William Lane Craig has made a list of objections to theistic conceptualism, though the main thrust of his writing is an attack on Platonism. He calls what I have named theistic conceptualism, *divine conceptualism*, but there is no real difference between the two theories. The points that Craig makes are important, so they will be quoted in detail here. Some may think that this is merely an intramural dispute between theists, and perhaps in a way it is. However, it should be relevant to everyone because here I hope to show that concepts, including ethical concepts, are best thought of as ideal objects in God's mind. This is something that philosophers who hold to rival theistic theories must deal with and is an important issue for non-theistic philosophers to grasp to fully understand the strengths of theism.

There are many different criticisms that Craig makes, and I will respond to the more important ones. In the end, antirealists such as Craig are not that far apart from theistic conceptualists.

Craig writes that divine (theistic) conceptualism gives rise to the following problem:

> Conceptualism requires that God be constantly entertaining actual thoughts corresponding to every proposition and every state of affairs. But this seems problematic. Graham Oppy complains that 'it threatens to lead to the attribution to God of

---

25. Which is a good thing, as otherwise philosophers would have to get jobs as produce managers at a grocery store, or some such thing.

inappropriate thoughts: bawdy thoughts, banal thoughts, malicious thoughts, silly thoughts, and so forth."[26]

Must God, for example, imagine himself to be thinking about all sorts of degrading and ridiculous activities? Craig thinks this is a problem because God must constantly think about all the above listed kinds of thoughts. As mentioned, if this is a problem, it is a problem for any believer in divine omniscience. Indeed, Craig's attack here seems to be less an attack on theistic conceptualism than on God's always thinking everything. Any believer in divine omniscience must acknowledge that God knows all about disgusting things, boring things, silly things, etc. After all, to think of something is not containing its approval, and God's condemnations necessarily talk about vile things. We can hardly say that God would condemn bad things that he does not know about.[27]

Craig then discusses an attempt to get around a difficulty that a theistic conceptualist might make, and that indeed, theistic conceptualist Greg Welty makes. This is to distinguish between the "aspectual shapes" of thoughts that God can have. Thoughts about what God can do are different from thoughts about what, for example, Napoleon could have done. So, God doesn't have to be thinking about himself as being engaged in some awful activities, though he would have to think about other creatures such as human beings being engaged in such activities, whether they are or not. And, of course, in thinking about acts with ethical import, God passes judgment on them based on his nature.

However, Craig thinks that this brings up even deeper problems. He continues,

> To take a simple example, the thought *The number of people killed in the attack was 66* and the thought *66 people were killed in the attack* have, on the customary criterion of ontological commitment, different ontological commitments. The former commits us to the reality of the number 66, whereas the latter, using the numerical term adjectively rather that substantively, lacks such a commitment. So which one is God's thought? If God thinks both, what are His ontological commitments? . . . [T]his same approach will wind up committing us to holes, lacks, and other unwanted commitments of ordinary language

---

26. Craig has another book on the same subject, much longer, wherein he delves more deeply and at much greater length regarding abstracta. Craig, *God and Abstract Objects*.

27. A personal note by Angus Menuge.

if God has, indeed, in Welty's words 'the full range of thoughts that we humans can have and will have'.[28]

This brings up several interesting issues. First, as all theists would or at least should admit, we do not really have a good understanding of how God thinks about things, so it is difficult to give a definitive answer on these matters. However, given perfect being theology, it is analytically necessarily true of God that he is omniscient, true by the very definition or concept of such a God, so in some manner he does know all propositions and their truth value. I do not think that God has epistemological commitments in the same sense that we do.

Second, what God thinks about numbers, holes, and everything else, depends upon their ontological status. If, for example, absolute creationism is true regarding numbers, then they do exist, and God would think about them as real entities. The same goes for everything else. God's thoughts about different entities depend upon the nature of the entities under consideration, and so the nature of God's thoughts will follow the nature of the objects he is thinking about. If we take that abstract objects are best thought of as concepts—ideal objects or concepts in the mind of God—this all becomes more understandable.

Third, Craig makes a move here that is rather problematic. He writes,

> Why in the world should we think that God is constantly thinking the non-denumerable infinity of banal and silly propositions or states of affairs that there are? Take Welty's own illustration of the thought that for any real number r, r is distinct from the Taj Mahal. Why would God hold such inanities constantly in consciousness? Or consider false propositions like *for any real number r, r is identical to the Taj Mahal*. Why would God keep such a silly thought constantly in consciousness, knowing it to be false? Obviously, the concern is not that God would be incapable of keeping such a non-denumerable infinity of thoughts ever in consciousness, but rather why He would dwell on such trivialities.
>
> Welty moves far too hastily from the fact that God is omniscient to the conceptualist view that all that God knows is occurrent in consciousness . . . Now I fully appreciate that God must have a conscious life much different than ours. Still, the proliferation in God's conscious thought of the silly and banal

---

28. Craig, *God Over All*, 87–88.

beliefs necessary for divine conceptualism seems pointless and makes conceptualism a less attractive option.[29]

Response to Craig

Several things may be said in response to this. First, the concept that God is not consciously entertaining all his knowledge all the time implies a temporalist view of God, which means that God is in time. If God were not in time, then he would have to know everything in his eternal existence, because there would be no other times that he could know things, and this would imply that God is not omniscient. This is not a problem for Craig who is a temporalist concerning God's present state, but the view that God does not actively entertain all his knowledge does seem to rule out the traditional view that God exists outside of time. Therefore, there is a cost to holding this view, as it narrows the options for the theist.[30]

Second, the view that God does *not* know always everything seems wrong to me. If God is the source of all reality, as theists hold to, then all propositions exist as part of God's nature. As I have stated above, and Craig agrees, we do not exactly understand how God thinks. That God is omniscient is something that we can understand about God. Questioning exactly how God knows things is, in a sense, an attempt to understand how it is *to be God*, and that is much more difficult. Certainly, this would be much harder to conceptualize than a visualization of what it is like to be a bat, or even a cat.

My view is that God sees everything at once in some unified vision, with everything in its proper place in the structure of both what is (reality), and what could be (possibility). Though this is a rather opaque saying, God is being himself, and thus there is nothing that escapes, or can escape, his purview. It is his nature to know everything, though again, being so different than we are, how he knows everything is quite mysterious to us.

Third, when choosing to actualize one world, it seems that God would have to know all worlds in order to be able to rationally choose one to actualize rather than any of the others. In addition, since God keeps the universe in existence at every moment that it exists, God would have to have exhaustive knowledge of the universe and everything in it. Since

---

29. Craig, *God Over All*, 88–89.
30. The relation of God and time is mysterious on any view.

at any moment, the universe is described by true propositions about everything in it, God will, by necessity, think about all sorts of disgusting and banal events. This is also true when God remembers what happened in the past, and what will happen in the future.

Fourth, suppose that I am wrong, and that Craig is right about this. Imagine that God exists temporally and does not always consciously entertain all thoughts. If this is true, why is it necessarily bad for the conceptualist? I do not see why the theistic conceptualist *as such* is necessarily bound to the view that God consciously entertains everything at every moment that he exists (which is, of course, eternally). The only thoughts that God would need to consciously entertain would be the information to create the universe when he created it, to sustain the universe, as it exists, and to foresee what will happen. He would know at every moment what he needs to know, though all other knowledge is at his disposal, so to speak.[31]

Craig gives an example about how human beings can know things like the multiplication table while not actually thinking about it. One does not usually consciously entertain the thought that 12 x 12 = 144, but one can think about it whenever the occasion arises. Therefore, on this model God could know everything while not consciously thinking about every jot and tittle constantly. God's mind could contain all the disgusting, banal, and silly thoughts even though he is not consciously thinking about them. Since all these truths still do exist eternally in God's mind, even though he is not consciously entertaining them, I see no reason why the conceptualist as such could not endorse this model. Any thought that God would need to think would still be there accessible to God whenever he needs them. What is there about the conceptualist model that makes it impossible for the conceptualist to adopt the theory that God does not always think about everything? Moreover really, how does this differ from the orthodox theistic antirealists, who must also hold that God is omniscient?

Therefore, these objections do not place an insurmountable burden on the theistic conceptualist. Indeed, here, it seems to me that Craig's position is not that different from that of the conceptualist. Both the conceptualist and Craig do not believe in abstract objects as they are properly considered to be, entities existing outside of God's mind. Further, both the theistic conceptualist and Craig believe that God is omniscient,

---

31. I asked Craig this question at a philosophy conference, and it seemed to me that he didn't give a successful response.

though their understanding of this may be different. However, there does not seem to be any reason why the conceptualist *as such* would need to deny Craig's notion that God does not always consciously entertain every proposition that exists within his mind.

Craig has another objection: that God's thoughts are concrete and therefore cannot legitimately be considered to be abstract objects. That God's thoughts cannot be Platonic abstracta may be granted, existing as objects outside of God's mind, though in many ways they are like them. Why could the divine thoughts not take the place of abstracta? This is, in fact, something that Craig considers, and that he moves to criticize. He expounds,

> [P]erhaps the conceptualist could say that divine thoughts can play *the role* of properties. In substituting God's thoughts for properties, Plantinga has suggested that particulars stand to God's thoughts in a relation analogous to exemplification . . . Thus, all brown things fall under God's thought of *brown*. Things which are brown resemble each other in virtue of falling under the same concept.[32]

> Intriguing as this suggestion might be, it is problematic. In the first place, concepts are not plausibly construed as concrete objects, for they are shared by multiple thinkers in a way that thoughts are not. Concepts seem to be part of the content of our thoughts. As such, they are plausibly abstract objects, if they exist at all.[33]

While it is true that concepts are not plausibly construed as concrete objects, it is not obvious that this undermines theistic conceptualism, or that it expresses a theory that is that much different from the antirealism that Craig holds. Can God's thoughts be plausibly thought of as being abstract objects? As was argued above, they do seem to be able to legitimately fulfill this role. For example, Platonic objects are usually considered aspatial, atemporal, necessary, and causally impotent.

This is quite like what ideal objects are in theistic conceptualism. For God thinks what he thinks eternally if he is thought of as being outside of time, or everlastingly if considered to be in time. Further, God also necessarily thinks what he thinks, at least regarding things like color universals. In addition, as almost everyone agrees, God is aspatial, so that the

32. Craig, *God Over All*, 91.
33. Craig, *God Over All*, 92.

thoughts he has do not exist anywhere, in a sense. Finally, though God is the paradigm case of a causer, for God causes everything else to exist, his thoughts do not themselves directly cause things. God knows what brown is, for the thought of brown exists necessarily in his mind, but only imperfectly in our minds. Our thoughts are in some sense limited copies or analogs of God's thoughts.

Concepts in the mind of God are not that different from abstract entities. They are both necessary, acausal, and spaceless. But what about atemporal? The traditional view is that God is timeless, but many, perhaps most philosophers and theologians today, believe that God exists within time. There is no room to go into this debate here.[34] If God is timeless, then the ideal objects that he thinks are also timeless. If, not, they still exist everlastingly and unchanging, which is quite close to what would be the case if God were to be considered to exist timelessly. They would necessarily exist forever unchanging in the mind of God. Only some indexical propositions, those whose truth-value depends upon existence at different times, would have changes regarding their truth status. Still, a statement as an ideal object would be unchanging in the mind of God. Only God's knowledge that it is true or false would vary depending on the day. So here too, ideal objects are like abstract ones.

Many philosophers believe that paradigmatically abstract objects are acausal.[35] These ideal objects in themselves do not cause anything. The same may be considered true with God's ideal objects. Though they are in a sense the basis for *God's* acting and causing anything (for God acts upon his knowledge), the ideal objects themselves do not act as the cause of anything. It is rather God, using his knowledge of the ideal objects and the situations in which they could exist, who acts and causes things to exist in the manner that they do.

So far, abstract entities and ideal entities sound quite close to being the same, with the one possible exception of existing in time, and even there the difference is not that great. Therefore, I think that we can coherently conceive of ideals objects in almost all their properties as being the same as Platonic abstracta, save that they exist in God's mind rather than

---

34. Two books that can serve as an introductory discussion to the God-in-time debate, may be found in Padgett, *God, Eternity, Time*; and Sansbury, *Beyond Time*.

35. Exceptions are Leslie, *Value and Existence,* and Williams, *Hating Perfection.* For a discussion of causal concerns about abstracta, see Cowling, *Abstract Entities,* 130–61.

independently in a Platonic heaven. *Ideal objects are thus concrete to God but seem abstract to us.*[36]

Many concepts are of physical things, like the blue ball example. So, while the concept itself is not physical, by its very nature, it is physical. So, though the concept itself cannot become physical, a physical object can be like the concept, only not in a mind.

Therefore, in the theistic conceptualism that I have been defending, God, using Craig's example, has the color of brown as a concept, and further, in some sense "sees" brown, just as one can in one's mind's eye, though in contrast, God would "see" it perfectly. My thinking of the color of brown matches, in at least some respects, God's thinking of brown.

Why is this a problem for the theistic conceptualist? Craig writes that concepts are abstract objects, if such things exist at all, and that since God's thoughts are concrete, they cannot serve in the role as abstracta. In response, whether we think of God's thoughts as abstract objects or not, God necessarily thinks about the color brown and brownness. Since God thinks brown, it is possible for it to be thought, and other minds with the requisite abilities, such as our own, can also think of the color brown. Some creatures, including normal human beings, have the concept of brown, and given theistic conceptualism, there is no other brown other than what is being thought necessarily by God and contingently by other minds. Which is to say, there is no abstract object of "brownness" that exists apart from any one's mind, though there is the necessary, eternal, possibility that creatures with the right kinds of minds can think of or picture brown. Frankly, this does not seem to be very different from what Craig himself believes. To what part of the above description regarding the existence of abstract entities would a perfect being theistic antirealist object? There seems to be none.

Since God eternally and necessarily thinks of universals such as brownness, and numbers such as two, and other similar abstracta, and since finite minds such as our own can also think at least some of these things, then abstracta are some of the thoughts in God's mind. They are not Platonic abstract objects, in an autonomous sense, but have enough of the characteristics of abstract objects that they can serve in the same role.

The fact that an indefinite number of minds can share the same concept provides a reason why we can all know the same concepts. That God

---

36. Angus Menuge proposed this idea to me.

eternally and necessarily knows all concepts by thinking them, and that our minds are made to be finite analogs of God's mind, means that we can know at least some of them.

Craig goes on to write,

> Moreover, as mental states, thoughts are characterized by intentionality—being about things—not by things' falling under them. My thought of redness is about redness; it is not itself redness, nor do things fall under it. This problem can be generalized. God's thought of the number 2 is about 2. But then His thought is not 2, but something distinct from 2. 2 is what He is thinking about. But He is not thinking about His thought; He is thinking about 2. Therefore, His thought cannot be 2.[37]

This seems to me to be a rather odd objection. Granted, that God's thought of the number 2 is not the number 2 itself, for it can also be thought of by an indefinite number of minds. In a way, that is sort of the point, for in theistic conceptualism there is no number 2 considered as an abstract autonomous object; rather all "abstract objects" can exist in minds. There is therefore on theistic conceptualism no such thing as the number 2 as an abstract autonomous object (though of course as was written above, it may legitimately be thought of as being an object in some sense because it is an object—grammatically speaking—of thought—one may think about it), and certainly not an object existing apart from God.

However, 2 necessarily exists as a concept in God's mind because God necessarily exists and necessarily has the nature that he does. Because 2 also has an essence (e.g., the natural number between 1 and 3, being an even number, being the square root of 4, being the smallest prime number), God will eternally and necessarily know it and all its essences. This would be the case even if God had not created a world.

So again, what is the problem? At the heart of the objection that Craig makes is the idea that if one holds that God's thoughts are what abstract objects really are, then they should have all the characteristics of abstract objects considered in a Platonic or absolute creationist manner, which they do not. Under theistic conceptualism abstract objects are considered as something *other* than abstract objects considered in a Platonic manner. They are ideas in God's mind that can also be thought by other minds. Because of this, they can solve some of the problems inherent in the Platonic or absolute creationist views.

---

37. Craig, *God Over All*, 92.

Craig's next objection is this,

> Furthermore, substituting the notion of falling under a concept for exemplifying a property seems to get the explanatory order backwards. Things are not brown because they fall under God's concept *brown*, in the way that things are brown because they exemplify *brownness*; rather, they fall under God's concept *brown* because they are brown. Thus, the relation of falling under a concept cannot do the work of exemplification. If this is right, then the conceptualist who wants God's thoughts to play the role of properties still has plenty of work cut out for him, if his view is to commend itself as an attractive option for theists.[38]

The way to take this is the reason that things are brown is because God has the concept both of *brownness* and of the individual item that God has created. If God necessarily exists as conceived in perfect being theology, then he has both the concept of *brown* and the concept of *brownness*. That is, he in his own divine manner "sees" brown, analogously to us when we see it either through perception or with our mind's eye, and he understands all the properties that both brown and brownness entail. Since God is the creator and sustainer of everything else that exists, he is the one that chooses to create the brown substance in the manner that it exists. Again, in theistic conceptualism, created objects are instantiations. In addition, God does so in accordance with his perfect understanding of what brownness is, and what it is like for something to be brown. So again, why is there a problem here for theistic conceptualists? Everything can be accounted for by the conceptualist.

Craig then goes on to write,

> Finally, consider mathematical sets. Plantinga suggests that sets be taken to be God's mental collectings. But this raises a problem. If sets are really particular divine thoughts, then how do we have any access to sets? The question here is not whether I have a causal connection with sets. Rather, it is that sets, the real sets, are locked away in God's private consciousness, so that what we talk and work with are not sets at all. When I collect into a unity all the pens on my desk, that 'set' of pens is not identical, it seems, with the set constituted by God's collecting activity. Since we have two collectings and since sets are God's particular collectings, the 'set' I form is not identical to the set of all pens on

---

38. Craig, *God Over All*, 92.

my desk. But if sets are determined by membership, how could they not be identical, since they have the same members?[39]

The answer to this objection seems to me to be this: sets, like numbers and colors, are things that can be thought of by many, indeed, an indefinite number of minds. God's mind is in this sense merely one of these minds that can think of these things, though of course it is the original mind upon which every other mind is analogous and depends upon. When theistic conceptualists speak of abstract objects as really being ideal objects in God's mind, what they are saying is that God's thoughts are the original and paradigm cases of these ideas, which any other thoughts are analogs of, and that these conceptions would exist even if no other such thoughts existed at all.

So, granted this, the answer to the question as to how we can know a set is exemplified by the set of pens on Craig's desk is that ultimately, God knows about the collection of Craig's pens, and thinks of this set by collecting the thought of them into the thought of that set. Since given perfect being theism, *human beings' minds are made in the image of God's mind*, we too are able to collect the thoughts of all of the pens that are on Craig's desk into a set, and the idea that we have of this set of pens will match the thought that God has of the set of pens on Craig's desk.[40]

---

39. Craig, *God Over All*, 92–93.

40. Gregg R. Allison writes, "[T]he past century of research into ancient Near Eastern literature has shifted attention to divine image-bearing as being primarily the function of exercising dominion over the created order." Allison, *Roman Catholic Theology*, 405. This may be true, but it is also the case that the functional attributes depend upon the ontological ones. That human beings are rational, moral, (at least part of the time), etc. means that they are fitted for the role in a way that rocks, mushrooms, and cats and dogs are not. For a recent discussion see Peppiatt, *Imago Dei*.. The doctrine of the imago Dei, that human beings are created in the "image and likeness of God," is an endlessly fascinating topic. Not only is it a central doctrine to Christian life and practice but also touches, perhaps even helps to form, every other doctrine of the Christian faith in one way or another. We do not think about God, in a Christian sense, as any other than the God who creates humanity in God's image. However, many of the details of this claim and what it means for human beings are left undefined by Hebrew and Christian Scriptures and it is not even mentioned in the creeds. This space leaves room for exploration. So, the quest for what it means for human beings to be made in the image and likeness of God has never ceased to occupy theologians, clerics, and the laity alike. Peppiatt charts the developments of the doctrine through the ages, summarizing each position and perspective up to the modern day. This volume offers a compact but rich overview of the various ways in which this doctrine has been and is understood as well as pointing readers to further questions for consideration. For other discussions of the divine image in human beings see Dockery and McAfee, *Created*, and Moreland, *The Recalcitrant Imago Dei*.

In other words, because human minds are to a certain extent themselves finite copies or analogs of God's mind, we can do some of the things that God can do. Naturally, we do not have perfect analogs of God's mind. We do not know everything, we can make mistakes, and we can learn or forget things, none of which God does. However, we can understand some things like God does, though not fully.

Therefore, it does not seem that theistic conceptualism is that much different from Craig's antirealism. Both agree that abstract objects in either the Platonic sense or that of absolute creationism do not exist. Both also hold that God as thought of in perfect being theology exists and is the foundation of everything else. With Craig's theory, though God is omniscient, he does not actively entertain every thought that he can. The rest are stored somehow in his memory. The theistic conceptualist as such may disagree with this, but, as far as I can see, need not.

What limits God's creativity? Undoubtedly God cannot create what is logically impossible. Even God cannot make round squares or make it so that 2 + 2 equals 137½. Further, God cannot make any natural numbers between three and four. Necessarily, four is a natural number rather than a color or geometrical shape. God is omnipotent, but this does not mean that God can create seven prime numbers between eight and nine. For God to do so would violate the law of non-contradiction and involve us in all sorts of absurdities. This law itself is based on the nature of God in perfect being theism, and God cannot deny his own perfect nature.

Therefore, when God creates, his choices are in some sense limited by the nature of the things that he conceives. Again, even God cannot make it so that red is a number rather than a color. The reason being is that the essence, that is, the essential properties of red, are such that it is necessarily a color, rather than some other kind of being. In creating, therefore, God is limited by the essence of the things that he desires to create. This logic applies to everything. If God wants to create a cat, then he must create a being that is also a mammal. Even God cannot create a reptile cat, a bird cat, or an insect cat. Cats by their very nature are mammals and have essences. The same reasoning may be applied to virtually everything that does or could exist. Everything exists as something and therefore must share in the essence of the kind of thing that it is.

Unless one wants to deny the laws of non-contradiction and identity, the above arguments are unassailable. Therefore, for both the theistic conceptualists and the group of antirealists who are also perfect being theologians, God creates everything else that he makes based on what he knows about the nature of the entities that he chooses to create. If God wants a world with red things in it, he cannot do so by trying to make red objects colored by the number two.

Human beings are made in the image of God, and on that basis, we have the ability to know some of the things that God knows. So, what is the difference between theistic conceptualism and theistic antirealism? The difference seems to me to be quite small. The only major difference seems to be that Craig thinks that God does not always actively entertain all the thoughts that are in his mind, while he states the conceptualist does. However, this does not seem to me to be true. That is, the theistic conceptualist as such might agree that God does not always entertain every thought, while the antirealist might on the other hand think that God does actively entertain every possible thought. These thoughts, when defined in terms of perfect being theology, seem to be the fundamental basis of both theistic conceptualism and of theistic antirealism.[41]

So, for the theistic antirealist regarding abstract objects, it may be asked where God gets his ideas of what he wants to create. It is apparent that they can only come from his mind. After all, for the orthodox antirealist, God creates everything and is omniscient. The only place God would go to for ideas to create (speaking anthropomorphically) is his mind. And this is what the theistic conceptualist would also say. If it is held that God didn't get the moral principles from his mind, then where did he get them? If he just made them up then we have a version of voluntarism, where God arbitrarily chose certain principles. But this goes against God's perfect goodness. It seems that God must have principles based on his nature, and these principles must be in his mind, which is theistic conceptualism. Craig himself writes, "God has created the universe according to a certain model which He had in mind."[42] This case sounds like a version of theistic conceptualism to me. Why not generalize it?

Indeed, theistic conceptualism and antirealism don't seem that far apart. Both agree that abstract objects as such do not exist. Both agree that God has ideal objects in his mind, for where else could he get the concepts to create the universe and everything in it?

It seems that the antirealist objections to Theistic Conceptualism have the flaw that they hold that the concepts in God's mind are just like

---

41. In my book, Parrish, *Knower and the Known*, 350, I have also referred to ideal objects as irreal objects when instantiated and conceptualized.

42. van Inwagen and Craig, *Do Numbers Exist?*, 238.

abstract entities in Platonism or Absolute Creationism. However, this is false. The point of having "abstract entities" being concepts is that it makes them different from the realist view of Abstracta. The fact that they are not literally abstract entities but rather concepts is the reason they can avoid the problems with both realism and antirealism regarding abstracta. They play many of the same roles but are ontologically different.

How does all of this relate to ethical truths? Just as things like the color of red and the number four have essences, so do ethical propositions, with the provision that some realist theory of ethics is correct—that there really are moral rights and wrongs, apart from what any finite mind thinks about them.

For example, it is part of the nature of pointless cruelty that it is morally wrong. This, given realism, is a necessary truth. So, just as red is necessarily a color rather than a number, and necessarily all red colored objects are both spatially and temporally extended, it is part of the nature of pointless cruelty to be evil. Someone cannot perpetrate pointless cruelty without doing something evil. This does, however, raise an important question.

The problem is the way in which evil is part of the nature of pointless cruelty, for it does not seem to be part of the definition of pointless cruelty to be morally wrong. As has been argued above, it is *not analytically true* that to inflict pain for no reason or to enjoy inflicting pain on some person or animal is morally wrong. It is here that we must see what difference God makes. God, by being the perfect being, is perfectly good. Although God does not have the same set of ethical duties that we have (he cannot steal because everything belongs to him), he affirms the ethical. It is this affirmation, consistent with God's nature, which is the *synthetic necessity* that gives the normativity to ethical propositions by necessarily affirming those that accord to his nature.[43]

---

43. The theory that *concepts* are what really exist, rather than abstract entities, may have bearing on other issues. For example, Actualism and Possibilism. *Actualism* is the theory that only actual things exist, while *Possibilism* holds that possible things also exist. Walter J. Schultz writes that given Possibilism, such statements as, "If it is possible for there to be a Loch Ness monster, then there is something that can be a Loch Ness monster" are true. Conceptualism holds that although "exists" may mean the same thing whenever used, what kinds of things that exist are quite different. There is the existence of extramental things, like my adorable dog Toffee, and there is the existence of the concept of Toffee. And of course, many concepts can be instantiated. So, what a conceptualist might say instead of the statement about the Loch Ness Monster and similar declarations, is something like, "If it is possible that the Loch Ness monster exists, there are concepts of the Loch Ness monster (in God's mind) that can be instantiated."

CHAPTER 11

Perfect Being Theism

IN THE LAST COUPLE of chapters, God was described as a perfect being. Is Perfect Being Theism any better in accounting for the existence of necessary ethical truths than naturalism and Platonism are? The short answer is yes. For the following discussion, the truth of theism will be assumed for the sake of argument, and we shall see how it can act as a basis for the existence of necessary ethical propositions. Initially, there are a couple of important points that will be discussed. The first is how it is possible for *ideal objects* to exist in the mind of God as the equivalent of abstract objects. The second is how the nature of God is such that necessarily ethics would flow from it. As was argued in the last chapter, God knows all propositions and affirms the truth of certain ethical ones, based on his nature. The God of perfect being theology can be the *secure foundation for a realist ethics*, in contrast to the other theories that have already been examined. After addressing the aforementioned important points, theological voluntarism will be critically examined.

GOD

To show that God is the firm foundation for ethics, the concept of God must first be examined. Although there have been innumerable concepts of God, the main one that has been accepted philosophically and theologically in Western civilization for the last couple of thousand years has

---

Schultz, "An Augustinian-Edwardsian," 194. Schultz uses different terminology, but this does not disagree with what he wrote. Concepts exist, but as concepts only until instantiated. Of course, this would take a lot more work to fully explicate.

been the classical concept of God.[1] However, even within this concept, there are variations. The view of God that I think is truest and best is *perfect being theology*. There is not a consensus on a thorough description of what a perfect being God would be like, but the main attributes are widely accepted. For example, there are differences of opinion as to if God is simple and whether or not God is in time.

So, the concept of God that will be employed here is that of perfect being theism—God conceived of as being the perfect or greatest conceivable or possible being. This view avoids some of the problems in the theories previously discussed. God's mind on this account is infinite, and indeed, in the account of perfect being theology, God is omniscient and therefore knows everything—including all putatively abstract entities. Further, God is, in perfect being theism, a necessary being who exists in all possible worlds.[2] God's necessity is not a brute fact, as we have seen Erik Wielenberg and many others claim. *Rather his necessity is analytically contained in the concept of God as the Greatest Possible Being. From this, it follows that he is omniscient, omnipotent, omnibenevolent, etc., in all possible worlds.*

God is Perfect

God conceived in perfect being theology is basically an Anselmian view of God, wherein God is considered to be that being which is greater than anything which could possibly be imagined, or, put simply, the Greatest Possible Being (GPB).[3] This is *maximal greatness* not just in the actual world, but also *in all worlds*, for God is understood to be a *necessary being*, existing in all possible worlds. Also, not only is God in perfect being theology considered a logically or absolutely necessary being, but he is also the *only* necessary, concrete being. Further, God is omnipotent, omniscient, and omnibenevolent in all worlds. In effect then, God is a perfect being, and necessarily so, who is perfect essentially, and could not be different than he is. Again, necessary existence is contained in the very

---

1. Rival views are the different varieties of Panentheism. See Cooper, *Panentheism*.
2. For a discussion of God's necessity and how it relates to the other necessary objects, see Davis, *Metaphysics of Theism*.
3. See Morris, *Anselmian Explorations*.

concept of God as the Greatest Possible Being.[4] God is a perfect being, and therefore is intrinsically, essentially, and infinitely good.

God is Personal

To be a perfect being, God must not only necessarily exist but also be a personal being. The reasons should be obvious. If God is omniscient, then he must know all things, including the truth about all propositions. Only a personal being can know propositions. An inanimate object cannot process concepts, nor can a living but non-sentient being such as an insect. Only persons can have language ability, and therefore the ability to understand propositions, as such. This is especially true regarding propositions of abstract ethical truths.

God is the basis for ethical truths

Therefore, conceived as a perfect being, God is both necessarily existing, and necessarily personal. With these attributes, he can serve as the basis for ethical truths. How should we then think about God as the basis for ethics? Even granting God's necessary existence and necessary personhood, how is it possible for God to serve as a basis for meta-ethics? Indeed, what else would be necessary for something to serve as a basis for meta-ethics, if there is anything else so necessary? This will take some sorting out to come to an answer.

One could say that ethical truths are truths that God affirms. For example, take proposition *T*, that it is wrong to torture innocent people, or anything for that matter, for fun. One can say that this ethical proposition is true because God affirms it and affirms it in all possible worlds. Since God exists in all possible worlds, and is a person in all possible worlds, this seems to be a plausible way for ethical propositions to be true, and necessarily true.

However, this is not the end of the story. For God must be both necessarily existing and necessarily person related for his affirmations to make ethical truths ethically true. God also must be good. This merely pushes the problem back a step. How and why do we think that God is good, and presumably necessarily good?

---

4. See Parrish, *God and Necessity*.

God is Good

To answer how and why God is good, we should look further at what ethical truths are. One way of looking at them is that they are part of what may be called goodness. That is, *to be ethical is to be good in some sense.* There are obviously different senses in which things are good, some of which have nothing to do with ethics. However, when looking at this on a fundamental level, it can be said that ethics is a form of goodness, and that to be ethical is to be good in a certain manner. Ethics is a necessary part of good and ethical people; people who are ethical are themselves necessarily good, when they follow true ethical principles.

The "good" here is not in the sense of utility, as in the manner that a computer is good for writing things.[5] Rather, it is in the sense of moral good. Other kinds of goodness include beauty. It seems obvious that true beauty is good, though a different kind of good than ethics. Indeed, in a sense, the goodness in beauty is more difficult to understand than ethical goodness. An ethical axiom, such as people ought to be treated with respect, is good in a clearer sense than the beauty of a mountain is good. Nonetheless, both beauty and ethical principles and behavior are aspects of goodness.

Therefore, ethical propositions are explicable, at least to a certain extent, by their participation in the concept of goodness. Ethical propositions looked at from this perspective are expressions of goodness. However, what may be considered goodness in itself? If ethical propositions are certain statements of goodness, what else may goodness be, in its essence? This question must be answered.

What is the essence of the good? A common way of answering this question is to say that the good is that which is sought for its own sake. As far as *ethical* good goes, the good is that which we *ought* to seek for its own sake. However, giving this definition of the good does not give us content: it does not tell us specifically what goodness is in itself.

So, what is *good* in actual content? This is not an easy question to answer, as we are dealing with primitive terms, terms that cannot be defined in words of something more basic. However, I would like to propose that ethical goodness is at least partially explicable in the concept of love, though it may not be entirely definable in this term. What this means will take a considerable discussion to make clear.

---

5. They are also good for causing high levels of stress when they don't work the way that you want them to.

Although love is today often thought to be an emotion, its primary meaning is wrapped up with that of will—to truly love someone is to *will* them good, whatever is good for them. It goes without saying that love can be for bad things. This is why love just in itself, without any qualification or context, is not automatically a good thing. People often love things that are bad or evil. In some extreme cases, people even love evil things because they are evil.[6] Therefore, a particular love is not automatically a good thing.

It should be noted that love is not the only concept with which we have this problem. If we define goodness in terms of something else than itself, we have the problem that just about anything else can be bad in some circumstances or at least used for bad things. Good health is a good thing but can be used by evil people to do bad things. The same can be said of anything that we can hold to be a good. In certain circumstances, good can be used for evil, and evil people in possession of good things are not themselves therefore made good.

We have here the problem that was noted by G. E. Moore.[7] He wrote that goodness is a simple, undefinable term. If goodness is this simple and undefinable, then it cannot ultimately be understood; for to be understood is to be explicable in terms of some other, more basic concepts. Yet, this seems difficult to believe, because goodness, in all of its varieties, is inextricably mixed in with all the other aspects of reality.

In an earlier chapter, we saw how there are different aspects of reality which cannot be completely defined or understood in terms of each other, yet they are all part of one reality, that are necessary parts of one another. A human being, for example, not only has the aspects that pertain to physical objects, but also necessarily has ones that pertain to mathematics, ethics, beauty, sociality, and so on. To just leave this as a group of separate concepts that are inexplicable ignores the problem of their necessary inter-relations—that they are necessary parts of one universe. There must be some fundamental principle that explains the different aspects of their natures and their inter-relations with each other.

We seem therefore to have a conundrum. If we define goodness in terms of love, we have the problem that not all loves are good. On the other hand, if we define goodness in terms of anything else, goodness

---

6. For a minor example of this, there is the story of Augustine and the pears. As a boy, he, and the gang he was with stole the pears simply because they knew it was wrong to do so. For an examination of this, see Melchert, *The Great Conversation*, 262.

7. Moore, *Principia*.

seems an empty concept that cannot be rationally located as an integral part of reality, human or otherwise. It is obvious that we cannot define, for example, love in terms of goodness, and goodness in terms of love.

It might be noted that the same problem arises whenever one attempts to define goodness in any other one term. To reduce goodness to any other concept must necessarily eviscerate the concept of good. To do so will merely make goodness into something else, which leaves out the essential concepts involved in goodness. Any such attempt at reduction will necessarily be a reduction that has a remainder of the goodness that leaves essential aspects of goodness out of the equation.

When one reduces some concept X to some other concept Y, unless the whole of X is analytically included in Y, then necessarily some aspect or aspects of X is left out. The reason is obvious. Unless all of X is included in Y as part of Y's nature, and X is in some sense reduced to Y, then those aspects of X that are not also aspects of Y will be left out.

What this means, besides other things, is that any attempt to reduce goodness or *the good* to some other concepts that themselves do not include goodness as part of their nature will necessarily leave out aspects of goodness, including, most likely, the essential nature of goodness itself. Therefore, *to reduce goodness without remainder one must reduce it to something that includes goodness analytically as part of its nature*, and, if this further concept is not identical with goodness, it must be broader than the concept of goodness.

Besides the concept of the reductive, there is also *necessary co-extension*. By this what is meant is that there are two concepts such that either they always necessarily exist together, or one cannot exist without the other, and one cannot be successfully reduced to another without remainder.

An example of this is a triangle. The concept of being a triangle necessarily includes the idea of being a geometrical figure having three angles, and three sides. The concept of having three sides is not identical, cannot be reduced to having three angles, though for a geometrical figure in Euclidean space composed only of straight lines, these two concepts will be necessarily co-extensive. There cannot be one without the other. Further, both tri-angularity and tri-sidedness are both analytically included in the concept of being a triangle.

Therefore, to reiterate, to successfully reduce goodness to some other concept entails that goodness must be included as part of that further concept or entity. The concept is analytically contained in the other. My response to all this is that Perfect Being Theism can bring this all together and give the answer to the most fundamental explanation of "good."[8] On PBT, God is the ultimate being, exists necessarily, and necessarily has the same nature in all worlds. In him, all good things have their origin. Though God has more attributes than just goodness, everything about him is good.

God is Omniscient

Are God's thoughts a part of God? My answer to this question is yes. God exists necessarily and knows everything necessarily. Thinking of the number seven for example, is part of God's nature. God would not be God without thinking of seven, and since God exists necessarily it is an aspect of his nature to think of the number seven. Thinking of the number is therefore an aspect of what God is. The definition of what God is involves that he thinks of the concept of seven and knows all of its properties and relations.

However, there is another element to this. Human beings can also think of concepts like the number seven, and countless other ones. The number seven is not an aspect of God in the sense that being omnipotent is an aspect of God. Other beings can think of seven, but only God can be omnipotent. The reason for this is that concepts are things that by their nature can be entertained by any number of thinking entities. There is therefore no problem with having both God and human beings thinking the same thought. Both God and humans, by their natures, can have concepts of certain kinds.

There is another question here. If what we think of as abstract entities are really concepts, and if no one is thinking of a particular concept, and it is not instantiated physically in something, does it really exist? If it doesn't exist, then how can it be thought of or instantiated? Travis Dumsday writes, "[W]hat exactly is the ontological status of the uninstantiated universals that actual dispositions necessarily (as part of their very identity conditions) reference? . . . *Prima facie* the moderate realist will resist attributing any reality to any uninstantiated universal."[9] And yet, it seems that they do have a kind of existence, "thin" though it might be, for they can be instantiated. A Platonist does not have this problem, nor does the

---

8. See my book Parrish, *God and Necessity*.
9. For more on Dispositionalism, see Dumsday, *Dispositionalism*, 733.

theistic conceptualist. In either theory, abstract entities do always exist, and do not have to be brought into existence out of nothing every time that they are thought of.

There is a problem for Platonism as to how Platonic objects become instantiated in the physical world, since the paradigm ones are thought to be acausal. The theist does not have this problem as God is a concrete being with ideas in his mind who can instantiate them. Another problem for Platonism is that some abstracta, such as phenomenal colors, seem only to be able to exist in minds, as was argued above. Thus, for example, orangeness can eternally exist in God's mind, though exactly how God knows or perceives things is a matter that we do not understand very well.

It seems clear that God can perceive orange and other colors eternally in his mind in some manner. So, phenomenal orangeness and greenness, and the other visual phenomenal aspects of reality can be thought of as existing in the mind of God. The same is true of the other phenomenal aspects of reality, such as sound, and touch and taste, and so forth, along with feelings and emotions. Does God eternally listen to Beethoven's ninth symphony?[10] It would seem so, though again how this happens is unanswerable to us. If so, how and in what manner? Again, answering these questions takes us beyond the limits of what we can say with certainty.

Other things that are not intrinsically phenomenal in the sense that has been used, such as geometrical shapes, seem to be easily understood as existing in God's mind. We can readily conceive of God as eternally and necessarily thinking, having a picture in his mind's eye, so to speak, of straight lines, triangles, circles, etc. In like manner, one can see a triangle either by looking at one, or else by having a mental image of one.[11] These and much else can be understood to exist in the mind of God without difficulty. There would seem to be an infinite number of things that are in God's mind's eye, though in which manner God truly perceives them is a mystery to us.

So, given that God has propositions in his mind and that he has phenomenal properties, is it plausible to think that other things can exist in God's mind? Yes, at least in the sense of God's knowing about them exhaustively. For example, take relations. There is a certain relation of

10. If so, does that mean that God must be in time? I do not think so, but this is an interesting question.

11. People with aphantasia cannot form mental images, or "pictures in their minds."

distance at this moment between my cat and me. The relation obviously cannot exist in God's mind, though he understands it, as my cat and I do not exist as mere thoughts in God's mind. It seems clear that the relationship itself cannot *be* in God's mind. However, God has knowledge of the distance between my cat and me at any specific time. Therefore, even though the relationship itself is external to God, it is nonetheless knowable by God. Perhaps, God also has a mental image of my cat and me but having at least propositional knowledge of the relationship would itself be enough for God to know the relation and hence the ideal object that it represents.

Other proposed abstracta are numbers and other mathematical entities. These, too, can be conceived of as being eternally existent in the mind of God. God, in perfect being theism, is, after all, considered to be infinite. This would include ethical propositions, as God's being perfect would also affirm all good truths and deny all bad ones.

Other concerns

Thus, the various ethical propositions are part of a web or system of such propositions, which may be dependent upon one or a few basic propositions, resembling *foundationalism* in epistemology. Another aspect is, as was mentioned in the earlier discussion of S and T, that some ethical propositions seem to be necessarily true in all circumstances, while others seem to be generally true but have exceptions. This factor also needs accounting, in any final theory of meta-ethics.

My general response is that some things are simply more important than others and thought so by God. People and other living creatures are intrinsically valuable, and to mistreat them for any response save to prevent a worse evil from happening is intrinsically wrong. Torturing sentient beings for fun thus is never right, while stealing to prevent innocent people from dying or greatly suffering may be the lesser of evils. There is therefore a hierarchy of goods, and sadly, in some situations, lesser goods need to be sacrificed to prevent a greater evil. The point is that persons are the ultimate good because God's essence is that of being personal. Animals are not as important but still should not be mistreated because they share some of the characteristics of persons, such as having feelings.

THEOLOGICAL VOLUNTARISM[12]

Theological Voluntarism is the idea that God is not constrained by the moral laws that he can decree. It should be noted that there is an ambiguity here. Theological voluntarism can have two basically different conceptions of the divine will. On the more moderate conception, God could will anything to be an ethical truth that he wanted, like mandating pointless cruelty, simply because there is nothing outside of him that could oppose him from doing so. However, God would not want to do so because things like pointless cruelty go against his intrinsic nature, which is essentially good. That is, God has the power to command anything, including pointless cruelty, but would never do so because this would go against his very nature. It might be said that this form of theological voluntarism is simply a version of *divine command* (or what I call divine nature) *morality*. Therefore, when I speak of theological voluntarism, it will mostly be in the more radical form as described below.

In divine command theory, God can make some ethical rules contingently. Though God could never command that T be right, he can make other rules unnecessarily. An example is that God could just as easily command that there be an eight-day week instead of a seven-day week. God's commands should be obeyed even though he could have legitimately made different ones.

On the more radical version, God is considered pure will. Goodness merely consists in obeying God, and the reason that we do that is not because God is pure goodness and we love the good; rather it is because God has absolute power over us, and we want to stay on God's good side, so to speak. This version was, according to some, held by some Christian thinkers like William Ockham in the Middle Ages,[13] and seems to be held by some Muslims today.[14]

---

12. For a brief exposition of and criticism of theological voluntarism, see Frankena, *Ethics*, 27–29.

13. For a discussion of theological voluntarism in the Middle Ages, see Adamson, *Medieval Philosophy*. However, "There's a wrinkle here: . . . Strictly speaking, God can't make murder right because 'murder is wrong' is true by definition and God doesn't contradict Himself. But He could make any sort of killing morally permissible, or even obligatory, by commanding it." Lutz and Case, *Is Morality Real?*, 56.

14. According to Reilly, in Islam God is unknowable. As he writes, "If God is pure will, then He is incomprehensible. There are two reasons for this. One is the doctrine of *tanzih*, which refers to God's absolute transcendence and utter incomparability. There is no correspondence at all between God and His creation . . . Comparison between God and man cannot be made because man is not made in His image or likeness . . .

It may be difficult to tell the difference between the two. For example, Gordon H. Clark wrote, "God . . . cannot be responsible [for evil] for the plain reason that there is no power superior to him; no greater being can hold him accountable; no one can punish him; there is no one to whom God is responsible; there are no laws which he could disobey."[15] This section could be interpreted in either way. It also seems to me that sometimes non-theists confuse the Divine Command Theory with Voluntarism in its more extreme version.[16]

There are few that hold to theological voluntarism in the west in its extreme forms. However, it is a possible position to hold, and, it is widespread in Islam, so it will thus be examined. This version of theistic ethics is, in fact, a form of antirealism, because ethical principles are merely God's decisions. In this case, we only obey God not because he is good and "ethical," but because he is the most powerful being in existence, and further, because he is ultimate reality. There exists nothing more fundamental than God and therefore there is no standard superior to, or more basic than, God's will.

Voluntarism is thus the philosophy that *will* is the ultimate nature of reality. When it comes to ethics, Voluntarism is the view that *God's will is the ultimate deciding factor*, as opposed to his purpose for ethical truths. Writes Mark Murphy on this matter, "To be a theological voluntarist with respect to some moral status is to hold that entities have that status in virtue of certain acts of divine will. But some instances of this view are metaethical theses; some instances of it are normative theses."[17]

Consider, for example, theological voluntarism of the more radical kind as being about the status of acts as obligatory or non-obligatory. One might hold that there is a single supreme obligation, the obligation to obey God. Every act that one might perform thus has its moral status as obligatory or non-obligatory in virtue of God's having commanded (or not) the performance of acts of that type. This is a common version of divine command theory, according to which are found all the obligations

---

The other reason follows as a simple conclusion from the incomprehensibility of the world as the direct and instantaneous product of the will of God. If the world cannot be understood by reason, how possibly could its Creator? What would be the point of access? God is incomprehensible *in himself* because pure will has no reason." Reilly, *Closing of the Muslim Mind*, 54.

15. Clark, *Religion, Reason*, 240–42.
16. As is done in the book Lutz and Case, *Is Morality Real?*, 54.
17. Murphy, "Theological Voluntarism," 1–2.

(even the mundane workaday dictums) that we are under. We are not to steal from each other, not to murder each other, and are to help each other out when it would not be overly inconvenient, etc. These obligations bind us because of the exercise of God's supreme authority over all the things that he created.

The view just described is a version of *normative* theological voluntarism. It is a normative view because it asserts that some normative state of affairs ("a must") obtains—namely, the normative state of affairs of *its being obligatory to obey God*. In addition, it is a version of theological voluntarism because it holds that all other normative states of affairs, at least those involving obligation, obtain in virtue of *God's commanding* activity.

Metaethical theological voluntarist views, by contrast, do not assert the obtaining of any normative situation. It is possible for one to be a metaethical theological voluntarist and to hold that no normative states of affairs obtain. Rather, metaethical theological voluntarists aim to say something interesting and informative about moral concepts, properties, or states of affairs; and they want to say something interesting and informative about them by connecting them to acts of the divine will. Metaethical theological voluntarists might claim that obligation is a theological concept, that the property of being obligatory is a theological property, or that obligations are caused immediately by divine will. In a real sense, moral obligation is thus reducible to God's will.[18]

In this book, the primary interest in theological voluntarism is in its metaethical views. Of course, metaethical views can, and in fact usually do, have normative implications. However, what is important here is *the basis for something being ethically right or wrong*. What is right or wrong is a different matter.

The question is, given voluntarism, how are ethical truths made to be ethical? "By God's will," is the reply that theological voluntarism gives. Why does this make these truths ethical? What property of God makes them so?

For any purportedly ethical truth, on the theological voluntaristic conception of God, it can only be because God wills it. Why does God will it? God's willing must be essentially arbitrary given radical voluntarism, so it cannot be based on any part of God's nature, other than his sheer will. This opens up this position to at least two objections.

---

18. Gordon Clark, *Religion, Reason*, 242.

Objections to Theistic Voluntarism

God's will considered to be arbitrary

First, since what God wills on this account is arbitrary, it is hard to see how just God's will could make it ethical. It is here where the Euthyphro objection to theistic ethics comes down hard. The Euthyphro objection puts forth a dilemma with two horns, so to speak, neither of which can be consistently held by a theistic ethic. As David Baggett and Jerry Walls write,

> [T]he first horn of the Dilemma suggests that God's commands determine the nature of goodness, and God's prohibitions determine what is bad. If God commands something, then it's good, in virtue of his commanding it (and his prohibitions determine what's bad in virtue of the prohibitions). To affirm this reply is to embrace "voluntarism" or the "pure will" theory of the good—a divine command theory of the good. The second horn of the Dilemma suggests that God's commands are what they are in virtue of God's choosing to command what is already good—this is a "nonvoluntarist" or "guided will" theory of the good. By "goodness" here we mean, unless otherwise indicated, *moral* goodness, which is one among other kinds of goodness, though a vitally important one and the focus of our current investigation.[19]

An answer to the second horn of the Dilemma has already been given in the section on Platonism—that morality is independent of God. On the first horn of the Dilemma, given radical voluntarism, God might just as easily have commanded cruelty rather than kindness, deceit as opposed to honesty, or theft instead of respect for other people's property.

This seems obviously wrong. There is a sense in which God, being the ultimate being, "could" have commanded cruelty. However, this is in the same sense that he could have willed that two plus two equal five. He could command this, for there is nothing to gainsay him. In another and more fundamental sense, though, he could not, for he would be contradicting his very nature. This presupposes that God does have a necessary nature, which is argued at length in chapter 12.

---

19. In their book, Baggett and Walls give an extensive refutation of the Euthyphro objection. Baggett and Walls, *Good God*, 33.

The willing does not necessitate the ethical

Second, just the fact that God wills something may mean that it ought to be done, but this by itself does not make the command ethical. Ethics, as already described, is composed of necessary truths. *On voluntarism, there are no necessary ethical truths*, as God could have made the opposite of any moral truth to be defined as ethical. In voluntarism, it seems that ethical truth is arbitrary, which cuts itself off from being necessary.

The only way it makes sense that God's will implies doing right is the following. Since God is omnipotent, whatever he wants done will be done. Since he has the power to determine everyone's fate, it behooves people to be on God's good side. This is the only way in which God's commands, just by being God's commands apart from any property apart from omnipotence of God, could be considered the "right" thing to do. However, ethics has fundamentally nothing to do with it.

An interesting question

It may be enlightening to consider a related question, though one that I have never seen considered anywhere else. Could there be voluntaristic aesthetics? That is, could something be considered beautiful just because God wills it to be so, say a big pile of rotting garbage? This is to deny that God could make beings who would think that whatever he declared to be beautiful was in fact so. God could make creatures, it seems, that would be so constituted as to consider things beautiful which we perceive are ugly, and vice versa, think that things are ugly which we enjoy as beautiful.

What is being asked here is if God could just command those certain things to be beautiful or ugly, and that they would then be so. It seems to me that no, even God could not make things beautiful just by ordering it. God is omnipotent, but even God cannot make necessary truths false.

To give an analogy, can God make it so that $2 + 2 = 137\frac{1}{2}$? It seems not, for to do so is to violate the law of non-contradiction. For God to violate the law of non-contradiction is to deny and contradict himself. Thinking of God as the Greatest Possible Being he must be purely rational. To deny the law of non-contradiction is to be irrational, which is a denial of God's very being. Therefore, God cannot make the basic laws of mathematics to be other than they are.

Similarly, it seems that God cannot just decree that a pile of garbage be beautiful, even though any sane human being thinks it is disgustingly ugly. Even God cannot do what is intrinsically impossible, for to do so ultimately means that he must deny his very nature, which is irrational in and of itself. He might make it so that some human beings think that a pile of garbage is beautiful, but then it seems that he could make some human beings think that two plus two equal five. However, he could only do so by making human beings flawed or broken in some respect. Therefore, though God can create any beautiful thing, he cannot create something ugly and then make it beautiful just by saying that it is so.

Similarly, it seems that God cannot make cruelty and deceitfulness good just by decreeing that they are so. In some sense it might be admitted that he could. God is the ultimate authority and makes whatever rules that he wants. In some sense, one might say, God could command all sorts of horrible laws, and then we and other creatures would be obligated to obey them. But this is not the correct way to think of God and goodness.

A better way

In contrast to voluntarism, the concept of God that is described and defended here is that of perfect being theology. In it, God is not just sheer will and omnipotence. There are no possible worlds where God commands that cruelty and deceitfulness are good in themselves. The final reason for this is that God cannot violate his essential nature. If God is essentially good, then he would never decree that cruelty is good, because being good, by his very nature he hates cruelty.

This is my answer to voluntarism, and to the Euthyphro objection to a divine command ethics. Ethical laws are indeed given to us and any other rational creatures by divine command, but the divine commands are not just based on God's will, but on his nature, which is constant throughout all possible worlds. God is essentially good, which means that he is essentially loving.

BACK TO GOD

God is Love

The question then becomes, "How can God be essentially loving?" This may seem to be an odd question. If God is perfectly good, then he must also be loving, for good persons love, and they love the right things. Indeed, it is difficult to imagine a personal being of any sort not loving some things.

However, the concept of God as a loving being seems prima facie to conflict with the concept of God as a being who is free. What is meant by this is that, with the standard conception of God, he was under no compulsion to create anything else besides himself. There was no necessity in his creating. However, if God exists without any necessary relation to anything besides himself, how can he be essentially loving?

One could argue that he might love himself. This may be true in a sense, but loving oneself is intrinsically different from loving another. It seems that self-love is quite different in both degree and in genre from other kinds of love. Besides, if all that God loved was himself, it would seem difficult to understand why God would create other things.

Unitarian and Trinitarian concepts of God

The difference here may be explained by comparing the Unitarian and Trinitarian concepts of God. In Unitarian systems, as in Islam, God is thought to be one being, and one person—though what kind of person God would be like is an interesting question. Indeed, in Islamic theology it might be asked if God can even be a personal being.[20] The point to be made here is that in Unitarian conceptions of God, God is intrinsically non-relational. Nothing exists by its nature except God. To have relations, God must create something. So, relations are not included in God as part of his nature. God is considered absolutely simple and alone. Thus, the theory of an essentially loving God becomes problematic. This will be examined in more detail in the next chapter.

This unitarian point of view is congruent with Muslims' belief in the absolute oneness of God. For them, Allah is absolutely alone and unique, and, therefore, unlike anything else that exists or could exist. Allah is held to be unknowable in himself. Human standards of rationality do not

---

20. Reilly, *Closing of the Muslim Mind*, 59–90.

apply to him. Most of what we supposedly know about Allah in standard Islamic thought is, 1) that he is omnipotent, and 2) what his will is for us.

The notion that Allah is unknowable seems to entail the notion that Allah is not a person. This by itself is difficult to understand, for since Allah allegedly inspired the Qur'an and makes laws human beings are supposed to follow, then in some sense the Muslim God must be a personal being. However, the notion that Allah is ultimately impersonal seems to be one that comes naturally to Islam, as Stanley Jaki has argued.[21]

In contradistinction, the Christian view of God is that of a personal being. Cornelius Van Til writes, "When we say that when we believe in a personal God, we do not merely mean that we believe in a God to whom the adjective 'personality' may be attached. God is not an essence that has personality; He is absolute personality."[22] It seems that being relational is part of the essence of being personal. If this is the case, then unitarian views of God have a problem explaining the existence of a personal God, while trinitarian views do not. The concept that God is personal is very important, for more than one reason. Herman Bavinck writes, "In point of fact, goodness, justice, wisdom, etc. have no existence in this world but as personal attributes . . . [N]ot only theology of all the ages but also philosophy in a good number of its interpreters has postulated the existence of a personal God."[23]

Further, though this is outside of the argument given in this book, this impersonalist view of God, Jaki also argues, caused a stillbirth of science in Islam.[24] It was the concept of the Trinity in Christianity, with three persons in one God, that prevented Christianity from having the same stillbirth of science.[25] If God is three persons, he cannot be impersonal. The laws of nature are contingent; they could have been different. Yet they seem to be consistent throughout space and time. And they are rational in the sense that these laws make for an understandable universe. It takes a personal being to choose the contingent yet consistent and rational. Therefore, a creating God cannot be impersonal. The same tendency toward impersonalism has also been noted in some Jewish theologies.

21. Jaki, *Science & Creation*, 192–218.
22. Van Til, *Systematic Theology*, 229–30.
23. Bavinck and Eglinton, *Philosophy of Revelation*, 110.
24. Jaki, *Science & Creation*, 192–218.
25. Jaki, *Savior of Science*.

Additional thoughts

There are two more points to be addressed here. First, William Lane Craig is a theistic antirealist. Does this make him a voluntarist of a radical nature? No, it appears not. It seems that Craig thinks that God is essentially good and loving, and therefore commands kindness instead of pointless cruelty. But, given antirealism, can Craig say that? It is uncertain that he can. On his view, where does God get his values if they are not conceptions in God's eternal mind?

This brings up the second question. Where then does God get the values that he commands? It would again seem to be by his very nature. Does this make Craig a theistic conceptualist of a sort? It seems to me that it does.

The other point is to briefly show that in several respects God is a better foundation for morality than are the Platonic abstract entities. For example:

(11.1) It is easier to see how people can *feel guilty* by disobeying God than by disobeying a Platonic abstract entity.

(11.2) It is easier to see how one can *repent* of one's wrong doings by asking forgiveness from God rather than from a Platonic abstract entity.

(11.3) It is easier to see how one can *receive forgiveness* from God than from a Platonic abstract entity.

(11.4) It is easier to see how God can *communicate ethical truths* to us than Platonic entities could. God can create us with minds with the ability to understand ethics, he can give us a conscience that helps us know them, and he can give us revelations as to what is morally right. Platonic entities can do none of these things. Atheists who are Platonic robust realists can only hope that evolution has somehow given us the ability to discern moral right from wrong and that any ethical knowledge gained will not dissolve in entropy.

The list could be extended, but these four examples illustrate the point.

In conclusion here, perfect being theism, which holds to the concept of a necessarily existing, morally perfect God, is a theory that gives an answer to why some propositions are ethical, and some are not. A perfect God can serve as the basis for all kinds of good, including the ethical. In fact, given the discussion above, it is difficult to see how any other kind of thing could be the foundation for ethics.

CHAPTER 12

The Trinity

THE LAST CHAPTER ARGUED that there is a concept of God wherein God could be the foundation of ethics. However, it was also noted that Unitarian conceptions of God have a problem here. At this point, the Christian doctrine of the Trinity becomes relevant. Thus, this chapter is about the concept of the Trinity, and how this doctrine relates to the goodness of God.[1] It also explores a different notion of God, that of absolute oneness.

THE CONCEPT OF THE TRINITY

Writing and thinking about the doctrine of the Trinity is rather difficult, and I undertake it with some trepidation. The concept of the Trinity is, in a sense, trying to understand the inner life of God, and this is the most difficult task of all. One might truly think that fools rush in where angels fear to tread. But sometimes even fools must try to do something. There are several reasons why this is such a difficult task.

One is simply that God is not only the greatest being who exists, but also the greatest being who possibly could exist. God is unique in important respects, and this makes it more difficult to grasp conceptually what God must be like.

---

1. Johnson, "Trinitarian Metaethical Theory vs Wielenberg." See also Bowne, *Principles of Ethics*, 200–204.

Knowing God

Another problem is that there is the notion of *divine ineffability*. Taken literally, whatever is called ineffable is completely inexpressible, in this case God. In this view, we cannot talk about God because we cannot really know anything about him. There are several problems with this. First, it is self-referentially incoherent; the whole notion contradicts itself. For it is saying of something that nothing can be said of that thing, in this case God. In other words, it is saying of God that we can't say anything about God.

Besides the fact that this is contradictory, it means that the concept of God is unknowable and hence useless.[2] Of what possible good or benefit is something about which we know nothing? Frankly none. Theologians who call God ineffable sometimes go on to say a great deal about God. The concept of complete ineffability should be discarded, and replaced with another term, that of incomprehensibility. What should be meant by this is *not* that God is totally incomprehensible, but that we will never understand God fully.[3] A complete knowledge of God is forever beyond the grasp of all finite beings—everyone other than God. However, this does not mean that we cannot know *anything* about God. We can and do know things about God; otherwise, theology would not only be in vain but could not even exist.

Univocal vs analogical knowledge of God

Sometimes what is meant by ineffability is that we can have no *univocal* knowledge of God. All our knowledge about God is *analogical*, many have said. What we mean by this is that we cannot use words when speaking of God in the same way that we do when speaking of other things. When one says a human being is good and that God is good, one

---

2. Bowne quotes Frederic Harrison on the doctrine of unknowability and religion. "To make a religion out of the Unknowable . . . is far more extravagant than to make it out of the Equator, for we know something of the Equator. It means much for sailors, geographers, astronomers, and has great significance for tropical life; but respecting the Unknowable our minds are a blank. We can only stare in empty wonder." Bowne, *Kant and Spencer*, 263–64.

3. Put just like this, the conclusion is less than awesome. For it is also the case that, for example, my diminuitive cat Squirt is also incomprehensible in that I will never know everything about her. Therefore, what must be emphasized is that God's incomprehensibility is infinitely more profound than my cat's.

does not mean that they are good in exactly the same way, for God is a very different being than we are. In contrast, univocal knowledge means that the words mean the same. In this sense, Alice's goodness can be the same as Beth's goodness, because they are both human.

There is no problem with analogical knowledge as such. The Bible often uses it to describe God. However, it seems to me that we cannot use only analogical knowledge of God; there must be more—a core of univocal knowledge. Otherwise, we have no way to understand how the analogical terms are used, having no frame of reference. Thence we would have no real knowledge of God. To give an example that I have used before, a good cat is different from a good human being, because cats are different from human beings. Nevertheless, we do understand what a good cat is like, because we have some univocal knowledge of cats. We understand that cats are little furry animals, and their being good is in being affectionate and not causing problems.

Therefore, our knowledge, including our analogical knowledge, must have a univocal core, if we are to understand how it is used. For example, one knows that $2 + 2 = 4$, and that Cleveland is in Ohio. God also knows that $2 + 2 = 4$, and that Cleveland is in Ohio. God knows how many people there are on a 43-man Squamish team.[4] There are, of course, important differences in God's knowledge of these things and ours. God knows them from eternity, while we learn them. God is never mistaken, while we can be. God understands all the implications of this knowledge, while we do not. However, the simple knowledge of the facts is the same. Hence, we can know some things about God.

There is another problem for the theory that all of our knowledge of God is analogical. By definition, a perfect God is omniscient. God knows everything that can be known. If all our knowledge is only an analog of God's, then our knowledge does not match his at any spot, and since God knows everything, we then know nothing—which is impossible, or we wouldn't be here having this discussion in an obscure philosophical treatise.

As Gordon H. Clark writes,

> "If God has the truth and if man has only an analogy, it follows that he does not have the truth. An analogy of the truth is not the truth; and even if man's knowledge is not called an analogy of the truth but an analogical truth, the situation is no better. An

---

4. A fictional sport created for Mad magazine in 1965. Actually, there are 42 players. The 43rd team member is a dummy.

analogical truth, except it contain a univocal point of coincident meaning, simply is not the truth at all."[5]

Without a univocal core, with only analogical knowledge, God is ineffable, or very close to it.

However, there is yet another approach taken by those who posit that we can have no real knowledge of God. As William Lane Craig and J.P. Moreland write,

> According to the doctrine of divine simplicity God has no distinct attributes, he stands in no real relations, his essence is not distinct from his existence, he just is the pure act of being subsisting. All such distinctions exist only in our minds, since we can form no conception of the absolutely simple divine being. While we can say what God is not like, we cannot say what he is like, except in an analogical sense. But these predications must in the end fail, since there is no univocal element in the predicates we assign to God, leaving us in a state of genuine agnosticism about the nature of God. Indeed, on this view God really has no nature; he is simply an inconceivable act of being.[6]

Craig and Moreland identify the problem of knowing God as a function of divine simplicity. I shall look at divine simplicity in more detail below.

My argument so far is that we *can* have genuine knowledge of God, without this being a threat to God's incomprehensibility. I think this is good news, as the idea of a completely unknowable God is utterly useless. Does God answer prayer? Did he create the universe? Does he will the good? All of these are unanswerable questions if God is unknowable.

Frankly, an unknowable God seems to me to be little different than atheism or at least agnosticism. Writes atheist George H. Smith on this, "Scratch the surface of a Christian and you will find an agnostic."[7] Atheist Ayn Rand wrote similarly: "God is that which no human mind can know, they say—and proceed to demand that you consider it knowledge . . ."[8]

---

5. Gordon H. Clark, as quoted in Weaver, "Man: Analog of God," 321–27. Weaver then goes on to write that human beings are analogs of God in the sense that we are finite imitations of God, so to speak, not that our knowledge is always analogical. A defense of univocity is in Clark, *Trinity*, 79–101, and Clark, *Christian View*, 309–12.

6. Moreland and Craig, *Philosophical Foundations*, 524.

7. Smith, *Atheism*, 50.

8. Rand, *For the New Intellectual*, 149.

Both of these are based on the notion that God is unknowable. Let me be clear here. The notion that God (or anything else for that matter) is completely ineffable is an irrational thing to believe. For one thing, it is incoherent, for one is saying of God or something else that it is unknowable, while claiming that one does know something about it—namely that it is unknowable. Unknowability and related notions must be strongly rejected. If God really were totally ineffable, then theologians ought to leave the seminaries and get jobs selling insurance, or truck driving, or skating for the roller derby.

This does not solve all the problems, however. A major issue in theology today is the notion of the Trinity. The debate that has been going on about this only directly affects Christians. Nevertheless, it also has implications for anyone pondering the concept of God.

Knowing the Trinity

What is the Trinity? Put simply, it is the idea that there are three persons in the one being of God. Linda Zagzebski argues for five distinguishing characteristics of a person. They are: 1) a rational nature; 2) subjectivity; 3) relations with other persons; 4) being free; and 5) incommunicability.[9] The last term needs some explication. She quotes an aphorism of Roman law: "A person is a being which belongs to itself and which does not share its being with another."[10] This last point is not true of the Trinity, in which I argue that the members all share being with each other.

It is, indeed, difficult to fully understand the Trinity, but as William Hasker wrote, "We have a name for those who make the Trinity easy to understand; we call them *heretics*."[11]

Three centers of consciousness

The concept of the Trinity that is being outlined here is that God is conceived of as existing as one being consisting of three different centers of consciousness. (Henceforth, COC will be used for centers of consciousness). There are, therefore, three different persons in God. This is taken to

9. Zagzebski, *Divine Motivation*, 193–96.
10. Zagzebski, *Divine Motivation*, 195.
11. Hasker, "How to Think," 105.

be both eternally and necessarily true. Reality could not exist in any other way than that this God exists. Each member of the Godhead knows the others necessarily, thoroughly, and perfectly, and is necessarily involved with the others. Each of the three persons is completely intermingled with the others and could not exist or act in any way without the others, a doctrine known as perichoresis. As Thomas McCall writes,

> I believe that divine revelation reveals that there is exactly one God who exists necessarily and who exists necessarily as triune; the Father, the Son, and the Holy Spirit are three fully divine persons who live in a perichoretic communion of holy love. By "fully divine" I mean that the divine persons are *homoousios*; each divine person has the complete divine essence and enjoys ontological equality with the other divine persons. By "divine persons" I mean necessarily existent entities who enjoy "I-Thou" relationships within the triune life. By "one God" I intend a wholehearted commitment to monotheism: there is exactly one God, and this one God exists as three persons.[12]

This is not the only concept of the Trinity. Other theologians, who also call themselves Trinitarians, reject the notion of three COCs in one God. The three persons of the Trinity are conceived as being constituted in some other manner. It is claimed that this is the historic belief of the church.[13] The concept of three COCs in the Trinity is sometimes said to have come about by misunderstanding, because in ancient times, what the word person meant is different from what it means today, leading to conceptual confusion.

On the other side of the debate, Matthew Barrett argues, "Separate, individual centers of consciousness and will may be true of created persons but cannot be true of divine persons, otherwise the Godhead would be divided."[14]

This may be called *the classic Trinity versus the social or relational Trinity debate*. On the classic side are those who deny three COCs, and, in contrast, those who affirm three COCs in God are sometimes called "social" trinitarians. Of course, one must be careful here, because different

---

12. See also his book, McCall, *Which Trinity?*

13. See for example, Holmes, "Classical Trinity," 25–48. Holmes states both that God is unknowable, and that God has one personality. Holmes, *Quest for the Trinity*, 200. This causes a problem. If God is unknowable, how can we know that he has one personality? See my comments on Molnar in the text below. Also see Peckham, *Divine Attributes*, 249–61, on the disagreements about what the early church believed.

14. Barrett, *Simply Trinity*, 57.

philosophers and theologians conceive, for example, of the social Trinity in different ways from others.[15] Their different definitions therefore muddy the picture.

Who is right? Obviously, this is a matter of opinion. However, several points should be made. First, if the three persons of the Trinity are not three COCs, what are they? Here, classic trinitarians do not seem to me to be very clear. Having three different somethings in God's being needs some explanation if they are not conceived of as being COCs. At present, calling them persons when they are not thought of as COCs is only confusing things. So, what are they?

I remember thinking as a boy as I sort of listened to sermons in church, that the Trinity must be composed of different COCs. I also think that the average churchgoer, to the extent that he or she thinks about the matter, thinks of the Trinity in a COC manner. If classic trinitarians think of the Trinity as something other than COCs, they should give them another name than "person" to stop confusing people and causing false beliefs. However, what would be put in their place is unclear, because if the members of the Trinity are not persons in the modern sense, it is unclear as to what they truly are.[16]

If the classical view of the Trinity is that there are not three COCs in the Trinity, does not this seem to be close to unitarianism? Even if there are three somethings, if there are not three subjectivities, which is part of what is now meant by the concept of person? Is there then only one subjectivity? If so, this seems to be a unitarian notion of God.

Further, Thomas H. McCall and William Hasker both present evidence that some thinkers in earlier centuries did reckon three COCs in God.[17] So it seems that the relational view may also have deep historic roots.

For me, it seems that the only way that a Trinity can be truly conceived of, wherein there are three persons in the Godhead, is that of three COCs. To hold otherwise seems to deny what is fundamentally meant by the concept of being a person. No doubt, divine persons are in many ways

---

15. Some examples are given in Molnar, "Classical Trinity," 69-95.

16. For another critique of simplicity see Craig, *Systematic Philosophical*, 2b:102-84, and Richards, *Untamed God*, 213-40.

17. McCall mentions Gregory of Nyassa, Richard of St. Victor, and Duns Scotus. Thomas Aquinas wrote that the persons of the Trinity loved each other. Elsewhere he mentions Athanasius. McCall, "Response," 58. William Hasker includes Augustine, Gregory Nazianzen, and Tertullian. Hasker, *Metaphysics*, 26-77.

different than human or other finite persons; but it seems that a basic element of the concept of "being a person" is that of being a center of subjective states, and for the Trinity to exist on this model, it seems there must be three distinct COCs in God's very being. However, there is some ambiguity in the notion of the term *distinct*. Distinct can mean apart, but it can also simply mean "different." This latter meaning is applicable here. I understand the persons of the Trinity to be totally united with each other. They are completely open to each other, having the same thoughts, and necessarily so. They have only one will and are completely equal to each other. There are, in *different senses*, three COCs and one COC, as they are completely united in all respects. It is true that there may be difficulty in understanding what the early theologians who formulated the creeds exactly meant by the word person. They may not have understood the terms in precisely the same way that we do today. Specifically, they may not have understood the term person as being something that inherently and necessarily contains the concept of a center of consciousness, a center of subjective states.

However, today the average person would think of persons like this as the center of a consciousness that contains such subjective states. Indeed, outside of theologians and philosophers, I believe that the average person will imagine a *person* in such a manner—it is a natural way to look at things.

Indeed, the average Christian would likely be quite surprised and upset to think that what he or she thought was a person was really something else entirely. That is, upon hearing that the members of the Trinity were not persons in the sense that they were not subjects of conscious states, the average Christian would think that this is not what they had thought of the Trinity as being. In effect, they would think that what they were hearing was really unitarianism, and not the traditional doctrine of the Trinity at all.

I am not saying that philosophers and theologians should entirely guide themselves in their thinking about God by what the average person in the pew thinks. Often what they think is uninformed and uncritical. Nonetheless, to move away from what the local churches and almost all their most informed members have taught for centuries is a dubious move at best. The nature of God is no trivial issue. When Christians pray to not only God but specifically to one of the members of the Trinity, they expect, indeed, take for granted, that it is a person to whom they are praying. It would do no good to pray to something else; only a person can understand a prayer and potentially act upon it.

Trinity vs Absolute Oneness

Imad Shehahedeh argues that the two separate concepts of *pure unity* versus *unity in Trinity* have resulted in large differences between the beliefs of the *Trinity* and *Absolute Oneness*.[18] Specifically, Shehahedeh writes that in Absolute Oneness concepts of God, there is no eternal relationship between persons, while in the Trinity there is. Because of this, God does not essentially have relations, making it difficult to understand how God can be a personal being. Indeed, the concept of God as being absolutely one, has led to the conception that all of God's attributes are identical with each other. This entails that God has, or is, just one property. That God's eternity is identical with his mercy, and his omnipotence is identical with his justice, and his omniscience is identical with his necessary existence. This makes no sense to me.

A couple of disturbing implications ensue. One is that taking God's attributes literally, they are in blatant contradiction to each other. The concept of God's mercy is not the same as the concept of God's eternity. To assert their sameness either means that the concept of God is contradictory and therefore impossible, or else that they do not mean the same thing as our concepts but are something different. A mercy that is absolutely identical to eternity is something we have no concept of. If one takes the route that the concepts are all something quite different from the ones we have, God becomes unknowable. Vern Poythress writes that this concept leads to God's being like a black hole, about which nothing can be known.[19]

Look at it this way: if God has one property which is both mercy and eternity, it may be asked if these two concepts are analytically and separately included in the one property. If they are, then they are not identical with each other, in which case there is more than one property. If they really are identical with each other, then they are not the same

---

18. Shehadeh, *God With Us*, vol. 1.
19. Poythress, *Mystery of the Trinity*, 441–42.

concepts that we recognize, in which case, what they mean to us is unknowable. And if all of God's attributes are like this, then God becomes unknowable.[20]

Trinity (with relations between three persons) vs God's simplicity

All of this is bound up with the concept of God's being absolutely simple, which apparently has been held by most theologians in the Christian tradition.[21] It should also be said that they may not have always meant the same thing by the word "simple."[22] As Jonathan Fuqua and Robert C. Koons write, "[T]he tradition of classical theism is not a uniform or homogenous one. Many contributors defend a strictly Thomist conception of divine simplicity . . . but others offer less extreme versions, including Anselmian . . . or Scotistic . . ."[23]

As I have argued, absolute simplicity also implies that all of God's properties are identical with each other. I have already critiqued this elsewhere and will not deal in great depth with it here.[24] If one were to hold this, then one has either 1) a contradiction, or else 2) God becomes unknowable. Mercy is conceptually distinct from justice, and both are conceptually distinct from omnipotence, omniscience, and necessary existence, which, in the simplicists' view, are indistinct from each other. Saying that each one is numerically identical with the others, then, is a contradiction. The tactic that avowers of absolute simplicity have sometimes used is to appeal to analogy. God's justice is analogous to ours, as is his mercy. They are not the same. The problem then is that we do not know what God is like. If God's mercy is so different from our concept of it, why can we rely on it?

A major part of the rejection of three COCs in God is based on the doctrine of divine simplicity. However, God has also been considered to

---

20. The Reformed theologian Charles Hodge made a similar argument. He wrote, "To say, as the schoolmen, and so many even of Protestant theologians, ancient and modern, were accustomed to say, that the divine attributes differ only in name, or in our conceptions, or in their effects, is to destroy all true knowledge of God." Hodge, *Systematic Theology*, 1:371.

21. Another critique of divine simplicity is Hinlicky, *Divine Simplicity*.

22. See especially the essays, Peterson, "Parting of God," and Peterson, "Sacred Monster."

23. Fuqua and Koons, *Classical Theism*, 2.

24. Parrish and Wartick, "Dilemma;" and Parrish and Wartick, "The Dilemma of Divine Simplicity: Part 2."

be a Trinity, so what is believed here is that God has absolute simplicity within a Trinity. Prima facie, this seems problematic, so it must be unpacked. Does acceptance of divine simplicity entail a rejection of there being 3 COCs in God? I am not trying to refute divine simplicity here but rather define it in a way that makes it defensible against various objections. First, I will describe and critique a traditional view of absolute simplicity—that all of God's attributes are strictly identical to each other, which is problematic. As Timothy O'Connor writes, "As is well known, this 'strict identity' theory faces severe theoretical problems."[25]

One of the best defenses of what is called the traditional view of simplicity is by James Dolezal, in his book, *A God Without Parts*.[26] In a later paper, he defends the doctrine of the Trinity in classical terms.[27] This next section will examine the latter specifically here.

Dolezal writes, "The divine persons do not divide or carve up the divine essence in any way, nor are they component parts of the Godhead. Nevertheless, there is a real distinction between the persons."[28] He goes on to write, "So far we have considered that real relation in God is not opposed to his simplicity inasmuch as accidentality does not belong to the proper character of relation and thus relation need not be construed as something really distinct from the divine substance itself."[29]

That there are no *accidental* relations or properties in God is an important part of Dolezal's thesis. What are accidental relations or properties? In defining the *accidental*, it is helpful to begin with the contrasting *essential*. Essential relations and properties are those that the being in question cannot exist without. For example, if my cat Squirt were not a mammal, she could not exist. Being a mammal is essential to her existence. In contradistinction, accidental properties and relations are ones that the being in question could exist without. In my cat's case, she could exist and not have the exact number of hairs that she has on her body at this moment.

In the case of God, Dolezal argues that all of God's properties and relations are essential and therefore necessary. Further, since God's existence is necessary, he has these properties in all possible worlds. What then is the Trinity precisely in Dolezal's estimation? He writes, "Indeed,

25. O'Connor, "Unity of the Divine," 124.
26. Dolezal, *God without Parts*.
27. Dolezal, "Simplicity."
28. Dolezal, "Simplicity," 7.
29. Dolezal, "Simplicity," 9.

there is no particular Father-essence, Son-essence or Spirit-essence: there is simply the divine essence subsisting according to three really distinct relations within itself."[30] Further, "As fully existing by virtue of the self-same divinity the divine persons cannot be distinguished by anything other than the opposition of their relations."[31]

What this thinking leads to is, "As such the three persons are nothing but the relations of paternity, filiation and spirated procession, and each of these relations is an act."[32] This sounds very strange, but Dolezal restates the point: "Rather, the persons just are the divine relations subsisting in the one act of God's existence and essence."[33] Also, "[T]he persons are relative in that their existence as persons is constituted by their relations, that is, in co-relation to one another."[34] It is important to note that Dolezal claims that this theory is not his alone, but that it represents an old and widespread concept of the Trinity.

Along with this explanation of the theory there is the following critique. First, what Dolezal, and Thomas Aquinas (and many others) are defending is the concept that God is absolutely simple. Now, part of the problem here may be terminological. That is, what the term absolute simplicity should really mean. The Trinity in the classic version that Dolezal represents holds that there are three persons in the one God. Given this, it is correct to say that there are three persons, not two, four, or fifty-seven. The persons are real; they are not just divisions of reason. However one wants to cut it, this seems to conflict with absolute simplicity, according to which there should only be one. Absolute means pure. Pure simplicity, with no distinctions within it at all. Again, this may be mainly a terminological problem, so I will not push it too far.

However, Dolezal writes in response to this problem, "While the distinction between God's persons and his nature may appear to undermine the strong classical account of simplicity, it has traditionally been argued by simplicists that it does not since it is not in fact *real*."[35] What is Dolezal talking about here? What he seems to mean is that God's person just *is* his nature. Since God is a necessary being, and has his properties necessarily, he exists as himself. God exists in all possible worlds and

---

30. Dolezal, "Simplicity," 11.
31. Dolezal, "Simplicity," 12.
32. Dolezal, "Simplicity," 13.
33. Dolezal, "Simplicity," 16.
34. Dolezal, "Simplicity," 17.
35. Dolezal, "Simplicity," 17.

exists as the Greatest Possible Being in every world. However, this does not by itself imply that there are no distinctions in God. Even if we were to agree to this point with Dolezal, there must still be distinctions between the persons of the Trinity, otherwise the Father would be numerically identical to the Son, and both numerically identical with the Spirit. This would be a denial of trinitarianism, contradicting strongly with the Athanasian Creed's powerful affirmation of the Trinity.

There are other problems with this concept of simplicity. According to these quotes from Dolezal, the classical view holds that the divine persons just *are* their relations. This is problematic for at least two different reasons. First, it seems self-evident that for there to be relations, there must be *things* related in some way. It makes no sense to think of relations as existing with no entities of any kind that serve the relations between. This is a mysterious issue, and it may possibly be the case that I am misunderstanding what Dolezal is saying, though what he writes seems clear. Alternatively, it may be argued that God is so different from us that what does not make sense in the world, still does make sense with God. Though agreeing that God is radically different from us in many ways (of course), I hold fast in denying that there could be any real substantive contradictions within the very being of God. To quote C.S. Lewis, "[N]onsense remains nonsense even when we talk it about God."[36]

Another major problem is that it seems impossible that a relation could be a person in any meaningful sense. It could be argued that the three persons of the Trinity are distinguished by relations, but that they are not only relations, since all three persons are also God, and have his non-relational attributes as well.[37] However, for the Trinity to be based on this, there would have to be three different sets of some of God's non-relational attributes, which again seems to go against absolute simplicity, so this doesn't solve the problem for Dolezal.

If we accept the idea that the Christian thinkers of long ago used the term "person" in a very different sense than that of the modern view, then it becomes difficult to understand what the three "persons" are like. That is, if all that we know is that there are relations between each other, it seems impossible to say anything meaningful about them. Further, how can persons as pure relations be omniscient, omnipotent, omnibenevolent, etc.?

36. Lewis, *Problem of Pain*, 28.
37. Suggested by Angus Menuge in discussion.

There is a further problem here. If there is only one COC in God, then where is it? It seems that the defender of absolute simplicity could have two answers to this. The first option is that it is the Father who has, or is, a COC. In this case, since there is just one COC then the Son, and the Spirit are radically different from the Father, which undercuts traditional notions of the Trinity drastically. The second option is that God's COC is in all three of the persons. However, this means that all three members of the Trinity are really one person, since in the modern concept what it means to be a person is to have a COC. Whatever the distinctions are between the members of the Trinity, these distinctions are not because they are different *persons* in any way like the modern sense of the word. What exactly the differences would be is very difficult to say.

Matthew Barrett, who is a defender of the classical view of the Trinity, also supports the notion that the three persons are completely equal. He writes,

> In our affirmation of simplicity . . . we learned that no one attribute of God can be kept from any one person of the Trinity. He is, after all, *simply* Trinity. As long as each person is a subsistence of the same divine nature, all three persons holding the same divine nature in common, and as long as God's nature or essence is identical with all that is within him (attributes), then whatever attribute we have in mind, it must be true of each person of the Trinity.[38]

> Yet we cannot forget that the persons of the Trinity are distinct according to their personal properties: paternity, filiation, and spiration.[39]

So, Barrett here espouses that the members of the Trinity are identical in their properties, except for their origin and their actions. Thus, they cannot be numerically identical with each other. I agree. However, if they are identical in almost all of their properties, but not the same thing, there are differences in the being of God. This is incompatible with absolute simplicity.

Additionally, if there is only one COC in God, then it seems to be impossible that the different members of the Trinity, however conceived, could have performed their roles by themselves. Such as, on this account, if they were one mind or COC, then all three would have been incarnated

---

38. Barrett, *Simply Trinity*, 279.
39. Barrett, *Simply Trinity*, 279.

on earth, been crucified, etc. Though they would all work together to achieve a goal, the contribution of each is different. Given that it is God whom we are investigating, this conclusion must be considered tentative. However, it does seem to follow from the premises.

One more response is to appeal to Aquinas and enlarge on the concept of divine relations. In the *Summa Theologica* Aquinas writes,

> "Now distinction in God is only by relation of origin . . . while relation in God is not as an accident in a subject but is the divine essence itself . . . Thus, it is true to say that the name 'person' signifies relation directly, and the essence indirectly; not, however, the relation as such, but as expressed by way of a hypostasis."[40]

This, however, does not explain how a relation can be a person, or what exactly is being related. Elsewhere, Aquinas wrote,

> "[I]n God a really existing relation has the existence of the divine nature and is completely identical with it . . . [so] a real relation in God is in reality identical with nature and differs only in our mind's understanding, inasmuch as relation implies a reference to the correlative term, which is not implied by the term 'nature'. Therefore, it is clear that in God relation and nature are existentially not two things but one and the same."[41]

I am not at all sure that this clarifies matters. For how can a nature and a relation be the same thing? By definition, a relation is between two or more things.[42] To maintain orthodoxy, there must be three persons in the Trinity, but they cannot be substances.[43] One can understand how something's nature includes relations, but there must be more to something than just relations. So again, it seems to me that if the terms are used univocally to the way they are among other beings than God, then contradictions arise. But if they are used analogically, which is the way that Aquinas thought they should be used, then, we simply do not understand what they mean. God becomes unknowable. This has some disturbing implications, including that personal is not a concept that should be applied to God.

---

40. Aquinas, Summa Theologica, I, Q. 29, a. 4.Bauerschmidt, Frederick Christian, *The Essential Summan Theologiae*, 57–62.

41. Quoted in Davies, *Thought of Aquinas*, 200.

42. But to avoid tritheism, though there are not merely relations, the persons of the Trinity cannot be thought of as substances in the Aristotelian sense.

43. Angus Menuge made this point in communication with me.

For example, Brian Davies writes about Aquinas, "[W]e may well ascribe to him a prima-facie willingness to look beyond the word 'person' as a way of explaining how there is distinction in God."[44] "[It] seems to me that he [Aquinas] would have been happy to look beyond the notion of person as a way of expressing how God can be three in one."[45] If there are not three persons in God, then what the vast majority of Christians have thought is wrong. Further, given the abstraction and merely analogical knowledge of God, that God may not be in any real sense a personal being, may well follow. And this destroys much of what is distinctive of Christian theism. One would no longer have a personal God.[46]

There is, of course, much more that can be said about these matters. Thomists and others will have responses to what has been written here. However, given the fundamental positions that they hold, it seems that the unknowability of God, and hence the non-personality of God, do logically follow from absolute simplicity. The concept of God as *absolutely* simple in all respects seems to me to be more the God of Plotinus than the God of the Bible.

Despite heroic efforts on the part of some theologians and philosophers to make sense of this, and the fact that the view has been very widespread, I simply do not see how the absolute simplicity view of God can work. I still hold to the notion of divine simplicity in a different sense, but it includes the notion of there being three persons in God. Simplicity is then simplicity in a real Trinity.

For me, the best notion of divine simplicity is that all of God's attributes are contained in the concept of God as the Greatest Possible Being. We can see some of these immediately. For example, being the GPB entails God's having aseity, being necessarily, omnipotence, omniscience, and omnibenevolence, among other attributes. These aspects are not identical to each other, but all of these attributes necessarily coexist in God. God's existence entails their existence, and they entail the existence of God and each other. On the other hand, that God is a Trinity is also analytically included in the concept of God, but it cannot immediately be seen that this is necessarily true. Still, we can see that being personal is included, and it seems that being a Trinity of persons is necessary to God's being personal. Also, if there is more than one possible world that

---

44. Davies, *Thought of Aquinas*, 201.

45. Davies, *Thought of Aquinas*, 202.

46. The rejection of a personal God is important in parts of Judaism. See Downey, *Maimonides's Yahweh*.

God could create, his knowledge and actions would vary from world to world. But in all worlds and possibilities, God is sovereign.

One more problem that will be brought up here is one that Dolezal admits in his book.[47] If God truly is identical with his nature, then he could not have been different in any respect from what he is. This entails that God could not have created things any differently than he has, for then his knowledge of them would be different. In short, this is the only world that could have been, and everything in it; every object, property, and event's existence is logically necessary, because nothing could have been otherwise. This contradicts the notion of God's having the freedom to create any world he wanted to. In short, there is only one possible world, the one we live in. A reason for accepting this is that if God had actualized a different world than ours, his knowledge would be different, and thus God would be different and absolute simplicity is denied. Nathan Greeley makes this argument, writing that there is no contingency in God, and, therefore, God cannot be other than he is, and so there are no other possible worlds where God knows that he has created different things than he did in this world.[48] To reiterate, there would be no other possible worlds, only this one.

Though God's necessarily actualizing of this world and no others may be a defensible position, it seems rather odd. The only plausible way to say that this is the only world that God would create is to say that this world is the best of all possible worlds. However, it is strange to think that God's absolute necessity depends upon his knowing that my cat has N numbers of hairs on her at this moment, and it could not possibly be otherwise. An alternative view is that God could have created different worlds other than this one, but that once he actualized this world, he does not change it.[49]

I will put the argument formally, showing that there are problems with saying that this is the only world that God would actualize.

(12.1) The premise: since God is simple, W, the world in which we exist, is the only possible one that he would actualize, and hence W is the only possible world.

---

47. Dolezal, *God without Parts*, 188–212.

48. Greeley, "Divine Simplicity," 214–43.

49. This seems to be consistent with the notion that God is immutable and impassable, that is, unchanging and unmoved.

(12.2) This is the only world that God would create, which we know because it exists.

(12.3) Given 12.1 and 12.2, and that God does nothing without a reason, it follows that God has a reason for preferring this world to all others.

(12.4) The reason that God would create only W is that it is better than all other worlds.

(12.5) This being the case, this world is the best of all worlds—and is the only possible one.

(12.6) But the idea that there is a best of all possible worlds seems implausible, and that W is the best one also seems implausible.

(12.7) If either of the suppositions of implausibility in 12.6 are true, then this cannot be the best of all worlds, and the argument that this world is the only one that God would create fails.

It is difficult to see how there could be a reason why W is the only world that God would create if it were not the best of all worlds. Suppose there is a set of worlds, S, whose worlds are equally good and are better than all other worlds. Were that the case, then there is no reason for God to prefer W to some other world in S, such as W', and God's choice to actualize W rather than W' is merely a contingency. In that case there would be other worlds that God could have actualized, in which case his choice of W is contingent.

I consider this argument to be plausible, but not decisive. Perhaps it is the case that this is the only world that God would create. A defender of the one possible world concept can argue that if W is the only world that God would actualize, then it must be the best of all imaginable worlds, though we cannot see why. It just seems implausible that it is. And if there are more possible worlds that God would create, then the doctrine of Absolute Simplicity fails.

In response to this the defender of the classical viewpoint may argue that whatever problems the classical viewpoint has, the "Social" or "Relational" trinitarian has it worse. For example, Paul Molnar argues that the concept of three COCs in one God is, or is close to, tritheism. He writes, "Yet according to the classical view of the Trinity, there is only one 'entity' because God *is* One Being, Three Persons. That is the mystery of the Trinity. It cannot be explained...because, according to the tradition, no one can explain *how* God can be One Being, Three Persons."[50] In other words, we really don't know, and indeed cannot know, what God is like in the Trinity. For Molnar, it is a total mystery.

However, Molnar then writes in response to McCall, "[I] believe his rejection of a 'single divine subjectivity' is a rejection of the unique unity and simplicity of the triune God."[51] Here Molnar seems to accept the existence of a single divine subjectivity. If so, then he thinks that he does know something about God's Trinity, which seems to contradict what he wrote in the quotation in the paragraph above. If Molnar thinks that the notion of three COCs in one God leads to tritheism, it may be responded that his view leads to Unitarians. Supporters of the one COC view will of course deny this, but it is questionable whether they can really do so and be consistent.

Adam Lloyd Johnson argues that classical trinitarians also support love among the persons of the trinity.

He writes, "Though classical trinitarians understand God to be a single divine subject, most of them also affirm that there are loving relationships between the members of the Trinity and that this same love is extended from the Trinity to humans."[52]

The problem here is that if God is one divine subject, one person, then how can there be loving relationships between the members of the Trinity. Would this not be a case of the single divine subject simply loving himself? This problem is worse if the members of the Trinity are thought of as being relations. How can relations love anything? Moreover, if there are three different loves in God, one for each member, is this compatible with absolute simplicity? Still, if Johnson is correct and classical trinitarians can acknowledge love between the members of the Trinity, then this makes the case stronger that God's goodness is founded on the love of the members of the Trinity.[53]

To fully explain this would take an entire book. Fortunately, I do not have to write one, because Adam Lloyd Johnson has already done so. In

---

50. Molnar, "Response to Thomas H. McCall," 146.
51. Molnar, "Response to Thomas H. McCall," 149.
52. Johnson, "Proposing a Trinitarian Metaethical Theory," 240.
53. Angus Menuge comments on this: "I also wonder if one cannot split the difference and think of one 3-dimensional consciousness? But the dimensions would need to not be parts (partialism) or modes (modalism)."

his book *Divine Love Theory*, he makes the case in detail that the divine Trinity is the basis of morality.[54]

Therefore, we should accept the concept of God as being simple in Trinity, while acknowledging that this means different things to different people. *Everything about God flows necessarily from his nature as the Greatest Possible Being.* With this concept in mind, we can readily understand why God is existing, omnipotent, omniscient, and omnibenevolent, and all of these are necessarily so.[55] These properties are not numerically identical, but they are all necessarily included in the concept of God as the Greatest Possible Being and are therefore necessarily coexisting. To be God is to be the Greatest Possible Being. These attributes are what God is, and necessarily so. We cannot see in the same way that God is three persons. Nevertheless, God's existing in three persons is just as necessary as his being all powerful, all knowing, and all good. God has all his attributes the same in all possible worlds, except for the difference of making different worlds, in which case his knowledge differs from world to world, but in every world, he knows everything. Further, the divine persons are in some ways like us, only infinite and perfect. There are three COC's in the one God.

Because of this difference, the Christian concept of a Trinity gives an answer to why God is essentially loving, while Absolute conceptions do not. To reiterate, for God to be the foundation of moral truths, God must be personal. However, for God to just be one person brings up the problem that being non-relational, God cannot be essentially loving. Therefore, there must be more than one person in God. This is not the entire doctrine of the Trinity, but it is a fundamental part of it. The persons are also necessarily united and completely open to and exist in relationship with each other.

As the above discussion shows, the Trinity is a difficult issue. First, the concept of just how three persons can all be one being is puzzling, though it has not been shown to be incoherent. Perhaps the basic difficulty with thinking about the concept of the Trinity is in attempting to know what it is like to actually *be* God; it is not just making statements about

---

54. The book is partly a rewrite of Johnson's doctoral dissertation. Johnson, *Divine Love Theory*. See also Baggett and Campbell, *Personal God*, 122–24.

55. In other words, I hold that God cannot be other than he is: omnipotent, omniscient, etc. For a contrary view, see Davis, *Logic*, 68–85; Kahane, "If There Is a Hole," 109; and Kraay, *Does God Matter?*, 109.

God. It is an attempt to explore the inner nature of the Greatest Possible Being, and this is bound to be difficult, perplexing, and mysterious.

To summarize, what is espoused here is that there are three COCs in God, but that they also interpenetrate each other and agree with each other, necessarily existing in community. This is the doctrine of *perichoresis*, which is an essential part of orthodox doctrine, wherein all members of the Trinity, as part of their nature, are mutually indwelling and interpenetrating each other. Since each person fully knows each other's mind, so to speak, all have the same thoughts, and have one will, there is therefore one fully integrated community. The community of the Trinity is thus both triune and fully united. This saves the important points that both the classical view and the social or relational view make. In essence, the Trinity has both three consciousnesses and a deep and necessary unity among them.

Argument that being a Trinity is necessary for God to be perfect

Sherene Nicholas Khouri has argued that for God to be the Greatest Possible Being (or as she states, the Conceived Being), then God must be necessarily relational. The Christian doctrine of the Trinity establishes this, while the Islamic doctrine of God's absolute oneness, or *tawhid* does not. She writes,

> Being perfect does not allow an attribute that is incompatible with perfection to exist. If being relational in all respects is a perfection, then it is better to have it necessarily than contingently... [A]n omniscient, omnipotent, and perfectly relational being who can maintain his relationality is more perfect that the one who cannot maintain his relationality (even if he chooses to) ... If an eternally relational divine being is better than a contingently divine being, and his relationality is compatible with the rest of his attributes, then perfect-being theology lies within the court of Christianity, and the doctrine of the Trinity, not the doctrine of *tawhid,* is the only model that shows God eternally relational.[56]

The Christian concept of God can thus be the Greatest Possible Being, while the Islamic God, and other unitarian gods, cannot. Indeed, it is difficult to see how a unitarian God could really love anything. Existing

---

56. Khouri and Habermas, *Triune Relationality,* 180.

of its own inner necessity, lacking necessary connection to anything else, why would it care about any other thing? A thing that cannot love cannot desire and, thus, lacks a reason for creating anything else. A self-sufficient unitarian God has no desire for relations—so why create?[57] What we really have here then is an impersonal idea of God.

Other philosophers have also written that the Trinity is necessary for God to be perfect. Stephen T. Davis defends what he names the social theory of the Trinity or ST in the following argument:

(12.8) Necessarily, God is perfect, and perfect in love (1 John 4:8).

(12.9) Necessarily, if God does not experience love of another, God is imperfect.

(12.10) Therefore, necessarily, God experiences love of another (12.1), (12.2).

(12.11) Necessarily, it is possible that only God exists (i.e., that God does not create).

(12.12) Necessarily, if ST is false, there is no 'other' in the Godhead.

(12.13) Necessarily, if God alone exists, and if ST is false, then God does not experience love of another, and thus is not perfect (12.2), (12.4), (12.5).

(12.14) Therefore, necessarily, ST is true (12.4), (12.6).[58]

There are critics of the argument. Dale Tuggy writes that what Davis is really assuming in (12.2) is that for God to be perfect, he needs to experience peer love, which of course only another God could have. To avoid polytheism, what is needed is the social view of the Trinity, which is three persons in one God. He writes, "There's a non-sequitur in Davis's reasoning. Were God to have 'missed out on something high and wonderful,' it doesn't seem to follow that there would be a 'deficiency in God.' Not all goods, not even all great goods, are such that their absence would render one imperfect."[59]

However, there is a similar argument to the one that Davis made that avoids Tuggy's criticism. It goes like this, given unitarianism:

---

57. Charles Schulz made this point in a private communication to me.
58. Davis, *Christian Philosophical Theology*, 65.
59. Tuggy, "On the Possibility," 135.

(12.15) Necessarily, God is perfect and perfect in love.

(12.16) Necessarily if God is not essentially loving, God is imperfect.

(12.17) Therefore, God is essentially loving.

(12.18) Necessarily it is possible that only God exists and that God does not create.

(12.19) If God exists alone, then God would not be essentially loving, for there would be nothing for him to love.

Therefore, to deny the notion of the three persons in the Trinity, even if the Trinity is conceived in some other way, negates the possibility of God's being essentially loving. One response to this is to hold that God must necessarily create a world. In other words, to be loving God must create other things to love. This is problematic for several reasons, one of which is that it makes a major attribute of God dependent upon created beings, which is a denial of classical and perfect being theism. In other words, on this view, to be loving, God had to create other beings.

Why would God have love in himself if he is only a single being who necessarily exists? The whole thing seems quite difficult to understand. A person seems only to be a full person if intrinsically relational. Necessarily, self-love is of a different kind of love from love-of-others. Loving someone else is at least loving someone because they are distinct from oneself. Indeed, in the case of God, what does it even mean that God—a solitary God—loves himself? Does not the concept of love entail a difference between a subject and an object?

On a Unitarian basis, God must create to love. Therefore, God *must* create other things to be loving and express love. However, were God to create, why would that make him loving, and if he were not loving, why would he create anything?

Of course, people can and do love themselves, sometimes inordinately. However, it is difficult to imagine a creature being loving apart from anything and anyone else. Perhaps this is all that can be said about this topic, but it seems to me that for God to be loving, there must be something other than a single person. To be a fully loving person, there must be another person involved; there must be an object of that love. At the very least, trinitarianism provides an explanation why God is loving, while unitarianism does not.

It may be objected that love between the divine persons in the Trinity would be so different from ours that it is difficult to conceive of as being love in any sense that we would recognize. While it should, of course, be admitted that we do not understand many things about God, especially how it is to *be* God, this does not mean that there can be no understanding at all.

Further, given standard trinitarian theory, the three persons all necessarily interpenetrate each other, and by loving each other, they are also loving the group and themselves. Thus, there is a basis for divine love that is available on a trinitarian basis, but that is not available on other models of God, specifically Unitarian ones, wherein God exists in all loneliness apart from any creation he makes. Robert Letham writes,

> Only a God who is triune can be personal. Only the Holy Trinity can be love. Human love cannot possibly reflect the nature of God unless God is a Trinity of persons in union and communion. A solitary monad cannot love, and since it cannot love, neither can it be a person. And if God is not personal, neither can we be—and if we are not persons, we cannot love. This marks a vast, immeasurable divide between those cultures that follow a monotheistic unitary deity and those that are permeated by the Christian teaching on the Trinity. Trinitarian theology asserts that love is ultimate because God is love, since he is three persons in undivided loving communion.[60]

Parenthetically, the concept of God as being a person is not only important in ethics, but in everything. Only a personal God, with understanding and the ability to choose, could create a contingent yet orderly and understandable universe.[61]

I believe this solves the Euthyphro problem, as was argued above. Indeed, in this theory of the intrinsically loving Trinity, God would never make evil laws, so the Euthyphro problem doesn't even arise. For if God is essentially loving in all possible worlds, there are no worlds where God will command cruelty for its own sake. Though God has some freedom to make some different rules, what they are, are limited by his goodness.[62] It is this goodness that expresses itself in different ways in various modal spheres—ethical goodness, aesthetic goodness, etc.

---

60. Letham, *Holy Trinity*, 539.
61. Jaki, *Science & Creation*; and Jaki, *Savior of Science*.
62. Hare, *God's Command*.

It should be noted that some philosophers have argued that a deity composed of a single person can still be intrinsically loving.[63] I strongly doubt it, and anyway, it is still true that the Trinity provides a natural and necessary way for God to be intrinsically loving, while a Unitarian view such as that of Islam may not. Indeed, a major reason for the differences between Christianity and Islam seems to be the Muslim's emphatic rejection of anything that compromises the sheer oneness of God.

I have posited that God is essentially loving and therefore loving in all worlds. There is one more objection to be addressed here. It has been argued that if ethics is based on God's necessary nature, it is still thinkable that if, *per impossible*, God were essentially evil, then we would be obligated to obey him. Thus, basing ethics on God's nature still leads to a Euthyphro dilemma.[64]

In response, this objection applies to all realist but non-trinitarian views of God. As has been shown, some philosophers base ethics on Platonic entities. Presumably, being abstract, they exist and have the properties that they do in all worlds. Luckily for us, these abstract entities entail kindness, honesty, etc., instead of their opposites. However, with the argument just given above, we could posit that even though absolutely impossible, if there were worlds where cruelty was commanded, we would be obligated to be cruel. However, considering God's necessary existence and nature, in this case we are dealing with the absolutely impossible and there are no possible worlds wherein God commands cruelty, so this objection is an empty and untenable one.

The Trinity, God's Goodness, and Normative Power

Standard trinitarian theory also shows how ethics has its normative power. If God has in some way created human beings for a purpose, then we have *telos* or goal. If God is perfectly good, then the purpose must be good. To follow God's law is therefore good, and goodness, by definition, is what should be done, and has normativity.[65]

---

63. Besides Dale Tuggy, Keith Ward also argues for this. Ward, *Christ and the Cosmos*. Ward writes, "Love within the Trinity does not seem to be anything at all like human love," 181. But the most basic part of love, knowing and appreciating the good in something, and having positive feelings for it, can be both human and divine.

64. Lutz and Case, *Is Morality Real?*, 176.

65. Morris, *Believing Philosophy*, 232–46.

To use a metaphor, God's goodness when he created the universe is like a light that is sent through a prism, and by doing so, breaks up into many colors. In the case of God, these colors are analogs of ethical, aesthetic, and other goods. How this happens is a difficult question and examination.

To reiterate, I agree with Adam Lloyd Johnson that *the Trinity is the key to understanding God's goodness and therefore is the basis of ethics.* However, I want to emphasize that it is the love of the members of the Trinity in this perichoretic union that specifically is a basis for all good, including ethical and aesthetic. By saying this, I am not saying that love is the only source of good in God. However, it is a very important, and perhaps the ultimate source of God's goodness, as any other goodness comes from the nature of the divine persons and their interrelationship.

Of course, if God is essentially loving, then the question may be understandably asked why there is so much evil and suffering in the world. If God is essentially loving, why is there so much misery in the world? The "problem of evil" is a classic argument against Christian Theism. There have been many responses to it. Due to limited space here, the reader will be encouraged to pursue this question in resources noted in the footnote.[66]

So why are there moral oughts? Because God is the ultimate good, and being so, he should be loved, and loving God involves doing things that he loves and which bring us closer to him. As John Hare writes, "We can be autonomous if we trust God to tell us to do what will in the end produce the highest intrinsic good, namely (as Scotus puts it) that we become co-lovers with God. So we carry out our obligations because God has made them obligatory, but also because we share this end with God."[67]

Finally, it should be noted that the notion of God as a personal God, which I have argued depends upon the doctrine of the Trinity, explains many things. Since God is personal, and human beings are made in the

---

66. There is a vast literature on the subject, with various worthwhile responses. See for example, Little, *God, Why*; Feinberg, *The Many Faces of Evil*; Rowe et al., *The Evidential Argument from Evil*; Johnson, *Calvinism and the Problem of Evil*; van Inwagen, *Christian Faith and the Problem of Evil*; and Welty, *Why Is There Evil in the World*. One book that explores the relation of ethics and evil from both a theistic and an atheistic position is Franks, *Explaining Evil*. For a debate on the subject see Sterba and Swinburne, *Could a Good God*. My own thoughts on the matter include the idea that creating humanity was worth it, even though we are a fallen race. See my book Parrish, *Atheism?*, 213–14.

67. Hare, *God's Call*, 118.

image of God, it can be seen why human beings have intrinsic value. Further, since God has a rational mind, and created the universe according to what is in his mind, and our minds are finite analogs of God's mind, we can know some of what he created. A personal God, which the Trinity guarantees, is philosophically very useful. Thus, Genesis 1:27, "So God created man in his own image, in the image of God he created him; male and female he created them," is one of the most important verses in the Bible. Saying that all human beings are made in the image of God gives intrinsic value to all human beings. The result has been that slowly and painfully, over the centuries, the concept that all human beings should be treated with respect has grown.[68]

---

68. Mangalwadi, *The Book*.

CHAPTER 13

Conclusion
The Best Reason for Ethics

WITH THE ABOVE THESES established, we can now move on to the conclusion of the book: that Christian Trinitarian Theism can provide a secure basis for normative ethical truths and that other systems cannot.

I have argued that one may divide metaethical theories into three types.

The first is strong or robust realist theories, where there are ethical propositions that both *necessarily exist and are true*. They exist independently of us.

Secondly, there are weak realist theories wherein true ethical propositions can be *derived* based on some factor of reality, such as reason, or human nature, or the desire for happiness or flourishing.

The last of the three divisions of metaethical theories is antirealism, where ethics is something that people *invent*. According to antirealism there is nothing that is truly right or wrong in itself. Instead, there are only preferences.

Atheists, as well as some theists, have different intuitions about the feasibility of combining some form of realism with atheism. Theists often think that without God, there is no chance of having truth in any form of ethical realism. Atheists, on the other hand, often seem to wonder why anyone would think that God would have anything to do with ethics. Even if God did exist, all he would do would be to affirm whatever theory we think is best.

According to what I have argued, in a sense both sides are wrong.[1] An atheist can be a robust realist if he or she is a Platonist. However, Platonism, at least regarding ethical propositions, seems to be extremely implausible. Atheists can also be weak realists and legitimately choose something like reason or happiness for the individual or society as the axiom that is the basis for an ethical system. The problem with weak realism is that there is no ethical *necessity* in accepting that axiom. Because it is before the system, it is an amoral choice that one does not have to buy into. It may be a plausible or reasonable choice, but it is not a necessary one. Seeing that there are several possible choices for an ethical axiom, there is no guarantee that any one of them will be a consensus choice. In any event, there is nothing *ethically* wrong in denying any of the moral axioms chosen.

I have further argued that we have good reason to think that a form of robust realism is true. This entails that some ethical propositions are necessarily and universally true. Ethical truths are in the form of propositions. This in turn means that they are either abstract objects or ideal objects in the mind of God. It has been argued at great length that they are not abstract objects in some Platonic sense. Therefore, they are ideas in the mind of God. Propositions are composed of concepts that are ordered in such a manner that they are at least potentially intentional. God knows all the propositions and their truth-values. Ethical propositions are true or false because God either affirms or denies them. Many ethical propositions are necessarily true because God necessarily affirms their truth based on his nature. God's nature is essentially loving because necessarily God exists as a Trinity, and the persons of the Trinity necessarily love each other.[2]

Hence, God necessarily affirms or rejects some ethical propositions based on God's and the propositions' necessary natures. *God is the Good, rather than just being good.* The loving nature of God is the ultimate good, and goodness itself. Many ethical laws flow with necessity from God's nature. Other ethical propositions are contingent because they are useful, not because they are necessarily true. In addition, God can rank the importance of ethical propositions so that if they conflict, one of them ought to be obeyed rather than the other. For example, stealing is morally wrong, but in a situation where one either steals or one's family starves

---

1. For a related view see Evans, *God and Moral Obligation*.
2. Copan and Taliaferro, *Naturalness of Belief*.

to death, the second (at least arguably) could overrule the first in this situation.

Human beings are finite analogs of God. Concepts are essentially things that can be understood by the requisite kinds of mind. God understands all propositions, while human beings understand only some. Ideal objects in the mind of God include concepts, which necessarily exist and can be grasped by any number of the right kinds of minds. Therefore, there is no problem with the fact that human beings and other personal creatures can grasp and understand concepts of ethics and moral choices. Thus, everything fits together in one system and all the parts of the system are explained. Other metaethical theories cannot do this.

In summary, I have argued that necessary moral truths exist, and for this to be, these truths must exist in the mind not only of a perfect being God, but a trinitarian one.

Bibliography

Adams, Robert Merrihew. "Divine Necessity." *Journal of Philosophy* 80 (1983) 741–51.
———. *Finite and Infinite Goods: A Framework for Ethics*. New York: Oxford University Press, 2002.
Adamson, Peter. *Medieval Philosophy*. Vol. 4. A History of Philosophy without Any Gaps. Oxford: Oxford University Press, 2019.
Allison, Gregg R. *Roman Catholic Theology and Practice: An Evangelical Assessment*. Wheaton: Crossway, 2014.
Allison, Henry E. *Kant's Transcendental Idealism: An Interpretation and Defense*. Revised and Enlarged ed. New Haven: Yale University Press, 2004.
Alston, William P. *A Realist Conception of Truth*. Ithaca, NY: Cornell University Press, 1997.
Altman, Matthew C. *A Companion to Kant's Critique of Pure Reason*. Boulder, CO: Westview, 2008.
Anderson, James N. *David Hume*. Phillipsburg, NJ: P&R, 2019.
Anderson, James N., and Welty, Greg. "The Lord of Non-Contradiction: An Argument for God from Logic." *Philosophia Christi* 13, no. 2 (2011) 321–38.
Angier, Tom, ed. *The Cambridge Companion to Natural Law Ethics*. Cambridge: Cambridge University Press, 2019.
Anselm. "Proslogium." In *St. Anselm: Basic Writings*, translated by S. N. Deane. LaSalle, IL: Open Court, 1962.
Aristotle. *The Basic Works of Aristotle*. 12th ed. Edited by Richard McKeon. New York: Random House, 1941.
Armstrong, David. "Naturalism, Materialism, and First Philosophy." *Philosophia* 8 (1978) 261–62.
Audi, Robert. *The Good in the Right: A Theory of Intuition and Intrinsic Value*. Princeton: Princeton University Press, 2005.
———. *Moral Perception*. Soochow University Lectures in Philosophy, Taiwan. Princeton: Princeton University Press, 2013.
Ayer, Alfred Jules. *Language, Truth and Logic*. 2nd ed. New York: Dover, 1952.
Baggett, David, and Marybeth Baggett. *The Morals of the Story: Good News About a Good God*. Downer's Grove, IL: IVP Academic, 2018.
Baggett, David, and Ronnie R. Campbell, Jr. *A Personal God and a Good World: The Coherence of the Christian Moral Vision*. Brentwood, TN: B&H Academic, 2024.
Baggett, David, and Jerry L. Walls. *Good God: The Theistic Foundations of Morality*. New York: Oxford University Press, 2011.

———. *The Moral Argument: A History*. New York: Oxford University Press, 2019.

———. "The Moral Argument." In *Contemporary Arguments in Natural Theology*, edited by Colin Ruloff and Peter Horban. London: Bloomsbury Academic, 2021.

Bagnoli, Carla. "Constructivism in Metaethics." *The Sanford Encyclopedia of Philosophy*. September 27, 2011. https://plato.stanford.edu/archives/spr2021/entries/constructivism-metaethics/.

Balaguer, Mark. "Moral Folkism and the Deflation of (Lots of) Normative and Metaethics." In *Abstract Objects: For and Against*, edited by José L. Falguera and Concha Martínez-Vidal. New York: Springer, 2020.

Bales, James D. *Communism and the Reality of Moral Law*. Nutley, NJ: Craig, 1969.

Barfield, Kenny. *Why the Bible Is Number 1: The World's Sacred Writings in the Light of Science*. Grand Rapids: Baker, 1988.

Barrett, Matthew. *Simply Trinity: The Unmanipulated Father, Son, and Spirit*. Grand Rapids: Baker, 2021.

Bauerschmidt, Frederick Christian. *The Essential Summa Theologiae*. 2nd ed. Grand Rapids: Baker Academic, 2021.

Bavinck, Herman, and James P. Eglinton. *Philosophy of Revelation: A New Annotated Edition*. Expanded ed, edited by Nathaniel Gray Sutanto and Cory Brock. Peabody, MA: Hendrickson Academic, 2018.

Beck, W. David. *Does God Exist?: A History of Answers to the Questions*. Downer's Grove, IL: InterVarsity Press, 2021.

Blackburn, Simon. *Essays in Quasi-Realism*. New York: Oxford University Press USA, 1993.

Blanshard, Brand. *Reason and Analysis*. The Paul Carus Lectures 12. LaSalle, IL: Open Court, 1964.

Bloomfield, Paul. *Moral Reality*. New York: Oxford University Press, 2001.

Bøhn, Einar Duenger. *God and Abstract Objects*. Cambridge: Cambridge University Press, 2019.

BonJour, Laurence. *In Defense of Pure Reason: A Rationalist Account of A Priori Justification*. Cambridge: Cambridge University Press, 1997.

Bowne, Borden Parker. *Kant and Spencer: A Critical Exposition*. Port Washington, NY: Kennikat, 1967.

———. *Principles of Ethics*. 1st Reprint. London: Forgotten Books, 2015.

Bradley, F. H. *Appearance and Reality: A Metaphysical Essay*. 2nd ed. Oxford: Oxford University Press, 1978.

Brandt, Richard B. *A Theory of the Good and the Right*. Revised ed. Amherst: Prometheus, 1998.

Braun, David. "Indexicals." *Stanford Encyclopedia of Philosophy*, Summer 2017. plato.stanford.edu/entries/indexicals/.

Brink, David O. *Moral Realism and the Foundations of Ethics*. Cambridge Studies in Philosophy. Cambridge: Cambridge University Press, 1989.

Brog, David. *In Defense of Faith: The Judeo-Christian Idea and the Struggle for Humanity*. New York: Encounter, 2010.

Budziszewski, J. *Written on the Heart: The Case for Natural Law*. Downer's Grove: IVP Academic, 1997.

Bueno, Octavio. "Contingent Abstract Objects." In *Abstract Objects: For and Against*, edited by José L. Falguera and Concha Martinez-Vidal. Studies n Epistemology,

Logic, Methodology, and Philosophy of Science, Synthese Library 422. Cham, Switzerland: Springer, 2020.

Burroughs, Edgar Rice. *The Chessmen of Mars*. Vol. 5. The Martian Series. New York: Ballantine, 1963.

Christensen, Scott. *What about Evil? A Defense of God's Sovereign Glory*. Phillipsburg, NJ: P&R, 2020.

Churchland, Patricia S. *Neurophilosophy: Toward a Unified Science of the Mind-Brain*. 9th ed. Cambridge: Bradford, 1996.

Clark, Gordon H. *A Christian View of Men and Things: An Introduction to Philosophy*. Reprint. Twin Brooks. Grand Rapids: Baker, 1981.

———. *Religion, Reason, and Revelation*. 2nd ed. Jefferson, MD: The Trinity Foundation, 1995.

———. *The Trinity*. Trinity Paper 8. Jefferson, MD: The Trinity Foundation, 1985.

Clark, Kelly James. "Naturalism and Its Discontents." In *The Blackwell Companion to Naturalism*, vol. 62. Blackwell Companions to Philosophy. Malden, MA: Wiley-Blackwell, 2016.

Clarke-Doane, Justin. *Morality and Mathematics*. New York: Oxford University Press, 2020.

Clouser, Roy A. *The Myth of Religious Neutrality: An Essay on the Hidden Role of Religious Belief in Theories*. Revised ed. Notre Dame: University of Notre Dame Press, 2005.

Cooper, John W. *Panentheism: The Other God of the Philosophers—From Plato to the Present*. Grand Rapids: Baker Academic, 2006.

Copan, Paul, and Charles Taliaferro, eds. *The Naturalness of Belief: New Essays on Theism's Rationality*. Lanham, MD: Lexington, 2018.

Copan, Paul, and Thom Wolf. "Another Dimension of the Moral Argument: The Voice of Jesus and the Historical Fruits of the Christian Faith." In *A New Theist Response to the New Atheists*, edited by Joshua Rasmussen and Kevin Vallier. Routledge New Critical Thinking in Religion, Theology and Biblical Studies. New York: Routledge, 2020.

Copp, David. "A Skeptical Challenge to Moral Non-Naturalism and a Defense of Constructivist Naturalism*." *Philosophical Studies* 126, no. 2 (2005) 269–83. https://doi.org/10.1007/s11098-005-2161-4.

Coppenger, Mark. *Moral Apologetics for Contemporary Christians: Pushing Back Against Cultural and Religious Critics*. Brentwood, TN: B&H Academic, 2011.

Cowling, Sam. *Abstract Entities*. New York: Routledge, 2017.

Craig, William Lane. "Eric Wielenberg's Metaphysics of Morals." *Philosophia Christi* 20, no. 2 (2018) 333–38.

———. *God and Abstract Objects: The Coherence of Theism: Aseity*. New York: Springer, 2018.

———. *God Over All: Divine Aseity and the Challenge of Platonism*. Illustrated ed. Oxford: Oxford University Press, 2016.

———. "Response to Van Inwagen and Welty." *Philosophia Christi* 21, no. 2 (2019) 277–86.

———. *Systematic Philosophical Theology*. Vol. 2b. Hoboken, NJ: Wiley-Blackwell, 2025.

Craig, William Lane, and Erik J. Wielenberg. *A Debate on God and Morality: What Is the Best Account of Objective Moral Values and Duties?*, edited by Adam Lloyd Johnson. New York: Routledge, 2021.

Cuneo, Terence. *The Normative Web: An Argument for Moral Realism*. New York: Oxford University Press, 2010.

———. *Speech and Morality: On the Metaethical Implications of Speaking*. Oxford: Oxford University Press, 2014.

Davies, Brian. *The Thought of Thomas Aquinas*. New York: Oxford University Press, 1993.

Davis, Richard Brian. *The Metaphysics of Theism and Modality*. Vol. 189. American University Studies, V Philosophy. New York: Peter Lang, 2001.

Davis, Stephen T. *Christian Philosophical Theology*. Oxford: Oxford University Press, 2016.

———. *Logic and the Nature of God*. Grand Rapids: Eerdmans, 1983.

Dembski, William A. *Being as Communion: A Metaphysics of Information*. Surrey: Ash Gate, 2014.

Dockery, David, and Lauren Green McAfee. *Created in the Image of God*. Nashville: Forefront, 2023.

Dolezal, James E. *God Without Parts: Divine Simplicity and the Metaphysics of God's Absoluteness*. Eugene, OR: Pickwick, 2011.

———. "Simplicity and the Status of God's Personal Relations." *Internation Journal of Systematic Theology*, 2013, 20. https://doi.org/10.1111/ijst.12016.

Dooyeweerd, Herman. *A New Critique of Theoretical Thought*. Translated by David H. Freeman and William S. Young. 4 vols. Phillipsburg, NJ: P&R, 1969.

Downey, Amy Karen. *Maimonides's Yahweh: Rabbinic Judaism's Attempt to Answer the Incarnational Question*. Eugene, OR: Wipf and Stock, 2019.

Dreier, James, ed. *Contemporary Debates in Moral Theory*. Malden, MA: Wiley-Blackwell, 2006.

Dumsday, Travis. "A Cosmological Argument from Moderate Realism." *The Heythrop Journal*, LXI (2020) 732–36.

Dumsday, Travis. *Dispositionalism and the Metaphysics of Science*. Cambridge: Cambridge University Press, 2019.

Egnor, Michael, and Denyse O'Leary. *The Immortal Mind: A Neurosurgeon's Case for the Existence of the Soul*. New York: Worthy, 2025.

Enoch, David. *Taking Morality Seriously: A Defense of Robust Realism*. Oxford: Oxford University Press, 2011.

Evans, C. Stephen. *God and Moral Obligation*. Oxford: Oxford University Press, 2013.

Evans, C. S., and Trinity O'Neill. "The Moral Argument." In *Contemporary Arguments in Natural Theology: God and Rational Belief*, edited by Colin Ruloff and Peter Horban. London: Bloomsbury Academic, 2021.

Falguera, José L., and Concha Martínez-Vidal, eds. *Abstract Objects: For and Against*. Cham, Switzerland: Springer, 2020.

Feinberg, John S. *The Many Faces of Evil: Theological Systems and the Problems of Evil*. Wheaton: Crossway, 2004.

Fisher, Andrew. *Metaethics: An Introduction*. New York: Routledge, 2014.

Flanagan, Owen, Hagop Sarkissian, and David Wong. "Naturalizing Ethics." In *The Blackwell Companion to Naturalism*, vol. 62. Blackwell Companions to Philosophy. Malden, MA: Wiley-Blackwell, 2016.

Flannagan, Matthew. "Divine Commands and the Euthyphro Dilemma: Some Naturalist Misperceptions." In *The Naturalness of Belief: New Essays on Theism's Rationality*, edited by Paul Copan and Charles Taliaferro. Lanham, MD: Lexington, 2018.

Foot, Philippa. *Natural Goodness*. Oxford: Clarendon, 2003.

Frankena, William K. *Ethics*. 2nd ed. Prentice-Hall Foundations of Philosophy. Saddle River, NJ: Prentice Hall, 1963.

Franks, W. Paul, ed. *Explaining Evil: Four Views*. London: Bloomsbury Academic, 2019.

Fuqua, Jonathan, and Robert C. Koons, eds. *Classical Theism*. New York: Routledge, 2023.

Gairdner, William D. *The Book of Absolutes: A Critique of Relativism and a Defence of Universals*. Montreal: McGill-Queen's University Press, 2009.

Gamwell, Franklin I. *The Divine Good: Modern Moral Theory and the Necessity of God*. Dallas: Southern Methodist University Press, 1996.

Garcia, Robert K., and Nathan L. King. *Is Goodness Without God Good Enough?: A Debate on Faith, Secularism, and Ethics*. Lanham, MD: Rowman & Littlefield, 2009.

Gibbard, Allan. *Thinking How to Live*. Cambridge, MA: Harvard University Press, 2008.

Goetz, Stuart. "The Argument from the Meaning of Life." In *Contemporary Arguments in Natural Theology*, edited by Colin Ruloff and Peter Horban. London: Bloomsbury Academic, 2021.

Goff, Philip. *Consciousness and Fundamental Reality*. New York: Oxford University Press, 2017.

———. *Galileo's Error: Foundations for a New Science of Consciousness*. New York: Pantheon, 2019.

Gordon, Bruce L., and William A. Dembski, eds. *The Nature of Nature: Examining the Role of Naturalism in Science*. 1st ed. Wilmington: Intercollegiate Studies Institute, 2011.

Gould, Paul, ed. *Beyond the Control of God?: Six Views on The Problem of God and Abstract Objects*. Bloomsbury Studies in Philosophy of Religion. London: Bloomsbury Academic, 2014.

Gould, Paul, and Richard B. Davis. "Modified Theistic Activism." In *Beyond the Control of God?: Six Views on The Problem of God and Abstract Objects*, edited by Paul Gould. Bloomsbury Studies in Philosophy of Religion. London: Bloomsbury Academic, 2014.

Greeley, Nathan. "Divine Simplicity: A Reply to Philosophical Objections." In *The Lord Is One: Reclaiming Divine Simplicity*, edited by Joseph Minich and Onsi Kamel. Leesburg, VA: Davenant, 2019.

Grice, H. P., and P. F. Strawson. "In Defense of a Dogma." In *Readings in the Philosophy of Language*, edited by Jay F. Rosenberg and Charles Travis. Englewood Cliffs, NJ: Prentice Hall, 1971.

Hale, Bob. *Necessary Beings: An Essay on Ontology, Modality, and the Relations Between Them*. New York: Oxford University Press, 2013.

Hare, John E. *God and Morality: A Philosophical History*. Malden, MA: Wiley-Blackwell, 2007.

———. *God's Call: Moral Realism, God's Commands, & Human Autonomy*. Grand Rapids: Eerdmans, 2001.

———. *God's Command*. Reprint ed. Oxford: Oxford University Press, 2018.

Hare, R. M. *The Language of Morals*. Oxford: Oxford University Press, 1964.

Hasker, William. "How to Think About the Trinity." In *Christian Philosophy of Religion: Essays in Honor of Stephen T. Davis*, edited by C. P. Ruloff. Notre Dame: University of Notre Dame Press, 2015.

———. *Metaphysics and the Tri-Personal God*. Reprint ed. New York: Oxford University Press, 2017.

Henry, Carl F. *Christian Personal Ethics*. Grand Rapids: Baker, 1977.

Hinlicky, Paul R. *Divine Simplicity: Christ the Crisis of Metaphysics*. Grand Rapids: Baker Academic, 2016.

Hodge, Charles. *Systematic Theology*. Reprint. Vol. 1. Grand Rapids: Eerdmans, 1979.

Hoffman, Donald D. *The Case Against Reality: How Evolution Hid the Truth from Our Eyes*. Westminster: Penguin, 2020.

Holland, Tom. *Dominion*. New York: Basic, 2019.

Holmes, Stephen R. "Classical Trinity: Evangelical Perspective." In *Two Views on the Doctrine of the Trinity*, edited by Jason S. Sexton. Counterpoints. Grand Rapids: Zondervan Academic, 2014.

———. *The Quest for the Trinity: The Doctrine of God in Scripture, History and Modernity*. Downer's Grove, IL: IVP Academic, 2012.

Huemer, Michael. *Ethical Intuitionism*. 2005 ed. New York: Palgrave Macmillan, 2007.

Hume, David. *An Enquiry Concerning the Principles of Morals*, edited by J. B. Schneewind. Indianapolis: Hackett, 1983.

Hunter, James Davison and Paul Nedelisky. *Science and the Good: The Tragic Quest for the Foundations of Morality*. New Haven, CT: Templeton Press, 2018.

Husserl, Edmund. *The Crisis of European Sciences and Transcendental Phenomenology: An Introduction to Phenomenological Philosophy*. Translated by David Carr. Evanston, IL: Northwestern University Press, 1970.

Husserl, Edmund, and Michael Dummett. *Logical Investigations, Vol. 1*, edited by Dermot Moran. Translated by J. N. Findlay. New York: Routledge, 2001.

Inman, Ross D. *Substance and the Fundamentality of the Familiar: A Neo-Aristotelian Mereology*. 22 vols. Routledge Studies in Metaphysics. New York: Routledge, 2020.

Jackson, Frank. *From Metaphysics to Ethics: A Defence of Conceptual Analysis*. Oxford: Clarendon, 2005.

Jaki, Stanley L. *The Savior of Science*. Washington, DC: Regnery Gateway, 1988.

———. *Science & Creation: From Eternal Cycles to an Oscillating Universe*. Lanham, MD: University Press of America, 1990.

Jakobsen, Martin. *Moral Realism and the Existence of God: Improving Parfit's Metaethics*. Briston, CT: Peeters, 2020.

Jeffrey, Anne. *God and Morality*. New York: Cambridge University Press, 2019.

Johnson, Adam Lloyd. *Divine Love Theory: How the Trinity Is the Source and Foundation of Morality*. Grand Rapids: Kregel Academic, 2023.

———. "Fortifying the Petard: A Response to One of Erik Wielenberg's Criticisms of the Divine Command Theory." *Philosophia Christi* 20, no. 2 (2018) 357–63.

———. "Introduction to the American Academy of Religion Panel Forum on Eric Wielenberg's Robust Ethics." *Philosophia Christi* 20, no. 2 (2018) 331–32.

———. "Proposing a Trinitarian Metaethical Theory as a Better Explanation for Objective Morality than Erik Wielenberg's Godless Normative Realism." PhD diss., Southeastern Baptist Theological Seminary, 2020. ProQuest (ProQuest 27959292).

Johnson, Daniel M. *Calvinism and the Problem of Evil*, edited by David E. Alexander. Eugene, OR: Pickwick, 2016.
Jollimore, Troy. "Impartiality." In *The Stanford Encyclopedia of Philosophy*, edited by Edward N. Zalta. Metaphysics Research Lab, Stanford University, 2021. https://plato.stanford.edu/archives/fall2021/entries/impartiality/.
Jones, Richard H. *Reductionism: Analysis and the Fullness of Reality*. Lewisburg, PA: Bucknell University Press, 2000.
Joyce, Richard. *The Myth of Morality*. Cambridge: Cambridge University Press, 2001.
Juhl, Cory, and Eric Loomis. *Analyticity*. New York: Routledge, 2010.
Kahane, Guy. "If There Is a Hole, It Is Not God-Shaped." In *Does God Matter?: Essays on the Axiological Consequences of Theism*, edited by Klaas Kraay. Routledge Studies in the Philosophy of Religion. New York: Routledge, 2020.
Kant, Immanuel. *Critique of Pure Reason*. Translated by Norman Kemp Smith. New York: St. Martin's, 1929.
———. *Foundations of the Metaphysics of Morals and What Is Enlightenment?* Translated by Lewis White Beck. Indianapolis: Bobbs-Merrill, 1959.
———. *Religion within the Bounds of Bare Reason*. Translated by Werner S. Pluhar. Indianapolis: Hackett, 2009.
Kauppinen, Antti. "A Humean Theory of Moral Intuition." *Canadian Journal of Philosophy* 43, no. 3 (2013) 360–81.
Khouri, Sherene Nicholas, and Gary R. Habermas. *Triune Relationality: A Trinitarian Response to Islamic Monotheism*. Downer's Grove, IL: IVP Academic, 2024.
Kinneging, Andreas. *The Geography of Good and Evil: Philosophical Investigations*. Edited by Jonathan Price. Translated by Ineke Hardy. Wilmington: Intercollegiate Studies Institute, 2009.
Kolakowski, Leszek. *Main Currents of Marxism: The Founders—The Golden Age—The Breakdown*. Translated by P. S. Falla. New York: W. W. Norton, 2008.
Koperski, Jeffrey. *The Physics of Theism: God, Physics, and the Philosophy of Science*. Malden, MA: Wiley-Blackwell, 2015.
Korsgaard, Christine M. *The Sources of Normativity*, edited by Onora O'Neill. Cambridge: Cambridge University Press, 1996.
Kraay, Klaas, ed. *Does God Matter? Essays on the Axiological Consequences of Theism*. Routledge Studies in the Philosophy of Religion. New York: Routledge, 2020.
Kratt, Dale. "A Theistic Critique of Secular Moral Nonnaturalism." PhD diss., Liberty University School of Divinity, 2023.
Kripke, Saul. *Naming and Necessity*. Malden, MA: Wiley-Blackwell, 1981.
Kulp, Christopher B. *Knowing Moral Truth: A Theory of Metaethics and Moral Knowledge*. Lanham, MD: Lexington, 2017.
———. *Metaphysics of Morality*. New York: Palgrave MacMillan, 2019.
Kvanvig, Jonathan L. *The Possibility of an All-Knowing God*. New York: St. Martin's, 1986.
Leslie, John. *Value and Existence*, edited by Nicholas Rescher. APQ Library of Philosophy. Totowa, NJ: Rowman & Littlefield, 1979.
Letham, Robert. *The Holy Trinity: In Scripture, History, Theology, and Worship*. Revised, Expanded ed. Phillipsburg, NJ: P&R, 2019.
Lewis, C. S. *The Abolition of Man*. New York: Macmillan, 1955.
———. *The Problem of Pain*. New York: Macmillan, 1971.

Linville, Mark D. *Is Everything Permitted?: Moral Values in a World Without God.* Atlanta: Ravi Zacharias International Ministries, 2001.

———. "The Moral Argument." In *The Blackwell Companion to Natural Theology*, edited by William Lane Craig and J. P. Moreland. Malden, MA: Blackwell, 2009.

Little, Bruce A. *God, Why This Evil?* Lanham, MD: Hamilton, 2012.

Loftin, R. Keith, ed. *God & Morality: Four Views.* Downer's Grove, IL: IVP Academic, 2012.

Lutz, Matt, and Spencer Case. *Is Morality Real?* New York: Routledge, 2023.

MacIntyre, Alasdair. *After Virtue: A Study in Moral Theory.* 3rd ed. Notre Dame: University of Notre Dame Press, 2007.

———. *Whose Justice? Which Rationality?* Notre Dame: University of Notre Dame Press, 1988.

Mackie, J. L. *Ethics: Inventing Right and Wrong.* Westminster: Penguin, 1977.

Maitzen, Stephen. "What Is the Difference Between Logical Necessity and Metaphysical Necessity?" *Ask Philosophers*, September 8, 2012. https://www.askphilosophers.org/?/4843.

Mangalwadi, Vishal. *The Book That Made Your World: How the Bible Created the Soul of Western Civilization.* Nashville, TN: Thomas Nelson, 2011.

Martin, Michael. *Atheism, Morality, and Meaning.* Amherst: Prometheus, 2002.

McCall, Thomas H. "Response to Stephen R. Holmes." In *Two Views on the Doctrine of the Trinity*, edited by Jason S. Sexton. Counterpoints. Grand Rapids: Zondervan Academic, 2014.

———. *Which Trinity? Whose Monotheism? Philosophical and Systematic Theologians on the Metaphysics of Trinitarian Theology.* Grand Rapids: Eerdmans, 2010.

McDowell, John. *Mind and World: With a New Introduction by the Author.* 2nd ed. Cambridge, MA: Harvard University Press, 1996.

McGinn, Colin. *Inborn Knowledge: The Mystery Within.* Cambridge, MA: The MIT Press, 2015.

———. *The Mysterious Flame: Conscious Minds in a Material World.* 1st paperback ed. New York: Basic, 1994.

McLaughlin, Brian. "Supervenience." In *Stanford Encyclopedia of Philosophy*. Stanford: Stanford University, 2018.

McNabb, Tyler Dalton. "Wile E. Coyote and the Craggy Rocks Below: The Perils of Godless Ethics." *Philosophia Christi* 20, no. 2 (2018) 339–46.

McPherson, Tristram, and David Plunkett, eds. *The Routledge Handbook of Metaethics.* New York: Routledge, 2017.

Meiland, Jack. "Category." In *The Cambridge Dictionary of Philosophy*, edited by Robert Audi. Cambridge: Cambridge University Press, 1995.

Meixner, Uwe. *Defending Husserl.* Frankfurt: de Gruyter, 2014.

———. *The Theory of Ontic Modalities.* Frankfurt: de Gruyter, 2006.

Melchert, Norman. *The Great Conversation: A Historical Introduction to Philosophy.* 7th ed. New York: Oxford University Press, 2014.

Melnyk, Andrew. *A Physicalist Manifesto: Thoroughly Modern Materialism.* Cambridge Studies in Philosophy. Cambridge: Cambridge University Press, 2003.

Mendelovici, Angela. *The Phenomenal Basis of Intentionality.* New York: Oxford University Press, 2018.

Mill, John Stuart. *Utilitarianism.* 2nd ed, edited by George Sher. Indianapolis: Hacket, 2001.

Miller, Alexander. *Contemporary Metaethics: An Introduction*. 2nd ed. Malden, MA: Polity, 2013.
Molnar, Paul D. "Classical Trinity: Catholic Perspective." In *Two Views on the Doctrine of the Trinity*, edited by Jason S. Sexton. Counterpoints. Grand Rapids: Zondervan Academic, 2014.
———. "Response to Thomas H. McCall." In *Two Views on the Doctrine of the Trinity*, edited by Jason S. Sexton. Counterpoints. Grand Rapids: Zondervan Academic, 2014.
Molnar, Thomas. *Sartre: Ideologue of Our Time*. New York: Funk & Wagnalls, 1968.
Moore, G. E. *Principia Ethica*. Monee, IL: Pantianos Classics, 2020.
Moreland, J. P. *The Recalcitrant Imago Dei: Human Persons and the Failure of Naturalism*. London: Student Christian Movement, 2009.
Moreland, J. P., and William Lane Craig. *Philosophical Foundations for a Christian Worldview*. Downer's Grove, IL: IVP Academic, 2003.
Morris, Dolores G. *Believing Philosophy: A Guide to Becoming a Christian Philosopher*. Grand Rapids: Zondervan Academic, 2021.
Morris, Thomas V. *Anselmian Explorations: Essays in Philosophical Theology*. Notre Dame: University of Notre Dame Press, 1987.
Murphy, Mark C. "Theological Voluntarism." *Stanford Encyclopedia of Philosophy*. Summer 2019 (June 2019). https://plato.standford.edu/archives/sum2019/entries/voluntarism-theological/>.
———. *God and Moral Law: On the Theistic Explanation of Morality*. Reprint ed. Oxford: Oxford University Press, 2016.
———. "No Creaturely Intrinsic Value." *Philosophia Christi* 20, no. 2 (2018) 347–55.
Nagel, Thomas. "What Is It like to Be a Bat?" *Philosophical Review* 83, no. 4 (1974) 435–50.
Narasimhan, Sakuntala. *Sati: Widow Burning in India*. New York: Doubleday, 1992.
Nietzsche, Friedrich. *The Geneology of Morals*. Translated by Horace B. Samuel. New York: Dover, 2003.
Nozick, Robert. *Invariances: The Structure of the Objective World*. Revised ed. Cambridge, MA: Belknap, 2001.
O'Connor, Timothy. "The Unity of the Divine Nature." In *Classical Theism: New Essays on the Metaphysics of God*. Routledge Studies in the Philosophy of Religion. New York: Routledge, 2023.
Oderberg, David S. *Real Essentialism*. New York: Routledge, 2008.
Olson, Jonas. *Moral Error Theory: History, Critique, Defence*. New York: Oxford University Press, 2014.
Oppy, Graham. "Naturalistic Axiology." In *Four Views on the Axiology of Theism: What Difference Does God Make?* Paperback ed. London: Bloomsbury Academic, 2022.
Oppy, Graham, and Kenneth L. Pearce. *Is There a God?* New York: Routledge, 2021.
Orr, James. *The Mind of God and the Works of Nature: Laws and Powers in Naturalism, Platonism, and Classical Theism*. Leuven, Belgium: Peeters, 2019.
Owen, H P. *The Moral Argument for Christian Theism*. London: Allen & Unwin, 1965.
Padgett, Alan G. *God, Eternity, and the Nature of Time*. Eugene, OR: Wipf and Stock, 1992.
Parfit, Derek. *On What Matters*. 3 vols. Oxford: Oxford University Press, 2011.
Parrish, Stephen E. *Atheism? A Critical Analysis*. Wipf and Stock, 2019.

———. "Defending Theistic Conceptualism." *Philosophia Christi* 20, no. 1 (2018) 101–17.

———. *God and Necessity: A Defense of Classical Theism*. Lanham, MD: University Press of America, 2001.

———. *The Knower and the Known: Physicalism, Dualism, and the Nature of Intelligibility*. South Bend, IN: St. Augustine, 2013.

Parrish, Stephen E, and J. W. Wartick. "The Dilemma of Divine Simplicity: Part 1." *Concordia Theological Journal* 2, no. 1 (2014) 13–22.

———. "The Dilemma of Divine Simplicity: Part 2." *Concordia Theological Journal* 2, no. 2 (2015) 71–84.

Paulsen, David Lamont. "Comparative Coherencey of Mormon (Finitistic) and Classical Theism." PhD diss., University of Michigan, 1975. University Microfilms International, Ann Arbor, MI (76-9485).

Peckham, John C. *Divine Attributes: Knowing the Covenantal God of Scripture*. Grand Rapids: Baker Academic, 2021.

Peikoff, Leonard. *Objectivism: The Philosophy of Ayn Rand*. New York: Dutton, 1991.

Peppiatt, Lucy. *The Imago Dei: Humanity Made in the Image of God*. Eugene, OR: Cascade, 2022.

Peterson, Derrick. "A Sacred Monster: On the Secret Fears of Some Recent Trinitarianism." In *The Lord Is One*, edited by Joseph Minich and Onsi A. Kamel. Leesburg, VA: Davenant, 2019.

———. "The Parting of God: Diagnosing the Fate of Divine Simplicity in Twentieth-Century Theology." In *The Lord Is One*, edited by Joseph Minich and Onsi Kamel. Leesburg, VA: Davenant, 2019.

Peterson, John. *Introduction to Scholastic Realism*. Vol. 12. New Perspectives in Philosophical Scholarship Texts and Issues. New York: Peter Lang, 1996.

Pinker, Steven. *The Blank Slate: The Modern Denial of Human Nature*. Reprint ed. London: Penguin Books, 2003.

Plantinga, Alvin. *The Nature of Necessity*. Revised ed. Oxford: Clarendon, 1979.

Plato. *Collected Dialogues of Plato Including the Letters*. 6th printing. Edited by Edith Hamilton and Huntington Cairns. Bollingen 71. Phillipsburg, NJ: Princeton University Press, 1971.

Plebani, Matteo. "Recent Debates over the Existence of Abstract Objects: An Overview." In *Abstract Objects: For and Against*, edited by José L. Falguera and Concha Martínez-Vidal. New York: Springer, 2020.

Pojman, Louis P. *Ethics: Discovering Right and Wrong*. 2nd ed. Belmont, CA: Wadsworth, 1995.

Porter, Steven. *Restoring the Foundations of Epistemic Justification: A Direct Realist and Conceptualist Theory of Foundationalism*. Lanham, MD: Lexington, 2006.

Powers, Lawrence H. *Non-Contradiction*. Studies in Logic: Vol. 39, Logic and Argumentation. London: College, 2012.

Poythress, Vern S. *The Mystery of the Trinity: A Trinitarian Approach to the Attributes of God*. Phillipsburg, NJ: P&R, 2020.

Pruss, Alexander R., and Joshua L. Rasmussen. *Necessary Existence*. Oxford: Oxford University Press, 2018.

Quine, Willard Van Orman. "Two Dogmas of Empiricism." In *From a Logical Point of View: Nine Logico-Philosophical Essays*. 2nd revised ed. Cambridge, MA: Harvard University Press, 1980.

Rae, Scott. *Moral Choices: An Introduction to Ethics.* 4th ed. Grand Rapids: Zondervan Academic, 2018.
Rand, Ayn. *For The New Intellectual: The Philosophy of Ayn Rand.* Paperback ed. New York: Penguin, 1961.
———. *The Virtue of Selfishness: A New Concept of Egoism.* 10th ed. New York: New American Library, 1964.
Rasmussen, Joshua. "An Argument for a Supreme Foundation." In *A New Theist Response to the New Atheists.* New York: Routledge, 2021.
———. *Defending the Correspondence Theory of Truth.* Cambridge: Cambridge University Press, 2014.
Rasmussen, Joshua and Felipe Leon. *Is God the Best Explanation of Things? A Dialogue.* Cham, Switzerland: Palgrave Macmillan, 2019.
Reid, Thomas, and Sir William Hamilton Thomas. *Reid's Essays on the Intellectual Powers of Man.* Charleston: Legare Street, 2022.
Reilly, Robert R. *The Closing of the Muslim Mind: How Intellectual Suicide Created the Modern Islamist Crisis.* Wilmington: Intercollegiate Studies Institute, 2010.
Ribeiro, Brian. "The Argument from Beauty." In *Contemporary Arguments in Natural Theology: God and Rational Belief,* edited by Colin Ruloff and Peter Horban. London: Bloomsbury Academic, 2021.
Richards, Jay W. *The Untamed God: A Philosophical Exploration of Divine Perfection, Simplicity, and Immutability.* Downer's Grove, IL: IVP Academic, 2003.
Richardson, Don. *Peace Child.* 4th ed. Ventura, CA: Regal, 2005.
Rieff, Philip. *The Triumph of the Therapeutic Uses of Faith after Freud.* Chicago: University of Chicago Press, 1987.
Rieff, Philip, and James Davison Hunter. *My Life Among the Deathworks: Illustrations of the Aesthetics of Authority.* 1st ed. Edited by Kenneth S. Piver. Charlottesville, VA: University of Virginia Press, 2006.
Rist, John. *On Inoculating Moral Philosophy Against God.* Marquette, MI: Marquette University Press, 1999.
———. *Real Ethics: Reconsidering the Foundations of Morality.* Cambridge University Press, 2002.
Ritchie, Angus. *From Morality to Metaphysics: The Theistic Implications of Our Ethical Commitments.* Oxford: Oxford University Press, 2012.
Rorty, Richard, Michael Williams, and David Bromwich. *Philosophy and the Mirror of Nature.* 30th Anniv. ed. Princeton: Princeton University Press, 2017.
Rosefielde, Steven. *Red Holocaust.* London: Routledge, 2010.
Rosenberg, Jay F., and Charles Travis, eds. *Readings in the Philosophy of Language.* Englewood Cliffs, NJ: Prentice Hall, 1971.
Ross, James. *Thought and World: The Hidden Necessities.* Notre Dame: University of Notre Dame Press, 2008.
Rowe, William L., Paul Draper, Richard Swinburne, et al. *The Evidential Argument from Evil,* edited by Daniel Howard-Snyder. Bloomington, IN: Indiana University Press, 2008.
Ruse, Michael. "Naturalist Moral Nonrealism." In *God & Morality: Four Views,* by R. Keith Loftin. Downer's Grove, IL: IVP Academic, 2012.
Sansbury, Timothy N. *Beyond Time: Defending God's Transcendence.* Lanham, MD: University Press Of America, 2009.

Sayre-McCord, Geoffrey, ed. *Essays on Moral Realism*. Ithaca, NY: Cornell University Press, 1988.

Scanlon, Thomas. *What We Owe to Each Other*. Revised ed. Cambridge, MA: Belknap, 2000.

Schmid, Joseph C. "Existential Inertia and the Aristotelian Proof." *International Journal for Philosophy of Religion*, September 3, 2020. https://doi.org/10.1007/s11153-020-09773-9.

Schroeder, Mark. "Frege–Geach Problem." In *Routledge Encyclopedia of Philosophy*. London: Routledge, 2016. https://doi.org/10.4324/9780415249126-L149-1.

———. *Noncognitivism in Ethics*. London: Routledge, 2010.

Schultz, Walter J. "An Augustinian-Edwardsian Metaphysics of Possibility for the Barcan Formula." *Philosophia Christi*. 24, no. 2 (2022) 191–215.

Schulz, Gregory P. *Wednesday's Child: From Heidegger to Affective Neuroscience, a Field Theory of Angst*. Eugene, OR: Wipf & Stock, 2010.

Scrivener, Glen. *The Air We Breathe: How We All Came to Believe in Freedom, Kindness, Progress, and Equality*. Epsom, UK: The Good Book, 2022.

Shafer-Landau, Russ. *Moral Realism: A Defence*. Oxford: Clarendon, 2005.

Shehadeh, Imad N. *God With Us and Without Us, Volume One: Oneness in Trinity versus Absolute Oneness*. Cumbria, UK: Langham, 2018.

Sidgwick, Henry, and John Rawls. *The Methods of Ethics*. 7th ed. Indianapolis: Hackett, 1981.

Sinnott-Armstrong, Walter. *Morality Without God?* Reprint ed. New York: Oxford University Press, 2011.

Smith, George H. *Atheism: The Case Against God*. The Skeptics Bookshelf. Buffalo: Prometheus, 1979.

Smith, Michael. *The Moral Problem*. Malden, MA: Wiley-Blackwell, 1994.

Smith, R. Scott. "Book Review: The Knower and the Known by Stephen E. Parrish." *Philosophia Christi* 18, no. 2 (2016) 518–22.

———. *Exposing the Roots of Constructivism: Nominalism and the Ontology of Knowledge*. Lanham, MD: Lexington, 2022.

———. *In Search of Moral Knowledge: Overcoming the Fact-Value Dichotomy*. Downer's Grove: IVP Academic, 2014.

Smith, Tara. *Viable Values: A Study of Life as the Root and Reward of Morality*. Lanham, MD: Rowman & Littlefield, 2000.

Smithies, Declan. *The Epistemic Role of Consciousness*. New York: Oxford University Press, 2019.

Spencer, Robert. *The Critical Qur'an: Explained from Key Islamic Commentaries and Contemporary Historical Research*. New York: Bombardier, 2022.

Sterba, James, and Richard Swinburne. *Could a Good God Permit So Much Suffering?: A Debate*. New York: Oxford University Press, 2024.

Taylor, A. E. *The Faith Of A Moralist*. The Theological Implications of Morality. London: Macmillan, 1930.

Trueman, Carl R., and Rod Dreher. *The Rise and Triumph of the Modern Self: Cultural Amnesia, Expressive Individualism, and the Road to Sexual Revolution*. Wheaton: Crossway, 2020.

Tucker, William. *Marriage and Civilization: How Monogamy Made Us Human*. Washington, DC: Regnery, 2014.

Tuggy, Dale. "On the Possibility of a Single Perfect Person." In *Christian Philosophy of Religion: Essays in Honor of Stephen T. Davis*, edited by C. P. Ruloff. Notre Dame: University of Notre Dame Press, 2015.

Van Cleve, James. "Brute Necessity." *Philosophy Compass* 13, no. e12516 (2018) 1–43.

van Inwagen, Peter. *Christian Faith and the Problem of Evil*. Grand Rapids: Eerdmans, 2004.

———. *Material Beings*. Ithaca, NY: Cornell University Press, 1995.

van Inwagen, Peter, and William Lane Craig. *Do Numbers Exist?* New York: Routledge, 2024.

van Roojen, Mark. *Metaethics: A Contemporary Introduction*. New York: Routledge, 2015.

Van Til, Cornelius. *An Introduction to Systematic Theology*. In Defense of the Faith, V. Phillipsburg, NJ: P&R, 1978.

Vitz, Paul C. *Psychology As Religion: The Cult of Self-Worship*. 3rd ed. Grand Rapids: Paternoster, 1994.

Walls, Jerry, and Trent Dougherty, eds. *Two Dozen (or so) Arguments for God: The Plantinga Project*. New York: Oxford University Press, 2018.

Ward, Keith. *Christ and the Cosmos: A Reformulation of Trinitarian Doctrine*. Cambridge: Cambridge University Press, 2015.

Ward, Thomas M. *Divine Ideas*. Cambridge: Cambridge University Press, 2020.

Weaver, Gilbert B. "Man: Analog of God." In *Jerusalem & Athens: Critical Discussions on the Philosophy and Apologetics of Cornelius Van Til*, edited by E. R. Geehan. Phillipsburg, NJ: P&R, 1974.

Wegner, Daniel M. *The Illusion of Conscious Will*. Cambridge, MA: Bradford, 2003.

Welty, Greg. *Why Is There Evil in the World (And So Much of It)?* Fearn, Scotland: Christian Focus, 2018.

West, John G. *Darwin Day In America: How Our Politics and Culture Have Been Dehumanized in the Name of Science*. Wilmington: Intercollegiate Studies Institute, 2007.

Whittle, Bruno. "There Are Brute Necessities." *Philosophical Review* 60, no. 238 (2010) 149–59.

Wielenberg, Erik J. "Reply to Craig, Murphy, McNabb, and Johnson." *Philosophia Christi* 20, no. 2 (2018) 365–75.

———. *Robust Ethics: The Metaphysics and Epistemology of Godless Normative Realism*. Oxford: Oxford University Press, 2014.

———. *Value and Virtue in a Godless Universe*. New York: Cambridge University Press, 2005.

Willard, Dallas. *The Disappearance of Moral Knowledge*, edited by Steven L. Porter, Aaron Preston, and Gregg A. Ten Elshof. New York: Routledge, 2020.

Williams, John F. *Hating Perfection: A Subtle Search for the Best Possible World*. Revised ed. Amherst: Humanity, 2009.

Williams, Richard N., and Daniel N. Robinson, eds. *Scientism: The New Orthodoxy*. New York: Bloomsbury Academic, 2014.

Williamson, Timothy. *Modal Logic as Metaphysics*. Oxford: Oxford University Press, 2013.

Wittgenstein, Ludwig, and Bertrand Russell. *Tractatus Logico-Philosophicus*. 471st ed. Translated by C. K. Ogden. Mineola, NY: Dover, 1998.

Wynn, Mark. *God and Goodness: A Natural Theological Perspective.* London: Routledge, 1999.

Yandell, Keith E. "God and Propositions." In *Beyond the Control of God? Six Views on the Problem of God and Abstract Objects,* edited by Paul Gould. New York: Bloomsbury, 2014.

Zagzebski, Linda Trinkaus. *Divine Motivation Theory.* New York: Cambridge University Press, 2004.

———. *Virtues of the Mind: An Inquiry into the Nature of Virtue and the Ethical Foundations of Knowledge.* Cambridge: Cambridge University Press, 1996.

Index

a posteriori, 83–84
a priori, 5n4
abortion, xiii, 75–76, 101, 112
Absolute, the, 64, 67, 236
absolute creationism, 4, 19, 66, 135n13, 141–42, 165–68, 170–97
absolute oneness, 213, 217, 225, 237
abstract entities, xiv, 4, 19–20, 23–24, 48, 51, 56, 63–72, 74, 77–80, 96–97, 106–10, 126, 135–36, 138, 141, 143, 148–52, 156–58, 161–63, 165–97, 198–205, 215, 241, 245
Adams, Robert Merrihew, 17n1, 78n32
Adamson, Peter, 207n13
aesthetic, 49, 58, 61–62, 124, 240, 242
Allison, Greg, 194n40
Allison, Henry, 52n9
Alston, William, 77
Altman, Matthew, 53n11
amoral choice, 46, 87, 120, 126–27, 245
analogical, 218–20, 231
Anderson, James, 45n23, 78–79
Anselm, 168
Anselmian, 159, 199, 226
antirealism, x, 2–3, 5, 7–8, 13–14, 18–20, 26, 52, 57–58, 65–67, 89–113, 114–20, 125–26, 128, 130, 133–34, 139, 147, 154, 244

Anya, 9
Aquinas, Thomas, 223n17, 228, 231–32
Aristotle, 29, 47–48, 231n42
Armstrong, David, 20–21
Athanasius, 223n17
Athanasian Creed, 229
Audi, Robert, 17n3, 58n22
autonomy, 34–37, 191, 242
axioms, ix, 15 n. 24, 16, 19–20, 63, 65, 87–88, 114–15, 120–26, 132, 136–37, 139, 201, 245
Ayer, Alfred Jules, 92n3, 94n7
Aztecs, 42–3
Baggett, David, 17n1, 155–56, 210, 236n54
Baggett, Marybeth, 156n36
Bagnoli, Carla, 115
Balaguer, Mark, 156
Bales, James, 17n1
Barfield, Kenny, 102n17
Barrett, Matthew, 222, 230
bat, 55, 187
Bauerschmidt, Frederick Christian, 231
Bavinck, Herman, 214
beauty, 47, 49, 61–62, 134, 153, 201–2
Beck, W. David, 17n1
Bentham, Jeremy, 121
Blackburn, Simon, 8n11, 94n7
blank slate, 33
Blanshard, Brand, 159n45
Bloomfield, Paul, 114n1

INDEX

Bøhn, Einar Duenger, 63n1
BonJour, Laurence, 108n25
bootstrapping problem, 178–80
Bowne, Borden Parker, 217n1, 218n2
Bradley, F. H., 143
Brandt, Richard, 121n15
Braun, David, 182
Brink, David, 60n26
Brog, David, 112–13
Brouwer axiom, 136
brute fact, 153, 158–9, 163, 199
brute necessity, 11, 15, 148, 153, 158–59
Budziszewski, J., 29n30
Bueno, Octavio, 16
Bundy, Ted, 60, 111, 116n7
Burroughs, Edgar Rice, 131n3
Campbell, Ronnie R., Jr., 236n54
Case, Spencer, 100n13, 110n31, 217n13, 208n16, 241n64
categorical imperative (CI), x, xiv, 3, 24, 45–46, 61–62, 121, 128–32
categories, xiv, 3, 8, 13, 18, 47–62, 104
chess, 13–14, 129–31
Christensen, Scott, 111
Churchland, Patricia S., 109n27
Clark, Gordon H., 208–9, 219–20
Clark, Kelly James, 21–22
Clarke-Doane, Justin, 120n14, 132
Clouser, Roy, 140n18
coherentism, 77, 127
consequentialism, 25, 39–40, 126
constructivism, 8, 115
contingent ethical truths, 139–40, 162
Cooper, John, 199n1
Copan, Paul, 17n1, 245
Copp, David, 116–7
Coppenger, Mark, 17n1
Cowling, Sam, 63n1, 64–67, 190n35
Craig, William Lane, 65, 67, 148–49, 152, 158, 165, 172, 184–96, 215, 220, 223
Culture, 6, 32, 41–43, 100–104, 112, 122–23, 139–40

Cuneo, Terence, 58–60, 133
Davies, Brian, 231n41, 232
Davis, Richard Brian, 66, 172, 199n2
Davis, Stephen, 236, 238
Dembski, William, 22n11, 49n6
determinism, 35–36
Dockery, David, 194n40
Dolezal, James, 169n13, 227
Dooyeweerd, Herman, 48–49, 51, 57, 61
Dougherty, Trent, 110
Downey, Amy Karen, 232n46
Drier, James, 114
dualism, 17, 22n10
Dummett, Michael, 68n15, 136n14
Dumsday, Travis, 204
Egnor, Michael, 36n8
egoism, 76, 93, 115, 118, 122, 126
eliminativism, 7, 90, 92
Emmeline, 9, 12
emotivism, 6, 91, 94, 98, 113
Enoch, David, 111, 133–34, 147, 163
equator, 65, 106, 136, 218n2
error theory, see nihilism
Euclid, 122–23, 132
euthanasia, xiii
Euthyphro dilemma/objection, x, xv, 210, 212, 240–41
Evans, C. Stephen, 17, 245n1
expressivism, 6, 95–96
externalism, 44–45
Falguera, José, 246n3
Feinberg, John, 242n66
Fisher, Andrew, 100
Flanagan, Owen, 23
Flannagan, Matthew, 17n1
flourishing, 3, 5, 14, 19, 27–29, 103, 116, 122, 244
Foot, Philippa, 15, 114n1
foundational principles, see axioms
foundationalism, 127, 206
Frankena, William, 207n12
Franks, W. Paul, 242n66
free will, 34–36
Frege-Geach problem, 91
Fuqua, Jonathan, 226
Gairdner, William, 6n6
Gamwell, Franklin, 17n1

INDEX

Garcia, Robert, 152n23
Gardner, Stephen, 113
Gershwin, Ira, 23
Gibbard, Allan, 8
God's mind, 4, 67, 69–70, 97, 141, 143, 166, 169–99, 205–6, 242
Goetz, Stuart, 21n7
Goff, Philip, 22n10, 144n6
Gordon, Bruce, 22n11
Gould, Paul, 66n8, 148n20, 172
Greatest Possible Being (GPB), 159n48, 168, 199–200, 211, 229, 232, 236–37
Greeley, Nathan, 233
Gregory of Nyassa, 223n17
Grice, H. P., 82n44
Habermas, Gary, 237n56
Hale, Bob, 9n18, 29n28
Hare, John, 17n1, 24n19, 77, 240n62, 242
Hare, R. M., 6, 94n7, 95
Hasker, William, 221, 223
Henry, Carl, 17n1
Hesiod, 104–5
Hinlicky, Paul, 169n13, 226n21
Hobbes, Thomas, 59
Hodge, Charles, 226n20
Hoffman, Donald, 54n13
Holland, Tom, 112n34
Holmes, Sherlock, 65
Holmes, Stephen, 222n13
Huemer, Michael, 17–18, 58n22, 92, 95–96, 133–34, 147, 163
Hume, David 17n4, 45n23, 53, 93, 107, 110
Hunter, James Davison, 38n11
Husserl, Edmund, 54n13, 55n19, 68n15, 136n14
hypothetical imperative (HI), 46, 128–30
Ideal Observer, 118–9
idealism, 52, 64, 67, 143, 177–78
indexicals, 168n10, 182–83, 189
ineffable, 218–21
Inman, Ross, 167n6

intentionality, 27, 29, 59–77, 107, 147, 149, 160, 175–76, 192, 245
inter-subjectivism, 6, 19, 90, 93
internalism, 44–45
intuitionism, 17–18, 58, 92, 96, 133, 197
Islam, 101, 207n14, 208, 213–14, 237, 241
Jackson, Frank, 25n20
Jaki, Stanley, 214, 240
Jakobsen, Martin, 5n5
Jeffrey, Anne, 143n3
Johnson, Adam Lloyd, 152, 217n1, 235–36, 242
Jollimore, Troy, 118
Jones, Richard, 22n12
Joyce, Richard, 89, 101n15, 104–5
Juhl, Cory, 82n42
Kahane, Guy, 236n55
Kant, Immanuel, 5, 24, 41, 47–48, 52–56, 82, 86, 110, 121, 127, 128
Kantian contractualism, 39–40
Kantian rules, 39–40
Kauppinen, Antti, 17n4
Khouri, Sherene Nicholas, 237
King, Nathan, 152n23
Kinneging, Andreas, 116n6
Kolakowski, Leszek, 34n4
Koons, Robert, 226
Koperski, Jeffrey, 79n37
Korsgaard, Christine, 8, 116
Kraay, Klass, 236n55
Kratt, Dale, vii, 79, 94, 148, 162n52
Kripke, Saul, 11
Kulp, Christopher, 58n22, 67n12, 133–34, 148
Kvanvig, Jonathan, 183
Laws
 natural, 29, 31, 76, 116n6, 131
 of identity, 11, 136n16
 of logic, ix, 15–16, 39–41, 43–44, 74, 78–79, 83n45, 132, 149, 151, 154n30, 159
 of nature, 81, 86, 130–31, 154n30, 162–63, 214
 of physics, 34–36

Leon, Felipe, 144n7
Leslie, John, 190n35, 8n16
Letham, Robert, 240
Lewis, C. S., 102, 229
Linville, Mark, 17n1
Little, Bruce, 242n66
Loch Ness monster, 197
Locke, John, 33, 107
Loftin, R. Keith, 152n23
Lobachevsky, Nikolai, 132
Loomis, Eric, 82n42
Lowe, E. J., 48
Lutz, Matt, 100n13, 110 n. 31, 207n13, 208n16, 241
MacIntyre, Alasdair, 6n6, 127
Mackie, J. L., 7, 100-102, 105-10
Maitzen, Stephen, 83n45
Mangalwadi, Vishal, 243
Marriage, 32-33, 42
Mars, 65, 78, 131n3, 136
Martin, Michael, 118n9
Mary, 179
materialism, 26, 35-36, 96, 109, 157
mathematics, 9-10, 12, 15-16, 43, 56, 75, 78, 81, 96-97, 107, 115, 120, 122-23, 131-34, 138, 149, 151, 158, 202, 211
McAfee, Lauren Green, 194n40
McCall, Thomas, 222-23, 235
McDowell, John, 8n13
McGinn, Colin, 55, 75n27, 108n26
McLaughlin, Brian, 27n25
McNabb, Tyler Dalton, 152n24
McPherson, Tristram, 2n1
Meiland, Jack, 47
Meixner, Uwe, 39n15, 55n19
Melchert, Norman, 202n6
Melnyk, Andrew, 146n9, 157n39
Mendelovici, Angela, 71n21
Menuge, Angus, vii, ix-xi, 23n14, 35n8, 176, 185n27, 191n36, 229n37, 231n43, 235n53
Mercury, 67
Mill, John Stuart, 121
Miller, Alexander, 2n1
modus ponens, 8-12, 44
Molnar, Paul, 222n13, 223n15, 234-5

Molnar, Thomas, 34n5
monism, 18
monogamy, 32, 101
Moore, G. E., 81n41, 85, 202
moral anarchy, 113, 127
Moreland, J. P., 172, 194n40, 220
Mormonism, 24, 71n20.
Morris, Dolores, 7n10, 241n65
Morris, Thomas, 199n3
Mount Rushmore, 67
motivation, 44-6
Murdoch, Iris, 87
Murphy, Mark, 17n1, 152, 208
mysterianism, 55
Nagel, Thomas, 55
Narasimhan, Sakuntala, 42
naturalism, 5, 7-9, 19-28, 42, 85, 107-10, 115, 118-19, 122, 125-26, 134, 143-48, 152, 157, 160-63, 198
necessary ethical truths, 84, 86, 142, 151, 163, 198, 218
necessity
    absolute, 3, 12, 29, 80, 85, 87, 123, 132, 146, 159, 233
    analytic, 82-83
    autonomous, 159n48
    metaphysical, 83-84, 107, 146, 160n51
    nomalogic, 81, 87-88, 146, 162
    synthetic, 76, 85-87, 160, 181, 197
Nedelisky, Paul, 38
Nietzsche, Friedrich, 89
nihilism, 2, 7, 66, 92, 96-99, 133
noncognitivism, 6, 91n3, 94-96
non-naturalism, 4, 21, 160
normativity, 8-13, 14-15, 28, 40, 49, 85, 110, 126, 197, 241
    norms, ix-x, 5, 8, 23, 58-60, 116, 148n17
Nozick, Robert, 55
noumenal, 52
O'Connor, Timothy, 227
O'Leary, Denyse, 36n8
objectivism, 8, 105, 107
obligation, ix-xi, 27, 45-46, 59-62, 85, 129-30, 208-9, 242

Ockham, William, 207
Oderberg, David, 10n19
Olson, Jonas, 101n15, 106n21
Oppy, Graham, 15, 153–54, 184
Orr, James, 166–67
Owen, H. P., 17n1
Padgett, Alan, 190n34
panpsychism, 22n10, 144, 176n19
Parfit, Derek, 5, 27, 39, 41, 119–20, 122
Parrish, Stephen, 12, 35, 37, 81, 109, 135n13, 146–47, 159, 162, 166, 172, 175, 196, 200, 204, 226, 242
Paulsen, David Lamont, 24
Pearce, Kenneth, 15
Peckham, John, 222n13
Peikoff, Leonard, 105n20
Peppiatt, Lucy, 194n40
Perfect Being God, *see* Greatest Possible Being
Peterson, Derrick, 226
Peterson, John, 67, 74n25
phenomenal, 38, 52, 54–55, 57, 69, 74, 136–38, 147, 169, 174–75, 177–79, 205
Pinker, Steven, 33
Plantinga, Alvin, 11, 29, 160n51, 189, 193
Plato, 64, 75, 104
Plato's Heaven, 66, 68, 78, 106, 191
Platonism, ix, x, xiv, 3–5, 8, 17, 19, 23–24, 64, 66, 68–70, 78, 106, 110n39, 119, 126n18, 141–42, 147, 148–63, 166–67, 172–73, 182, 184, 192, 197, 204–5, 210, 245
Plebani, Matteo, 65
Plunkett, David, 2n1
Pluto, 170, 184
Pojman, Louis, 36n9
polygamy, 32–33, 101
Porter, Steven, 167n6
positivism, 55, 66
Powers, Lawrence, 48
Poythress, Vern, 225
prescriptivism, 6, 91, 94, 133
Pruss, Alexander, 9n18

quasi-realism, 8
queerness, argument from, 100, 105–8, 110, 162
Quine, Willard Van Orman, 82
Rae, Scott, xiii n1
Rand, Ayn, 105, 122, 220
Rasmussen, Joshua, 9n18, 77, 110n29, 136, 144n7
rationalism, 5, 19–21, 24–26, 29, 117–18, 122, 134
Rawls, John, 121n15
realism
 strong/robust, x–xi, 3–5, 14, 17, 20–24, 61, 88, 113–14, 118–20, 124, 126, 128–40, 141–64
 weak, 2–5, 8–9, 13–14, 19–20, 26, 46, 87, 90, 92, 113, 114–27, 128, 134, 137, 147, 244–45
Rebekah, 135n12
reductionism, 6, 20, 22, 25–28, 29, 90–91
Reid, Thomas, 56n21
Reilly, Robert, 94n6, 207n14, 213
relativism, 5, 6n6, 90, 100–101, 134
Ribeiro, Brian, 153
Richard of St. Victor, 223n17
Richards, Jay, 223n16
Richardson, Don, 101
Rieff, Philip, 112n38, 113, 153
Riemann, Bernhard, 132
Rist, John, 152n22
Ritchie, Angus, 8
Robinson, Daniel, 111n32
Rorty, Richard, 54n12
Rosefielde, Steven, 34n4
Rosenberg, Jay, 73n24
Ross, James, 10n19
Rowe, William, 242n66
Ruse, Michael, 99–100
Russell, Bertrand, 55n18
Sansbury, Timothy, 190n34
Sarkissian, Hagop, 23
sati, 42
Sayre-McCord, Geoffrey, 60n26
Scanlon, Thomas, 8, 39–41
Schmid, Joseph, 153

Schroeder, Mark, 91n3, 94n7, 95
Schultz, Walter, 197n43
Schulz, Charles, 238n57
Schulz, Gregory, 26
Scotistic, 226
Scotus, John Duns, 223n17, 242
Shafer-Landau, Russ, 133, 148
Shehadeh, Imad, 255
Sidgwick, Henry, 121n15
simplicity, 169–70, 220, 223n16, 226–30, 232–35
Sinnott-Armstrong, Walter, 114n1
Smith, George, 220
Smith, Michael, 5n5
Smith, R. Scott, 17n1, 115n4, 167, 172, 175
Smith, Tara, 105n20
Smithies, Declan, 52
Speaks, Jeff, 159n48
Spencer, Robert, 42
Squirt, 67, 170, 218n3, 227
Sterba, James, 242n66
Strawson, P. F., 82n44
strong realism, *see* realism, strong
subjectivism, 6, 18–19, 26, 61, 89–90, 92–93, 100, 134, 276
Swinburne, Richard, 242n66
Tacitus, 112
Taliaferro, Charles, 245
tautology, ix, 15, 55, 75, 81–82, 158
Taylor, A. E., 17n1
theistic antirealism, x, 165–66, 184–88, 191, 196, 215
theistic conceptualism, x, 4, 20, 67, 70–71, 106, 135 n. 13, 141, 143, 164–67, 172–75, 180, 184–85, 188–96, 205, 215
Tertullian, 223n17
Toffee, 67, 197n93
Travis, Charles, 73n24
Trinity, x, 214, 217–43, 245
Trope theory, 67, 141
Trueman, Carl, 127
Trump, Donald, 170
Tucker, William, 32

Tuggy, Dale, 238, 240n63
unitarianism, 223–24, 238–39
universals, 23n13, 48n5, 64, 68, 77–78, 107, 135, 141, 150, 161, 167, 171, 174–75, 177, 189, 191, 204
univocal, 218–21, 231
utilitarianism, 85, 118, 121–22, 126–27
Van Cleve, James, 159n48
van Inwagen, Peter, 148n19–20, 170, 196, 242n66
van Roojen, Mark, 44, 95
Van Til, Cornelius, 214
Vitz, Paul, 112n38
voluntarism, 4, 6, 93–94, 134, 142, 196, 198, 207–12, 215
Walls, Jerry, 17n1, 110n30, 155–56, 210
Ward, Keith, 240n63
Ward, Thomas, 169n12
Wartick, J. W., 226
weak realism, *see* realism, weak
Weaver, Gilbert, 220n5
Wegner, Daniel, 36n8
Welty, Greg, 78–79, 116, 185–86, 242n66
West, John, 29n29
Whittle, Bruno, 153n26
Wielenberg, Erik, x, 133–34, 148, 152–63, 199
Willard, Dallas, xiii
Williams, John, 190n35
Williams, Richard, 111n32
Williamson, Timothy, 149n21
Wittgenstein, Ludwig, 55n18
Wolf, Thom, 17n1
Wong, David, 23
worldviews, 3, 42, 103–5, 119, 124–26, 134, 162
Wynn, Mark, 62n28
Yandell, Keith, 142, 148n20
Zagzebski, Linda Trinkaus, xiv, 59, 87, 221
Zeno's paradoxes, 51

www.ingramcontent.com/pod-product-compliance
Lightning Source LLC
Chambersburg PA
CBHW071243230426
43668CB00011B/1566